Investigating Corporate Fraud

To Greg, Daisy, Maggie and Molly Harris.
Out of sight, but never out of mind.

Investigating Corporate Fraud

MICHAEL J. COMER

GOWER

Published by
Gower Publishing Limited
Gower House
Croft Road
Aldershot
Hants GU11 3HR
England

Gower Publishing Company
Suite 420
101 Cherry Street
Burlington VT 05401–4405
USA

Michael J. Comer has asserted his moral right under the Copyright, Designs and Patents Act, 1998, to be identified as the author of this work.

British Library Cataloguing in Publication Data
Comer, Michael J.
    Investigating corporate fraud
    1. Corporations–Corrupt practices 2. Fraud 3. Fraud
    investigation
    I. Title II. Maxima Group Plc
    364.1'63

ISBN 0 566 08531 3

The Library of Congress Control Number: 2002104531

Typeset in 9 point Stone Serif by IML Typographers, Birkenhead, Merseyside and printed in Great Britain by MPG Books Limited, Bodmin.

Contents

List of Figures and Tables

FIGURES

TABLES

'It was definitely the perfect fraud . . . unfortunately they hired the perfect investigators.'

'We can't touch him, he has a reasonable expectation of privacy.'

Preamble by Spot the Dog

For those unlucky humans who were forced to read *Corporate Fraud III* rather than eat up their greens, it's me again. For those that didn't, I should introduce myself. My name is Spot, and I am a dog. Unlike most humans, who avoid him, I have been close to Mr Comer for over ten years. Excluding his family, which has little option, I have stayed loyal to the pipe-smoking, mercurial ex-guru longer than any living creature, and it's a record in which I take considerable pride: a living monument to my patience and understanding of an increasingly irascible, elderly investigator.

In Mr Comer's favour – and there is not much else – he, with his colleagues in Maxima Group Plc, are probably among the best corporate fraud investigators in the world. Even some lawyers admire them, and *The Lawyer*, on 3 September 2001 said (at the time):

> A leading UK Law Firm typically uses Maxima, whose Chief Executive is former senior Customs & Excise investigator Mike Comer, for a number of large banks, FTSE 100 companies and private organisations. The company is frequently employed by the firm to carry out anti-counterfeiting and copyright protection work for Microsoft in Europe, Africa and the Middle East.

> A source, who is familiar with Maxima said 'Their work is done very quickly, effectively and behind the scenes. They're changing the whole process of investigation and that's why they're so attractive. They get the evidence so quickly that the other side can do nothing but negotiate their way out of it.' These guys have very advanced techniques where almost nothing can be hidden, wiped or destroyed.

This is a really amazing tribute, because many lawyers regard investigators as 'plods' or worse. When Mr Comer read *The Lawyer* article, he had to be brought round with smelling salts. He could not believe that anyone would say anything nice about him, and even I have to admit that praise in his direction is very unusual.

Mr Comer was asked to write this book by Gower, mainly because the Chinese edition of *Corporate Fraud III* is a best seller. For most people, the Chinese version is far more understandable than the English (or, more truthfully, *almost* English) original and at a sales price of 65p a copy, it is a bargain. I have a feeling that the Chinese find the book cheaper than wood, and are using it in their stoves to cook chow mein and very tasty bones.

Mr Comer thought long and hard before putting pen to paper or fingers and thumbs to the keyboard on this book. He was worried on two counts. The first was that it would alert fraudsters to the methods that might be used to investigate them. This problem quickly vaporized when it was drawn to Mr Comer's attention that nobody reads his books, and thus there was no danger of it alerting anyone. If you are reading this, you must be a really sad bastard.

Some readers may not like the cartoons or Mr Comer's focus on the male gender when referring to humans and humanoids. But these are Mr Comer's hallmarks, and he is unlikely to change at his age. As far as sexual discrimination is concerned, it is of no consequence to him because he has long forgotten the difference. He tells everyone that crooks should not have all the fun, and that he would investigate fraud even if he were not paid fortunes for doing so. He is another really sad bastard, so if you are still reading this, you should get on well together.

Mr Comer's style of writing is a little unusual for what is supposed to be a serious text-book. I agree that having a dog write the foreword is unconventional and not everyone's cup of tea. Personally, I don't get a lot of requests to write stuff like this, but I am open to offers. From time to time, Mr Comer uses Anglo-Saxon words and makes disrespectful comments about politicians, lawyers and other people who don't have to work for a living. He asks for forgiveness: it is just his nature and he cannot resist beating a dead donkey to death. I have noticed that this is a failing of a lot of investigators.

Mr Comer has asked me to thank Mike Williams for doing the cartoons. Thanks also go to a number of brilliant managers and lawyers for whom Maxima has worked on some excep-tionally successful cases, especially Miles Flint and Jonathan Pearl at Sony, Ron Warmington and Jane Wexton at GE Capital, Gary Miller and Dan Morrison at Mishcon de Reya, Guy Martin at Peter Carter Ruck & Partners, Mike Hart, Tom Cassells and Paul Friedman at Baker & McKenzie, Jeremy Carver at Clifford Chance, Nick Valner at Eversheds, Peter Warner at Europay, Ken Matthews at TNT, the late and much missed George Carman QC, plus many others whose names Mr Comer cannot remember, probably because they do not pay their bills or are rude to him. But one thing you should note in view of Mr Comer's opinions about lawyers: he has a lot of them as friends, and some even say they like him. I am not so sure about this, but he believes it.

Mr Comer also wants to thank the Forensic Accountants in the big accounting firms, for making Maxima look even better than it is, and the sponsors of the 'Partners In Crime Initiative' which fell flat on its ass. This confirmed that the 'initiative' of passing fraud inves-tigations from the police to selective investigation firm members of the Confederation of British Industry was nothing more than a shimmy by British politicians to divert attention away from their appalling record in the corporate fraud area. For once, Mr Comer was right, and he will never let anyone forget it. He is also right about the Human Rights Act, the Data Protection Act and the Regulation of Investigatory Powers Act, as time will tell.

Mr Comer thanks his ex-colleagues in Maxima – especially Mr Ex, who is living proof that speed isn't everything, and Rod Burge, Senior Consultant, who has demonstrated that it is possible to live successfully with a split personality. Rod (for that's what I call him) is both an ex-senior Scotland Yard detective and a lawyer, and is never sure until he gets out of bed in the morning which one will prevail during the day. He spends a lot of time arguing with him-self, and of course, the lawyer in him usually comes out on top, and when it doesn't, always appeals. Rod has worked hard on most of the difficult charts and ticklish legal issues, but is absolved of Mr Comer's interpretations of them. Rod insisted I say this.

Rod has also asked me to make it clear that nothing in this book is a substitute for specific legal advice, and that neither he, me, the author, the publishers nor anyone else remotely connected can accept any liability for any errors, omissions, oversights and so on. This is fair, as our royalties are for the National Society for the Prevention of Cruelty to Children, and they do not deserve to be punished for our mistakes.

Finally, Mr Comer would like to acknowledge Tim Stephens, Maxima's ex-Research

Manager, who has mounted a determined crusade to enforce the Data Protection Act by changing passwords on company computers without telling anyone. Tim is the ultimate access controller, and a thoroughly good bloke.

Anyway, enough of this *dog*gerel. I hope you find this book useful. It is meant to tell you what you can and should do when you suspect fraud. As a minimum, I suggest you read the chapter on 'Essential Planning and Policy Areas', as it could just save your ass if your organization suspects fraud.

If you have any questions or comments, you can contact me or – in my absence on walkies – Mr Comer on <comer@btinternet.com>.

Yours aye *(I am told this how the real toffs sign off)*

Spot

'Dog napping, you said; crime of the decade, you said – what a joke!'

General Background

1 *Introduction*

Shit Happens, and So Does Fraud

GOOD COMPANIES: EFFECTIVE MANAGERS

Contrary to popular belief, fraud happens to good companies and to effective managers. Companies like Barings Bank and Deutsche Morgan Grenfell, which were devastated by very serious internal dishonesty, were well managed. Their failing was that they reacted ineffectively when suspicions were first aroused, and tried to solve the problem by ignoring it. Fraud becomes disastrous, mainly because the reaction is ineffective.

OBJECTIVES OF THIS BOOK

This book is to help make sure that, if you suspect fraud, you react swiftly and effectively, get your money back, recover all of your costs and interest, punish the offenders so that you establish a deterrent to others, and return to work as quickly as possible.

The book is divided into three parts:

- general background on fraud investigations
- annotated checklist for investigating fraud
- appendices.

There are overlaps in some parts, but these are unavoidable.

PLANNING AND THE DEADLY SINS

Most victims have no policies and plans for reacting to fraud, and thus, in panic and disarray, make mistakes from which they never recover. The 'Deadly Sins' of fraud investigation are explained on pages 9–27. They demonstrate that the time to get plans in place is *now* – before the worst happens.

Condemning the Innocent

No employee can guarantee that fraud will not take place in the operations under his control. In fact, it would be untenable to maintain control systems that eliminated all risks, and even if it were possible, the resulting lack of trust and bureaucracy would make life intolerable. Trust and effective management are symbiotic, and fraud is the result when the former is abused.

Often the best and most hard-working employees are the easiest to deceive. This is because they are so focused on their primary work that they do not have time to pay attention to details that appear unimportant until too late. It is easy to be wise after the event, and fraud is always concealed in the detail.

Fraud can best be prevented by good people asking the right questions at the right time.

SCOTLAND YARD DEFRAUDED OF £5 MILLION

Anthony Williams, despite having no accounting qualifications, was the Deputy Director of Finance at New Scotland Yard, and responsible for managing a sensitive account used for funding anti-terrorist activities. Over a five-year period, he stole around £5 million, concealing his dishonesty by false vouchers for payments to informants and aircraft hire. In fact, about 70 per cent of expenditure from the account went directly into Williams's pocket – among other things, to buy a castle in Scotland, where he lived like a king.

Fraud can happen to anyone at any time.

Types of Fraud

Fraud is defined as: 'any dishonesty through which one person intends to gain an advantage over another'. It is committed by people exploiting processes with the intention of getting their greedy hands on assets, both tangible and intangible. Fraud can be prevented by secure processes, and by ensuring that people with access to them are honest. This is easier said than done, failures will occur, so reactive plans are the safety net. This book is about such plans.

We live in a world in which dishonesty is on the increase, and it affects everyone. Evasion of tax, social security frauds, public sector dishonesty, false insurance claims and credit card frauds are the obvious tip of the iceberg. They tend to be very common, but with a low unit value, and they are a public scandal. Corporate fraud is a much more serious problem. It tends to be less common, with a high unit value, and it takes victims by surprise.

Although most corporate victims survive, fraud devastates the careers of honest managers, puts jobs at risk, and undermines people's confidence in business. Publicity – especially when the fraudster escapes unpunished – encourages others, and the problem spirals out of control. Fraud is a nasty business.

There are five main categories of corporate fraud (see Figure 1.1):

- **Corruption** – meaning the payment or receipt of any unauthorized benefit to or by an agent (usually an employee) for doing, or not doing, anything in relation to his work. Examples include:
  - acceptance by an employee of cash for influencing a decision made on behalf of his employer
  - payment of club membership for an employee of a supplier in return for favourable treatment

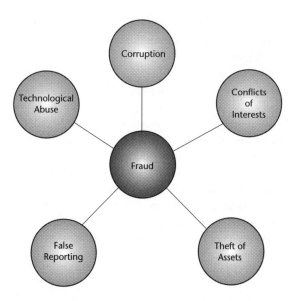

Figure 1.1   Main types of corporate fraud

- indefensibly lavish entertaining of or by an employee with the possible intention of influencing a decision.

- **Conflicts of interest** – where agents (again usually employees) have private, undisclosed interests that could interfere with their work and fiduciary obligations to their principals. Examples include:
  - engaging in part-time work or consultancy, without permission
  - using sensitive company information for personal benefit, including inside dealing
  - drug or alcohol abuse, which affects work performance.

- **Theft of assets** – including the unauthorized removal of intellectual capital and information. Examples include:
  - theft, embezzlement, false accounting and deception
  - theft or misuse of proprietary information
  - malingering and theft of time paid for by the company
  - commercial deception by suppliers, customers and others.

- **False reporting or falsifying performance** – this includes both the creation of false reports and suppression of material information. Examples include:
  - submitting false accounts to conceal inadequate performance or to qualify for a bonus
  - using false accounts to deceive investors, bankers, a stock exchange or a third party
  - manipulating financial results
  - suppression of regulatory and other breaches and false reporting; examples include: falsely reporting compliance with environmental, anti-discriminatory or other regulatory requirements; fraudulently concealing violations of money laundering, health and safety, Human Rights or other regulations.

- **Technological abuse** – including unauthorized access to computer systems, implanting viruses or other malicious code, and sabotage. Examples include:
  - accessing computer files without authority
  - unauthorized Internet browsing
  - computer-related fraud.

The most reliable statistics (and few statistics on fraud are better than a guess) show that on average companies lose between *2 per cent and 5 per cent of turnover* through fraud. Most practitioners believe this is a conservative estimate.

Far too many organizations are woefully unaware of the risks of fraud. Managers mistakenly believe that it is an unlikely, nebulous problem that will never affect them. In fact, fraud is highly predictable and conforms to well-established profiles. It is also contagious. The circumstances in which it occurs are easily identifiable, the most likely indicators being management apathy and cultural weaknesses, such as a focus on short-term gain over principles.

Who are the Fraudsters?

Fraud involves dishonesty by employees, customers, suppliers, agents, others in whom trust is placed, and competitors and ex-employees. Most are motivated by greed and a belief that their dishonesty will not be detected. These days, organized criminal syndicates are heavily involved in corporate fraud, and so are professional con men. Without being paranoid, the list of potential opponents is virtually unlimited. But the good news is that the greatest strength is an honest, principled workforce trained to ask questions and to react effectively when things seem out of place.

Basic Measures: Now!

THE PRINCIPLES

Obviously, prevention is better than cure, and a few simple measures can reduce the likelihood that an organization will be victimized by fraud.

RISKS APPRAISAL AND COMPLIANCE

Firstly, all employees should be trained so that they understand the risks in the operations under their control. This can be achieved through a process of *Control Self-Assessment* (see <http://www.mc2consulting.com>), through which employees review risks and controls, and agree between themselves on the improvements necessary. Risks may also be identified by internal auditors or specialist consultants.

Secondly, all organizations should have continuing intelligence on the sorts of frauds that occur in their sectors and the people who might commit them. The modern Internal Audit Department (or Corporate Security function) should take on intelligence responsibilities by routinely searching news services (such as *Reuters' Business Briefing*), the Internet, and liaising with other organizations so that risks can be avoided.

It is also very important that compliance responsibilities are understood and that awareness spreads through the bloodstream of the organization. These days, there are simply so many laws, rules, regulations and guidelines that compliance cannot be left to luck or sporadic advice from some old buffer remote from the workforce.

If the organization does not understand its compliance obligations, it is easy to make mistakes – and if these are concealed, very serious problems can result. In fact fraud and concealment of failure to comply with laws, rules and regulations can be regarded as almost equal dangers.

DEFINE VALUES AND FRAUD POLICY

More than twenty years ago, the Treadway Commission (see <www.coso.org>) identified the importance of setting the 'tone from the top' of the organization, and the principle is even more important today. Every organization should set out a clear statement of its core values, and make sure these are followed by employees and third parties with which it deals through its 'extended enterprise'.

It is also vital that larger organizations have a policy on fraud and specified processes covering sensitive issues that can arise in investigations, such as:

* human rights
* interception of communications
* data protection
* computer misuse
* privacy.

The organization's policy on prevention, detection and investigation should be specified in procedures in the cold light of day, rather than being guessed at in panic in the heat of the moment. The important principles are discussed on pages 97 *et seq.*

PREVENTIVE CONTROLS AND OWNERSHIP

The third measure is to maintain effective controls and these fall under the four headings shown in Table 1.1.

To a high degree, controls are compensatory and weaknesses in one area can be solved in

Table 1.1   Types of preventative controls

Type of control	Examples of what is achieved
Physical security	Limited access to premises and assets
	Separation of responsibilities
	Accountability
Policy and process control	Limited access, authorization, balancing and audit trails in accounting and other processes
	Processes for conducting investigations
Due diligence	Validating the integrity of people and organizations before placing trust in them; it should be remembered that every asset and every process is secure if access is only granted to honest people
Technical controls	Physical and logical controls in computer, communications and other infrastructure assets and processes

others. For example, weak process controls can be reinforced by strict integrity validation of those who have access to them.

Every asset and every process must have a designated owner who has the authority for control and the responsibility for failure. This balance between authority and responsibility is critical. The most common reason for control failures – and thus fraud – is that the person who has the authority to improve controls is able to avoid responsibility for failure. He thus has the luxury of doing nothing and, when the disaster inevitably occurs, of blaming someone else.

The cow grows fat under the eyes of the owner.

Lack of ownership and ambiguity between authority and responsibility is especially evident in matrix management systems and in organizations that pride themselves on being empowered; confusion reigns supreme and, in this atmosphere, fraud flourishes.

REACTIVE CONTROLS

Not all frauds can be prevented, so monitoring processes to quickly identify problems act as the safety net. The most important of these is the subject of this book, and focuses on the correct reaction to the first suspicions of dishonesty

RECONSTRUCTIVE CONTROLS

These come into play when preventive and reactive controls fail. They enable the organization to recover, and include contingency plans, backup and insurance. In the fraud area, Fidelity and Computer Crime policies are important, but many organizations do not understand what cover they have or how it is activated. We will return to the key insurance issues in Part 2.

SPECIFICATION OF CONTROLS

Controls can only work when they are specified. This means that they must be set out in writing, in manuals, checklists, flowcharts, on forms, and made known to everyone who is meant to comply with them. They must be supported by good leadership, effective supervision and powerful audit, so that they function as specified. This is all basic stuff, but too many victims of fraud overlook them.

Conclusion

It is usually best to be wise before the event, but lessons can always be learned from the failure of others. Chapter 2 examines fraud's deadly sins.

2 *Deadly Sins*

Blind Pugh's Law

Many (if not most) organizations are woefully unprepared when they discover the symptoms of fraud. Within hours of suspicions being aroused, the investigation is irreparably compromised through incompetence, panic, disbelief, ignorance or, more often, because the managers put in charge of getting the money back were preoccupied with protecting their own backsides.

Because of such fatal failings:

- 85 per cent of fraud victims never get their money back.
- Most investigations flounder, leaving the victim to defend against itself counter-attacks by hostile parties.
- 30 per cent of companies that fail do so as a result of fraud.

This chapter recommends, if you have not already done so, that you develop a policy and simple procedures for reacting when suspicions are first aroused. Obviously, it is much easier to persuade managers to agree policy and procedures in the abstract, where they cannot have any reasonable objection to valid principles, than it is to convince them to take appropriate action in the heat of the moment, in a case in which they are emotionally involved. A policy cuts out the panic and eradicates erratic decisions.

If This were to Happen to You . . .

As usual, you, as Marketing Director for Nice Grub International Ltd, arrive at the office on the 8.15 a.m. train from Cheam and open your mail:

Date as postmarked

Dear Sir,

You should know that for the past four years Robin Blind, your Marketing Manager, and his assistants have been working a scam. They have been selling food products which have been returned by your customers for destruction because they were stale and past their sell-by dates.

Basically, what Blind does is to remove the correct sell-by dates, replacing them with new labels to make it appear that the food is fresh when it is not. The product is then sold to your usual customers, and then on to the public. THESE PRODUCTS ARE DANGEROUS, and I know that at least one person has died from food poisoning as a result. Blind has made at least a million for himself, and his little pals have made the same. I have all the evidence, and I want £5 million to keep quiet.

Contact me with your agreement to pay by placing the following advertisement in the Personal Column of the *Coulsden Weekly News*:

'Muncher come home quickly: Love Mum.'

Also give me a mobile number on which I can contact you.

If you do not do this, keep a lookout on the papers, as I am sure that Rupert Murdoch, Max Hastings and Private Eye will be interested. God knows what will happen to your company from there on.

Yours ever

Muncher

PS Be careful on your office telephone, as Robin has bugged it and knows all about your 'little personal indiscretions': know what I mean?

Now what do you do? Without a plan, the most likely reaction would be to take an extended visit to the bathroom and then panic – and you would be right. Good planning and an effective policy are the answers to fraud's deadly sins.

Each sin is illustrated with cases taken from the real world, although identities have been changed to protect the idiotic and gullible. Each sinful section summarizes the lessons to be learned.

Sin 1: Looking After Their Own Nuts

Employees responsible for managing operations in which fraud took place are made responsible for investigating it.

Putting inexperienced, ignorant, possibly culpable and sometimes crooked employees in charge of an investigation that could result in their own shortcomings being exposed is like asking the monkeys to distribute peanuts equally. Inevitably, some animals will lose their nuts.

THE BANK MANAGER

A major financial institution was defrauded of over £100 million, mainly through fraudulent project financing loans to a group of companies that we will call Snaffle Inc., managed by Robin Crooke. Snaffle Inc. was, in fact, a front for organized criminals with no legitimate business. Mr Joe Snow, Head of Credit, had approved the original advances without making adequate checks, but was put in charge of what he described as a 'credit workout'. He confidently reported to his directors that there would be no problem getting the money back. He appeared relaxed; but inside, his stomach was churning.

Joe's delay in recognizing the obvious – which is typical, and an example of self-deception – allowed the crooks to make a safe escape and to hide their funds even more deeply than they already had. When he realized this, he told no one, but looked in the *Yellow Pages* and retained a firm that claimed it could trace hidden assets: 'Breaking through the veils of off-shore tax havens is our speciality,' proclaimed the advert. Joe liked the sound of this, as a bit of 'hanky panky' did harm to no one.

The asset tracers first obtained (albeit illegally) the itemized telephone billing records of Snaffle Inc. and its directors, and tracked banks they had called. The asset tracers then telephoned these banks, posing as, among other things, accountants, bankers, lawyers, doctors and priests, and asked for confirmation that Snaffle Inc. 'was good for £10 million' or whatever amount took their fancy. Based on these unreliable and illegal findings, they advised Joe that Snaffle Inc. had funds at banks in Switzerland, Germany and the Isle of Man.

Joe was delighted, retained the small firm of lawyers where his daughter was a trainee solicitor, and asked the partners to seize the monies which the asset tracers had identified. Although the firm had little litigation experience, Joe thought that recovery would be simple. Initially, so did the lawyers. Joe thought passing business to them would improve his daughter's career.

After a few promising meetings, the lawyers said there was no 'evidence' on which to base a seizure order, and that, in any case, they would be totally unable to use the information gained by the asset tracers. Joe did not understand what they meant by the word 'evidence' – after all, the asset tracers had reported there was money to be had, so what was the problem?

The lawyers explained, and cautioned Joe that mere acceptance of the illegally obtained bank information and telephone records exposed him to criminal charges of deception, or worse. The colour drained from Joe's face – he did not like the idea of jail. He was so worried that he took his file home and burned it in the garden.

Things were now getting serious, and Joe called in the bank's Head of Inspection, insisting that he should report the case to the police so that they could track the disappearing debtors and get the bank's money back. The Inspector, being junior to Joe and something of a creep, complied without demur. 'Yes, of course, Joe,' he said, and rushed off without any real idea of what was expected of him. There was nothing unusual in his being confused, and he could not wait to get transferred out of inspection into what his wife said was a 'proper job', where he could lord it over customers, play golf, and have lots of lovely long lunches. He did not like being an inspector.

A few weeks later, the police reported

that they had traced Robin Crooke, and when Joe heard this, he insisted that the Head of Inspection should do the same. 'If PC Plod can trace him, anyone can,' Joe said. The inspector did as he was told, and using the dodgy asset tracers, tracked Robin to a villa in the Algarve, where he was living with his latest girlfriend and her fat and ugly mother.

Joe and the Inspector ambushed Robin in his Algarvian retreat as he was just about to barbecue a pig. Robin was not pleased by the appearance of the uninvited guests, and threw them out. The badly crestfallen Joe stood on the drive of the villa shouting obscenities and making threats which were less than veiled. Robin came out and hit him with a shovel. The distinguished Head of Credit was rushed to hospital with a broken arm and hurt pride.

When the police investigating the fraud heard what had happened, they warned Joe that he should not have approached witnesses or defendants, and that he would be reported for attempting to pervert the course of justice. Joe felt battered and bruised, but he still reported to his managers that the 'case was focused' and that he was 'confident the full amount would be recovered'. Deep down, he knew differently, but his managers were desperate to swallow the sort of news they wanted to hear, and did not ask questions. Besides that, if Joe was prepared to take the responsibility, why should they worry?

From this point, the case went from bad to worse; the police dropped the prosecution, and the bank eventually had to write off its losses. While Joe was living out his detective fantasies, other business went down the tubes, and the bank faced a string of new losses. But irony of ironies, Joe was promoted to a new position in Asia and, no doubt, will live happily ever after. We saw him the other day, and he looked happy enough, in spite of the scar left by the shovel.

COMMENTS AND LESSONS: SIN 1

Everything is easier to get into than to get out of. The reliability of people and organizations in whom trust is to be placed should be checked before a commitment is made. The checking should be independent and professional.

The person potentially responsible for a loss should never be allowed to investigate it. There are two reasons for this:
- The investigation must be independent – this protects both the organization and the line manager in whose area dishonesty is suspected.
- Line managers must concentrate on their routine business.

Advisers who offer the impossible or who agree to break the law should be avoided at all costs. In fact, every organization should select and screen the advisers it might need to use in an emergency *now*, before the disaster strikes.

Not all people working in inspection, audit, security and investigations either like, or are good at, the job. Make sure you have professional advisers available to you.

The police are not debt collectors.

Once you report a case to the police, do nothing to impede their investigations.

Sin 2: Driving an Investigation on Costs

Conflicts of interests of the type previously described are made even worse when the department in which fraud is suspected has to absorb legal and investigative costs.

This sin arbitrarily misdirects the investigation and allows the perverse or protective manager to starve it of funding, thus ensuring his deficiencies are not exposed.

ESCORTS GALORE

An investigation was moving along just fine, driven by a team of external lawyers and consultants reporting to a director of a bank. He had been very positive throughout, and the team was confident it would recover many millions of dollars under fidelity insurance. Then the client's support suddenly disappeared. Invoices from the lawyers and consultants were not paid, and the director's deputy questioned every line of enquiry and its cost.

Before long, the case ran out of steam and then collapsed. The director blamed the consultants for the failure, saying that they were 'too greedy, had lost focus and were going nowhere'. His managers accepted this excuse, since they didn't like paying consultants either.

A few months later, the real reason for upsetting the lawyers and consultants emerged. It appears that one evening, the main suspect working for the bank called on the director and warned him that if the investigation continued, some very fruity photographs and tape recordings of his sexual misbehaviour with escorts whilst overseas on the bank's business might materialize.

The director was terrified and wanted to comply, but did not wish to put his neck on the line by terminating the investigation. However, he achieved the same result by not paying the advisers' bills and by nitpicking, causing them to withdraw.

The bottom line was that suppression of the director's indiscretions cost the bank $20 million. But the problem has not really gone away, and if the shareholders were to ever discover the truth, all hell would break loose.

When personal interests conflict with fiduciary responsibilities, the usual loser is the victim organization. Bad guys protect themselves first.

COMMENTS AND LESSONS: SIN 2

Investigations should be driven by objectives and a clear action plan based on the principle of finding the truth, the whole truth and nothing but the truth in the most cost-effective way. At the start of an investigation, it is likely that the victim sees less than 10 per cent of the picture. When actions are driven primarily by a desire to avoid costs, the investigation will fail.

When an investigation is successful, costs can be recovered. For example, it is more cost-effective to spend £200 000 on an investigation which recovers £10 million than it is to spend £20 on one that recovers nothing.

However, costs should not be incurred if the best available professional advice (not subjective guesses by inexperienced employees) indicates that potential recoveries are not worth the effort.

The costs of investigations and recoveries should – at least initially – be charged to a central overhead, and not to the budget of the department in which the dishonesty occurred.

As a general rule, legal, investigative and recovery costs amount to 10 per cent of the funds defrauded. There are, of course, exceptions, but this is a good yardstick.

The best advisers are those who tell you when you are wrong.

Sin 3: Personal Financial Interests

To protect their own rear ends or to conceal their culpability, some managers wilfully fail to respond to the symptoms of fraud.

The line manager who is put in charge of investigating a case which could result in his censure is in an impossible position. In such circumstances, the only loser is the organization which employs him.

THE CHAIRMAN OF THE AUDIT COMMITTEE

At a 1998 fraud seminar, a delegate – who was a very senior representative of a leading listed company – approached one of the speakers after the close of the day's session. He explained to the speaker and the seminar organizer that he was Chairman of his company's Audit Committee, and that in the past few weeks he had received reliable information that the company had been defrauded of at least £100 million.

The alleged scam was based on the purchase of land for building development in an emerging country. He said he had told no one, and had avoided the last two Board meetings because he could not bear to face people he was sure were dishonest. The Chairman was obviously a nice, ethical man.

The Chairman said he had been told that a group of his company's senior managers had set up a trust in Switzerland which had taken an option to buy the land from the real vendor for £60 million. Then, based on false reports from compliant surveyors and architects, they had convinced their colleagues on the Board that the company should buy the land for £160 million. The case to justify the purchase was, apparently, very convincing, and well within the company's investment criteria.

The land was duly bought, with the switch deal through the Swiss trust making the senior managers a cool £100 million profit. However, a year later the company discovered that the land was totally unsuitable: the gradients and subsoil were such that the actual building densities were less than 50 per cent of those indicated in the proposal to invest.

The Chairman said that the legal position in the countries concerned was very clear, and it was equally clear that at the end of the financial year the loss would have to be reflected in the company's accounts.

He asked what he should do. The speaker said he would be happy to make a few background checks without charge, and these confirmed the Chairman's suspicions. The Chairman asked for a written proposal for the speaker's company to carry out a detailed investigation. This was faxed to him the next day.

A few weeks went by before the Chairman responded. His letter concluded:

> It will be difficult for me to get your proposed appointment approved by the Board, as the Managing Director, Deputy Managing Director and Executive Director are three of the five persons now under suspicion and 'delicate investigation'. The fourth suspect is the General Manager who resigned suddenly, apparently on the advice of his superiors with the purpose of frustrating our enquiry trail. I don't have the financial authority as Audit Committee Chairman to make the appointment proposed. What should I do?

The speaker answered that he should resign immediately, to try to minimize his personal liabilities. The seminar organizer, who had been in regular contact with the Chairman, responded:

> Resigning is out of the question, as he is not a wealthy man. What is your alternative approach? I detected that he was somewhat offended and flabbergasted by your suggestion of his resigning. Are you jesting?

The speaker's response to this was that the recommendation was not a joke and that the Chairman was sitting on a timebomb: '. . . if he does not do something now and the case becomes public, he could be in a very serious personal position. I suggest that he consults a lawyer without delay.'

This was the last to be heard of the case, and over a year has passed. The Chairman is still in place, drawing his fees and, as far as we can see, the land is valued in the company's published accounts at £160 million.

But sooner or later the house of cards must fall. Who knows, as we only get to know of concealments that fail? The Chairman may escape with his life intact, but he may not. If the public shareholders ever heard about the case, they would be less than delighted, as the write-off of the useless land would reduce the company's market capitalization by 15 per cent.

COMMENTS AND LESSONS: SIN 3

The difference between a supermarket trolley and an Audit Committee member has been described thus: 'The first has a mind of its own, but the second holds more booze and food.' Audit Committees must be effective.

Personal financial interests should never be permitted to interfere with an employee's fiduciary duties.

Senior managers who take decisions to favour their private interests or personal career development render themselves impotent in all other cases.

Sin 4: Giving in to Blackmail

In most serious cases, crooks counter-attack and make threats to harm the victim. These are mainly bluffs, but when they are not, the allegations must be faced head-on.

Impotence is especially obvious when senior managers knowingly break the law.

THE SOVIET CASE

A few years ago the Marketing Manager of a major top-class European company made a presentation to the Directors, urging them to authorize his proposed visit to Moscow to see if there was a market for its products. A few weeks later, the manager made a further presentation, supported by colourful overheads, diagrams and projections. There was only one problem, he explained, which was that a senior Russian official wanted a one-time bribe of £1 million.

Being good, honest, trustworthy members of the business community, the Board took about ten seconds to approve the payment. The manager then explained that the Former Soviet Union was short of hard currency, and that for the first few years the company would have to keep its prices very low. Shipments went forward, and everyone was pleased – presumably on the basis that what it lost on margin it made up on volume.

Then, out of the blue, the company's subsidiaries in India and Pakistan complained that products were flooding the local markets at prices with which they could not compete. Investigations established that product destined for the Former Soviet Union had been diverted. The manager was interviewed, and readily admitted that he had never visited Moscow, and had no plans to do so; that he had kept the £1 million for himself, and that he had helped himself to another £4 million from the sales of product in India and Pakistan.

The directors were more than shocked at such affrontery, and bayed for his blood. They soon modified their views when the manager told them he had tape recorded the Board meeting giving him approval to pay the bribe, and coolly asked the Directors what they intended to do about it. The response, unsurprisingly, was 'Nothing.' He is now working as an auditor for a leading European organization.

COMMENTS AND LESSONS: SIN 4

Integrity cannot be slightly compromised.

Employees asked to act dishonestly, supposedly in the company's interest, are its most serious liability.

Once a manager gives in to blackmail, he is forever compromised.

What an organization loses on profit is not made up by turnover.

Risks and rewards vary inversely. It is critical that high risks are compensated through effective contingency plans.

Sin 5: Unrealistic Expectations

Managers who have no experience of fraud and watch too much television believe that investigations are easy, fast, cheap and must be successful.

Everyone believes himself to possess a gargantuan intellect, to be an excellent driver and lover, very good-looking, witty and kind – and a super fraud investigator. Of these, the last is the most dangerous delusion. Investigating fraud is a difficult job, best reserved for specialists.

FLAPPER LTD

Flapper Ltd had been defrauded of £20 million on an investment in an emerging country. Retained lawyers and forensic accountants were making steady progress, but it was a difficult and dangerous case, with organized crime involvement. Tom, the senior line manager, was less than impressed, and decided to take matters into his own hands.

He told his Board: 'These people are deliberately dragging things out. It may be good for their fees, but not for us. I am getting on to this myself.'

Ignoring expert advice, he went to the country concerned, and to make matters worse, took his wife along, 'to see a bit of rough'. They booked into the capital's best hotel (which is not saying much), and Tom set about seeing the crooks and generally stirring the pot. One morning, someone telephoned his hotel, and told

him that if he was not out of the country on the next flight, he would be dead.

Tom had learned from television that 'when the going gets tough, the tough get going' and he – a Rambo fan – was not about to be put off by a few local toerags. He hired a guard company for protection, and continued about his business. That night, on returning to his hotel, there was a note that his wife had been kidnapped and that she would be released only when Tom had boarded the next plane for home. He reported the case to hotel security, local management and the police, and they all urged him to comply. Even Tom recognized he had no option. Although he did as instructed, he never saw his wife again. Cynical readers might ask if this was a ploy to get rid of his missus, but we think not.

COMMENTS AND LESSONS : SIN 5

Investigations can be:
- easy, fast and cheap, but not successful
- fast, easy and successful, but not cheap
- successful, but not cheap, fast or easy.

Wise people never bite off more than they can chew.

Line managers manage lines: investigators investigate.

The determination and violence of fraudsters should never be underestimated.

The fact is, most managers do not understand fraud – but that does not prevent them making expert pronouncements on its finer details. This makes it imperative that fraud awareness is promoted through training courses and in bulletins prepared by Audit and Security. When line managers know the score, they are less likely to act irrationally. When they have to comply with a Fraud Policy, the risks are reduced even further.

Sin 6: Falling for Bad Advice

The advice the victim takes in the hours after discovery determines the outcome of an investigation.

Few companies have the foggiest idea to whom they would turn to advise them in a difficult investigation. Appointments made in the heat of the moment can determine the outcome, and there is some dreadful advice about.

THE FRAUD ADVISORY PANEL

The FAP is at the leading edge of the Institute of Chartered Accountants' (ICAEW) fight against crime. In 1998, the Panel, headed by a top solicitor and staffed by a team of nine Fraud Gurus, published a handbook called 'It's Fraud – The Threat to Business'. Practice Note 6 set out guidelines for conducting investigations, and suggested the following first steps:

• **Gather and protect the evidence.**
✓ GOOD, but do so without alerting the suspects.

• **Decide whether to tell the suspect he is being investigated.**
✗ WRONG. The first move you take should surprise the crooks, with the object of catching them in an act they cannot legitimately explain, allowing the investigators to seize the initiative.

• **Consider suspension on full pay while the investigation continues.**
✗ WRONG, especially if you have not already decided to carry out a full investigation.

• **Then decide whether a full investigation is justified.**
✗ WRONG. It is a bit late to think about this when the suspect has already been alerted, and possibly suspended.

The advice borders on the nonsensical, and is compounded later in the handbook by equally unwise recommendations. However, to be fair, the Practice Note was not issued following our suggestions. Given the undoubted skill of the panel members, it has to be assumed that either they did not have time to check the handbook as thoroughly as they would have liked, or they fell for the Cynic's First Rule on Committees, which concludes that:

The aggregate IQ of a committee varies inversely with the number of its members.

Simply stated, this means that the more people there are on a committee, the dafter it is.

Maybe it is a bit unfair to criticize when the Fraud Gurus were giving free advice in a hurry. They might be much more effective when the fee clock is ticking away, or all of the bad advice could have been a double-bluff to lead crooks into a false sense of security.

In most cases, bad advice frightens victims into believing that because of such things as the Data Protection Act, the Human Rights Act, the Privacy Act, European laws, the Curvature of Bananas (Going Straight) Bill, and other rules, regulations, laws, guidelines and edicts, they are helpless in the fight against fraud. This is not so, but in every serious case of fraud, the advice of top-level specialists is justified.

COMMENTS AND LESSONS: SIN 6

Every organization should have expert resources available to investigate fraud. It is generally more cost-effective to have these in house and to retain consultants for specialist tasks in particularly difficult cases, or where additional resources are essential.

Advisers should never be selected in the heat of the moment. Any organization which does not have internal resources should test the market and prepare a list of consultants – showing the names of qualified individuals – before the event, as part of its Fraud Policy.

Managers should listen to what consultants advise, but if they want eggs, they should not buy a goat.

Many people who are supposed Fraud Gurus have little practical experience. Their advice is as valuable as a Trappist monk's pronouncements on breakdancing.

At the other end of the scale, there are investigators who cut corners or behave illegally, with dire consequences for their clients. The asset tracers discussed in Sin 1 are an example, but there are plenty of others:

THE PHARMA CASE

The Head of Security for a pharmaceuticals company was concerned that its products were being counterfeited, and he retained a small firm of private investigators to look into two competitors based in the Eastern Mediterranean. The investigators were arrested as they were about to leave the country, and were found to be in possession of documents allegedly stolen from the offices of the counterfeiters.

The police later established that the offices had been broken into, and the men received stiff jail terms. The Head of Security tried to buy the men's silence, but this did not work and they made serious allegations of complicity against him and his employer. He was fired, and his company's trademark enforcement efforts were left in tatters.

All professional investigative or forensic accounting firms have clear policies on the standards they will maintain, and most likely will be members of appropriate professional organizations. Even so, great care must be taken (even with reputable firms) where subcontractors are used.

THE *MAIL ON SUNDAY*

In December 1991, the *Mail on Sunday* reported: 'The two Britons arrested by the Swiss last month on charges of illegally spying on Swiss companies are under investigation by the British police for similar activities.

In particular, the police are investigating an alleged attempt they made to plant a bugging device inside a computer software company in Poole, Dorset. The Metropolitan Police Fraud Squad has gathered information from Swiss and Dorset Police.

The two men are Christopher Clark, a 27-year-old private detective who has his own agency in Cricklewood, North London, and businessman Antony Blythe, aged 44. It is now known that they were on an assignment for Kroll Associates, the leading US-based corporate investigations agency, for a fee of £1000 per day plus performance-linked bonuses.

MORE COMMENTS AND LESSONS: SIN 6

The cheaper the advice, the more expensive the consequences.

No organization should use its own external accountants to investigate fraud, because if the investigation is successful it may prove negligence by their audit practice. This is a serious conflict of interest.

Sin 7: Relying on Old Friends

Managers may assume that friends will help them in times of trouble.

It is true that fraud can bring out the worst in people, and this is particularly so when large financial exposures are threatened; then it is every man for himself.

BARINGS: DECEMBER 1995

In December 1995, in response to being sued for $1 billion for permitting the bank's collapse, Coopers & Lybrand issued writs against eight of Barings' former managers, alleging that if they '. . . had performed their duties, Leeson would not have been able to incur loss making trades, and such unauthorized trading would have been discovered and should have been brought to an end'.

Various former directors were blamed for introducing a matrix management system, and for not permitting an investigation into Mr Leeson's activities.

You cannot blame the auditors for protecting their own positions, and no doubt most people would do the same. The point is that relationships break down under pressure. The relationship with insurers may also suffer when a serious fraud is uncovered.

COMMENTS AND LESSONS: SIN 7

External auditors should not be retained to investigate suspected fraud, as they may end up suing the victim's directors and officers for contributory negligence.

When the going gets tough, the tough first look out for themselves.

FIDELITY INSURERS ARE HERE TO HELP YOU

Fidelity insurance should be the final safety net against major fraud, yet it is more often a trampoline. No insurer likes to pay out, and this is understandable. If there is any defect under the policy, cover will be denied, often for one of the following reasons:

- There is no proof that the dishonest employee intended to gain for himself.
- He is not really an employee.
- The claim falls under the loan, trading or other esoteric exclusion.

One of the most difficult objections to deal with is that the employer had prior knowledge of the employee's dishonesty and failed to notify the underwriters. The policy terms vary, but generally cover is immediately invalidated when someone not in collusion with the employee learns of any prior dishonesty and fails to notify insurers. Thus if an employee tells you tomorrow that as a child he stole someone's bicycle and you do not report it, the employee's cover may be out of the window. The exclusion on some policies is more specific, and the dishonesty has to be work-related.

But if you catch Johnny Smith fiddling his expenses and decide to issue him with a written warning without telling the underwriters, his cover could be withdrawn. If he subsequently defrauds his employer of £100 million, that loss may not be insured.

You should never expect an easy ride from insurers. As one told the *Inside Fraud Bulletin* about computer crime insurance: 'It is a bloody wonderful policy with lots and lots and lots of premium income and absolutely no coverage.' The cynical view of this underwriter is not representative, but it should serve as a warning.

Finally, under most policies, the underwriter is entitled to all of the victim's rights and is therefore able to take legal action – effectively in the victim's name – against anyone potentially liable. Thus the underwriter may sue the victim's external auditors, bankers, advisers, and its directors and officers.

Threats of such actions are a disincentive to the victim's pursuit of a claim, since ultimately they could lead to the underwriter reimbursing the victim organization for the loss whilst making an equivalent recovery from the personal funds of its directors and employees. If, for this reason, the victim drops the insurance claim, it and its directors and officers are liable to shareholders in a dreadful no-win conflict.

MORE COMMENTS AND LESSONS: SIN 7

When fraud is discovered, it is each man for himself, and don't expect any favours.

Although fraud is a corporate problem, the personal future of good employees may be on the line.

Problems are best avoided.

Everything that could threaten a future claim should be reported to underwriters.

Standard subrogation clauses in fidelity insurance policies are dangerous and, where possible, should be amended.

Sin 8: Wilful Blindness

Through lack of experience, determination – or sometimes for worse reasons – employees fail to recognize or react even to blatant symptoms of fraud.

One of the greatest sins has been left towards the end, and that concerns the unwillingness of some managers to accept the truth. It is well known that people who are kidnapped develop a rapport with the kidnappers. This is known as the 'Stockholm Syndrome', a phrase coined after a failed 1973 bank robbery in the Swedish capital in which four hostages were taken.

The quartet resisted efforts to liberate them, and one actually later got engaged to one of the captors. In fraud, there is 'Blind Pugh's Law', when victims stubbornly close their eyes to the obvious.

THE SNOW JOB

In the course of general research, Maxima gathered evidence that a senior manager of the British subsidiary of a Continental European company had been taking kickbacks of £6000 a month for the past five years as a reward for permitting a vendor to overcharge by at least £1 million a year.

The evidence was conclusive, consisting of copy invoices from two dummy companies set up by the manager and paid by the vendor, and copies of bank documents and the vendor's calculations of its overcharging.

Maxima checked with its lawyers, and their advice was to inform the victim's parent company at the highest level, and to pass over the evidence without any obligation. As Maxima did not know anyone at the parent company, it checked with other contacts, and an introduction was made to the Chairman.

To say that he was far from pleased at the news would be the grossest understatement. In immaculate English, he said: 'I don't like to hear about these things in my company. Why are you speaking to me about this?'

Maxima explained the evidence, and that it had been advised by its lawyers that the right and proper thing to do was to tell him. He clearly did not agree, and said: 'We are divided into functional businesses in this company, and I will speak to the manager concerned, and if he is interested, he will contact you.' Maxima reiterated that it was prepared to pass over the information through its lawyers without obligation. But everything went silent.

Months went by until a multi-million-dollar bid was made for the European parent company. Maxima was approached by its lawyers, and through its own advisers handed over the evidence without charge or obligation. It should have been sufficient for the company to recover at least £6 million and to rid itself of a very crooked senior manager. A year has gone by. The acquisition was completed, and the dishonest manager remains in place.

COMMENTS AND LESSONS: SIN 8

Not everyone can be convinced to do the right thing: this is especially true when the convincing is needed in the heat of the moment.

A Fraud Policy reduces the risks of perversely making bad decisions in the heat of the moment.

Sin 9: Blind Pugh's Law II

Once the suspicions of fraud have been aroused, there is a two-way obligation to resolve them: firstly, to the company to get the money back, and secondly, to clear people wrongfully suspected.

The first step is to establish the facts. The following case relates to poor or weak investigative processes. Sometimes, the greatest obligation is towards the person wrongly suspected.

THE BRAND MANAGER

Allegations were made against a senior and very successful brand manager to the effect that he had taken bribes for passing business to an advertising agency. His managers decided not to probe the allegations, believing incorrectly that an investigation would result in adverse publicity. However, they transferred the manager to low-level work, but refused to explain why. He became depressed, and killed himself. At the inquest, the facts were revealed, the allegations were proven to be false, and the employer was heavily censured for its lack of action.

In this case, the company's decision not to investigate cost the life of a good employee, and it is usually the organization and honest employees that suffer the most.

COMMENTS AND LESSONS: SIN 9

Suspicions must be resolved by first establishing the facts.

Problems are not solved by ignoring them.

Sin 10: Going for Fool's Gold

Providing the crook will pay some of the money back and resign, some foolish managers are prepared to let the matter drop.

In some cases, as part of the deal, they will provide the crook with a nice reference so that he can defraud future employers.

The short-term attraction of grabbing back some money blinds managers to the long-term damage to the deterrence of dishonesty.

THE AGREEMENT

In 1997, a major company lost £5 million through a fraud perpetrated by a senior manager. He was caught by accident, and offered to pay back everything which had been stolen. The agreement between him and the company was drafted by lawyers as follows:

THIS AGREEMENT
is made this _____ day of _____
one thousand nine hundred and ninety eight

BETWEEN
XYZ Limited whose registered office is at
123 High Street, Nowhere
("The Employer") and;
Bill Thief of 3 The Close, New Town
("The Employee")

WHEREAS
A   The Employee has admitted to fraudulently obtaining benefits in relation to his duties with the Employer

B   The parties have agreed that no action will be taken to prosecute or inform third parties of such admissions, including the police

Despite the fact that the agreement was meant to be strictly confidential, many employees soon learned of it, and were horrified. To a few others, it was an invitation to defraud.

COMMENTS AND LESSONS: SIN 10

Short-term decisions based on expediency usually corrupt principles.

In fraud, a bird in the hand is worth nothing in the bush.

If a crook offers to pay back what he has stolen, take it – but continue with the prosecution.

Deterrence is critical to good control.

'We can do them fast and good but not cheap, or cheap but neither fast nor good.'

Sin 11: Failing to Recover

By not making every effort to establish the truth, victims forfeit the chance of recovery.

The first step in every investigation must be to find the truth. When this principle is ignored, serious consequences can result.

BANKERS

An American bank incurred bad debts of over £30 million when one of its customers filed for bankruptcy and disappeared. The bank officer who had handled the account reported that the debts were irrecoverable. Subsequent investigations revealed that the officer had received kickbacks of around £50 000 from the borrower on an earlier and paid-up loan. A substantial recovery, plus interest, was made from the bank's fidelity insurers.

COMMENTS AND LESSONS: SIN 11

In all but exceptional cases, there are always viable methods of recovery. Effective investigation identifies these.

If you don't look, you don't find.

Sin 12: Ultimate Gullibility

Managers will find every reason for not prosecuting – and if they can't find one they will make one up.

GOD'S LITTLE WONDER

Tommy Taylor stole £100 000 from ABC Ltd and admitted his sins to his manager. If anyone was facing a term of imprisonment, Tommy was – until God intervened. The day after making his admissions, Tommy and his tearful wife saw the Head of Personnel and explained that he had a terminal illness and was unlikely to live for more than a few months. A letter from his doctor – backed up by very bleak test results – confirmed the tragic news.

Human Resources, being nice loveable types, recommended that Tommy be allowed to resign and die in peace. Any idea of prosecuting him was abandoned. In fact, he was given time (something of an irony under the circumstances) to repay.

A few months later, Tommy appeared on a national television show (*The Gladiators*), and was a picture of health. God had miraculously intervened with a miraculous cure, and six years later, Tommy is still alive and well, and probably still cherishing the letter supposedly from his doctor and test results that his wife had dutifully forged on her laptop computer.

Such miracles happen between the time the crook is detected and excused. If medical practitioners were able to identify what metaphysical changes take place in the bodies of crooks between detection and absolution, all health problems would be solved

COMMENTS AND LESSONS: SIN 12

Excuses should always be investigated.

The hardest line possible should always be taken with crooks as a deterrent to others.

Benefits of a Fraud Policy

An effective Fraud Policy and defined processes for handling investigations can eliminate all of the deadly sins and achieve the victim's objectives.

If you don't have a policy, now is the time to get one. It will be too late when it happens.The essential aspects are set out in Chapter 5.

'That was always your problem, Comer – too bloody self-opinionated!'

3 The Criminal and Civil Law in England

Introduction

THE HEALTH WARNING

This chapter provides a working-class overview of the English legal system, explaining the practical legal problems faced in fraud investigations, and their solution. It contains two serious health warnings. Firstly, it is cynical – bordering on reactionary – and if you like reading *The Independent*, or believe in the Tooth Fairy, you won't like what follows. Secondly, it contains a sort of pseudo-legal opinion by a non-lawyer, and, worse still, suggests what you can – rather than the usual can't – do. In short, it is disgraceful, and is akin to allowing the hospital janitor to carry out brain surgery with a buzz saw. So let's buzz away, but please remember that what follows is not a substitute for specific legal advice, and that for every law or rule there is at least one alternative of equal strength.

POLITICAL INTERESTS

People involved in fraud can be viewed as being divided into five distinct groups. The first are the English politicians who come into the world full of vision, principles, goodness – bordering on sainthood – and mature rapidly to the age of 12, and then stop. They can be distinguished from European politicians, who reach their peak of maturity at the age of six. Whatever their ethnic background, politicians soon realize that their main goal in life is to stay in power. To do this, they must avoid making real decisions, and appease the masses. This is easy, providing they don't make rude remarks about the European Union, David Beckham or interfere with *Coronation Street*. The only serious blip on the political joy screen arises because the European smelly-socks keep insisting that new laws be introduced to conform with some esoteric convention or right. This must be an irritating inconvenience, and an interference with long, philosophical lunches at Langan's or weekends in Cowes.

There are two common threads to recent legislation regarding fraud. The first is that companies – and their managers – are being held to ever higher standards of compliance, while the necessary tools are being removed. If you want simple examples, just look at money laundering or human rights laws, regulations, rules and procedures. The second point is that the application of the criminal law to fraud has been eroded to the point of being a joke. Victims have to fend for themselves, and that is why they need to retain good lawyers and investigators and turn to the civil law.

DRACULA IN CHARGE OF THE BLOODBANK

The second group vaguely interested in fraud consists of senior civil servants, heads of quangos, some main board directors, the confederations and associations, drafters of rules and regulations, senior government officers and judges in the European Court of Human Rights.

These well-meaning people are sometimes referred to as 'Mandarins' or 'Sir Humphreys', and they give life to the machinations of politicians. A lot of these inscrutable men live in Cheam, Surbiton or Islington, have two children named Tarquin and Amanda-Jane, and take their vacations in Tuscany. Some even drive Volvos, or worse still, Citroen C5s, in the mistaken belief that they are environmentally friendly.

Unfortunately, both children and parents have no idea what life is like in the real world – how criminals think or live. They show boundless compassion to criminals, while totally ignoring the plight of victims. The result is that legal guidelines and regulatory interpretations are even weaker than the laws on which they are supposedly based. For a classic example, see the OFTEL guidelines issued after the European Court of Human Rights case involving Allison Halford (*Halford* v. *UK* 1997) which is discussed in detail on pages 44–45.

THE GREAT UNWASHED

The third group is made up of the great unwashed: the police, the security services, Customs & Excise, public and private investigators, and commercial managers. These poor blighters have to try to maximize profits, secure jobs and contain crime while being shackled by political and interpretative weakness and misguided do-gooding. They are often viewed by the other groups in the same 'below stairs' category as butlers and maids, but are nice to speak to momentarily at the Christmas party. Chances are, if you are reading this, you fall into this sad group, so remember you are not alone, and *don't give up*.

CROOKS AND CHATTERERS

The fourth group is made up of crooks, who live on their wits, are streetwise, and basically don't give a damn about the laws and the smelly-socked, chattering classes who want to give away the rights of good people and organizations. Through weakness and apathy, society is playing into the hands of the fraudsters, and by the time the truth is realized, it will be too late.

LAWYERS

The last group, of course, consists of lawyers (Bless!). Some are excellent – almost bordering on super-human – and a few are just awful. The golden rule on major investigations is to have the best, toughest, case-hardened litigation lawyers on your side. This is priority one, and it cannot be said often enough.

CRAP ADVICE

In a recent £20 million fraud case, a Queen's Counsel, a barrister and a solicitor pronounced and agreed:

- An investigations report, marked 'Strictly Confidential. For Legal Advice and In Contemplation of Legal Proceedings' and produced for the sole purpose of obtaining legal advice, had to be disclosed to the opposition.
- The victim company should maintain 'the marginal moral high ground' by not seeking to apply for Search and Freezing Orders against the accused.

- Orders against third parties for disclosure (Norwich Pharmicals, in this case) were 'uncharted territory', and virtually impossible to obtain.
- They could not present critical evidence to the judge 'as it would be beyond his capability to understand it'.

The client and the aging investigator were both flabber and gasted at such ill-informed and pompous nonsense. The Counsel was fired, and more sensible alternatives appointed.

In most cases, bad lawyers get away with bad advice because clients and the great unwashed are afraid to challenge them. This is a mistake, and lawyers have the same frailties as normal human beings, and the same ability to flannel when they don't know the answer. So don't accept everything a lawyer (or even, for that matter, an investigator) says as gospel. The good news is that judges in the English courts (and especially the High Court) are mostly superb.

Structure of the English Courts

The English courts are structured as shown in Figure 3.1.

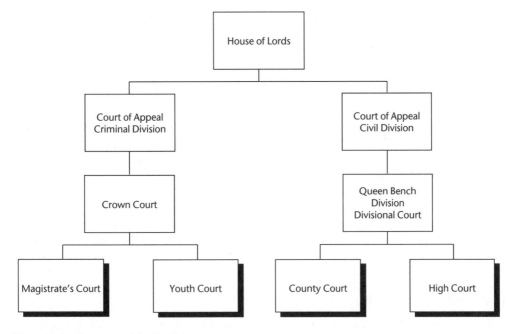

Figure 3.1   Structure of the English courts

Obviously, the main division is between the civil and criminal courts. The significant features are discussed below. The English legal system is adversarial, and rests on three pillars. The first is that the court should hear the whole truth. The second is that innocence should be presumed. The third is that those involved in proceedings should be able to obtain unvarnished advice from their lawyers in total confidence under the cloak of *legal professional privilege*.

The Criminal Law

SCOPE

Fraud victims have rights of recovery under both the civil and criminal law, although many completely overlook the former, and thus reduce their chances of recovery.

The criminal law is defined by statute or practice, and breaches can result in punishment being imposed by the State, including imprisonment, restraining orders and financial penalties. Examples of crimes include theft, murder, treason, robbery and fraud. Also, *attempts* to commit crimes are usually punishable under the criminal law. The principal focus of the criminal justice system is to punish and deter but, judging by recent cases, this is not always obvious.

HOW ACTIONS ARE STARTED AND PROCESSED

Most criminal prosecutions are undertaken by government organizations, such as the police, Customs and Excise or Inland Revenue, but are usually based on a complaint by a victim. The suspect may be arrested or summonsed to appear in court on a specified date. The prosecution is managed by an official body such as the Crown Prosecution Service (CPS), the Serious Fraud Office (SFO) or a regulatory agency.

A victim may also start a private criminal prosecution by applying to a magistrate's court for a summons, requiring the accused to appear at a set date and time. Private prosecutions are both rare and hazardous, and may be taken over and abandoned at any time by the Director of Public Prosecutions.

Even when criminal prosecutions are successful, any financial penalties are paid to the government, not to the victim. Equally, the costs of the prosecution are borne by the State. Thus, in criminal prosecutions, the State takes control, and the victim assumes a secondary position.

Some important differences between the objectives of fraud victims, and the police and public prosecutors are described in Table 3.1.

In most cases, to get their money back, fraud victims have to take civil actions or negotiate. However, it should be noted that from 1 November 2000, the Criminal Proceedings Amendment Act (CPAA) 2000 permitted fraud victims to apply to the police – through their lawyers – to inspect their case files. The extent to which any evidence obtained can be used in civil proceedings is, as yet, unclear.

STANDARDS OF PROOF

To succeed with a criminal complaint, the prosecution has to prove – to the satisfaction of

Table 3.1   Different objectives of police and civil investigations

Police prosecution (or Regulatory Agency)	Victim company's objectives
The police aim at a successful prosecution on a number of specimen charges.	The victim needs to establish the full extent of the loss to maximize its recoveries.
The police are not concerned with making financial recoveries.	This may be a top priority for the victim.
The police expect unrestricted access to evidence in the possession of the victim.	The police have to release all evidence in their possession to the defence. This can seriously compromise the victim in civil actions.
A lack of resources usually means the investigation will not be completed quickly.	Delay always acts against the interests of the victim.
Public prosecutors will not usually proceed with the case unless the chances of success are overwhelming, and in the public interest.	The victim may start a case to obtain injunctions or discovery of evidence with a view to a negotiated settlement.

the magistrate, jury or judge – all of the elements of the offence and the accused's responsibility, 'beyond reasonable doubt'. This is an extremely high standard, and any benefit of the doubt is given to the accused. It is usually critical to show that the accused acted with 'guilty knowledge' or intent. There are some criminal offences where proof of guilty knowledge is not required, and these (such as failing to submit a tax return, not registering with the Information Commissioner or using a television without a licence) are referred to as 'absolute offences'. They have little relevance for corporate fraud cases.

Juries, being constructed of those who are insufficiently sharp to avoid being called to this noble service, often find the evidence in complicated fraud cases too difficult, and thus fail to agree on a verdict – much to the delight of the accused. This is life.

The trial judge will determine what evidence is and is not admissible, applying a rule of 'fairness' (Section 76 of the Police and Criminal Evidence Act 1984). If evidence has been obtained illegally, for example by making threats or promises to a defendant, the judge may still admit it, but may make adverse comments that reduce its significance. This makes it imperative that investigators understand and comply with the laws and evidential procedures, and act fairly.

PENALTIES IN CRIMINAL CASES

If the defendant pleads, or is found, guilty, the magistrate or judge will impose what he believes is the appropriate financial, custodial or other sentence, having regard to the seriousness of the offence, previous convictions (which are not made available to the jury prior to its decision being reached) and any pleas in mitigation. The latter are often a work of art, and victims of corporate fraud should try, through their counsel, to ensure that the most extravagant excuses are refuted. They should also press for financial compensation, although in criminal cases this is always limited.

The Civil Law

SCOPE

The civil law deals with such things as breaches of contract and other wrongful acts or *torts*. Most frauds result in breaches of the civil law, and remedies can be sought in addition to criminal prosecution. It is important to recognize that the civil and criminal paths to recovery are not mutually exclusive but, in fact, complement each other. The primary focus of the civil law is to put the victim back into the position he would have been in but for the wrongful act. It is a bit like a TV sports action replay, but damages can be substantial.

Examples of civil law violations include:

- breach of employment or other contracts
- negligence
- breach of fiduciary duties
- fraud.

Also, attempts to commit a breach of contract, conspiracy, or failure to act as agreed may be actionable under the civil law.

Civil actions may be brought to obtain compensation or injunctive relief, preventing the continuation of an undesirable act (such as trespass), requiring a person or company to perform a specific act (such as complying with a contract) or to disclose evidence. Civil courts cannot impose custodial penalties except for perjury or contempt of court.

HOW ACTIONS ARE STARTED

Routine actions

Civil actions are normally commenced by private citizens, government agencies and organizations issuing a Claim Form through their lawyers setting out the nature of the complaint. The Claim Form obviously gives the defendant notice that trouble is brewing, and allows him to take defensive steps, including interference with witnesses and hiding his assets.

Pre-emptive actions

The law recognizes that people accused of wrongful acts – and especially fraud – are unlikely to make a full and frank disclosure in the normal course of events. It is therefore possible for claimants to carry out a pre-emptive strike by asking a High Court or other judge – *ex parte*, without the knowledge of the third parties involved – to issue orders of the type described in Table 3.2.

Pre-emptive orders are often the first indication a defendant has that civil action has been started, and they are intended to take him by surprise.

The claimant's lawyers have to convince a judge sitting in camera that an order is justified, and this requires a 'good arguable case'. Most English judges are well versed in fraud, and realize that the evidence available to support an application is likely to be less than complete. In fact, if the evidence were sufficient, there would be no need for a pre-emptive order.

Unfortunately, bad lawyers are detached from the real world, and believe that pre-emptive orders should only be applied for when there is already overwhelming evidence.

Table 3.2   Main types of civil orders

Type of order	When used	Directed against
Freezing Order *Previously referred to as a* *Mareva Injunction*	To preserve assets To locate (discover) assets and to prevent their dissipation	Defendants
Search and Seizure Order *Previously referred to as an* *Anton Pillar Order*	To enter and search premises for evidence where there are grounds for believing it might be destroyed	Defendants
Production Order (in various shapes and sizes)	To require the production of evidence	Defendants and witnesses

DETACHMENT AND STREETWISE

Two senior barristers were sipping port in their club. 'Do you really think, Jenkins, old boy, that we are privileged and divorced from reality?' 'I don't think so,' said Jenkins, 'I go shooting every weekend and I speak to my butler, Smith, and my valet, Tom and my clerk, Peters. They are pretty ordinary folk, working-class even, and I seem to get on frightfully well with them.' 'I see,' said Carnaby-Smythe, 'Why don't we experiment by getting the bus back to Chambers and see how we get on?' Jenkins was always game for a lark, and said: 'What a great idea.'

After a few more ports, the distinguished barristers stagger out to the Number 58, going east, bus stop. Carnaby-Smythe leaps out, limbs akimbo, in front of a Number 42 going west, and flags it down. 'Driver, my dear friend, please take us to number 3 King's Bench Walk, on the east side of Middle Temple, just past the flower pots, without delay, or better still "toots weet".' The Afghan driver, who in any case was having a bad day, responded: 'Piss off, you old fart.'. 'Well,' said Carnaby-Smythe, 'that appears to prove the point. He seemed to treat us as ordinary folk.'

Until the human rights stuff came on the scene, judges would apply what was known as the *Cyanamide* test, and decide whether it was just and reasonable to grant an order. Now the judgment is more likely to be based on the notion of 'proportionality', which means that the relief requested should be commensurate with the seriousness of the case.

Courts usually require the claimant to enter into an undertaking on costs, so if the action is unfounded, the defendant is not damaged. Because of the checks and balances applied by good litigation lawyers and the judges themselves, there are very few cases of pre-emptive action that go wrong. However, if they do, the claimant can be heavily penalized for costs.

A *Search and Seizure Order* allows the claimant and his legal advisers to enter and search premises under the control of the defendant or third party, and to recover evidence that would normally be available on discovery. If the defendant refuses to co-operate, he can be held in contempt of court and imprisoned. Search and Seizure Orders are executed by the claimant's lawyers (accompanied by a specified number of assistants, investigators and representatives) by simply appearing on the defendant's doorstep. The order will also specify the name of a *supervising solicitor*. He will be from an independent firm, and his job is to ensure that that order is executed fairly, and that the defendant complies.

'It's disgusting. They're not even on fees!'

The Defendant has a reasonable period to take legal advice, during which he can refuse to admit the claimant's representatives, including his solicitor. This is usually a critical period, because it allows the defendant to conceal or destroy evidence. In practice, the supervising solicitor should seek immediate access, but again this can be a problem if there are a number of defendants in the premises and only one supervising solicitor, as he cannot watch them all. This aspect calls for very careful planning (see page 140).

Freezing Orders, which are often obtained in parallel with Search and Seizure Orders, compel the defendant to disclose and preserve any assets which may, in due course, be recoverable by the claimant. They may also require the defendant to disclose under oath all of his income and assets. This is usually a very productive exercise and puts the crook in considerable difficulty.

Production Orders can be issued against the defendant's bankers, financial advisers and others from whom the claimant believes useful evidence can be obtained. They are very powerful weapons in the fight against fraud.

FURTHER PROCESSING

In the last couple of years, the civil process has been streamlined (based on the Civil Procedure Rules) and involves statements of truth, discovery, interrogatories (written questions and answers) and submissions by both sides before trial. Such exchanges of evidence ensure that there should be few surprises at trial. There is often a mediation stage, when the judge will try to bring the sides together to reach a settlement before trial.

Despite the improvements, proceedings are very slow and costly, and take on a life of their own as both sides take increasingly intransigent positions. Thus the main practical benefit of civil proceedings is to discover evidence and to bring the parties to negotiation. A full-blown trial should be avoided, almost at all costs. The better litigation lawyers are excellent negotiators.

Before litigating, dig two graves.

STANDARDS OF PROOF

To succeed with a civil case, the claimant has to prove his case on a 'balance of probabilities', and may succeed where a parallel criminal prosecution fails. This is an important distinction.

Trial judges are rightly concerned with the issue of fairness, and this is essential when injunctive relief or pre-emptive orders are being sought. The claimant must present all of the relevant information – whether it is good or adverse – and if he fails to do so, the injunction will fail.

It is critical that courts are not misled. If they are, the claimant can be penalized very heavily. Thus the judge should be advised at the earliest possible opportunity of anything that is unusual or could cause a problem.

PENALTIES IN CIVIL CASES

Penalties in civil cases can include recovery of all losses, interest, costs and damages which are normally payable to the claimant. However, both parties are responsible for legal and other costs, and the loser may have to compensate the winner. This can be a serious disincentive – and, in fact, the party with the largest purse usually has the advantage.

ST MERRYN MEAT AND OTHERS V. HAWKINS AND OTHERS QB2001

In this case, injunctions were granted on the basis that evidence had been obtained by intercepting the Defendant's office telephone. It subsequently transpired that this was untrue and that his home telephone had been tapped illegally, which the court viewed as a possible infringement of his rights to privacy under Article 8 (2) of the Human Rights Act.

The Judge discharged the orders, not because of the Human Rights violation, but because he had been misled. It is possible that had he known the truth from the outset, he would have maintained the orders.

Discovery and Disclosure

IN CRIMINAL CASES

In all criminal cases, the accused has a fundamental right against self-incrimination, and is not usually required to answer questions or produce evidence that could be against his interests – but there are exceptions. For example, if the police execute a Search Warrant, any documents or other stuff recovered can be produced in evidence, although the accused is under no obligation to explain them. However, under the Criminal Justice and Public Order Act 1994, if a person, when questioned, fails to mention any fact relied on in his defence, the court may draw such inferences as appear proper.

In England, people accused of crimes are required to provide details of any alibi they intend to develop in their defence. For example, if a robber claims that he is innocent and at the time of the alleged offence was at ballet classes, he is required, before trial, to produce details of the witnesses and other evidence he plans to call to support his alibi. The object of this is to prevent the prosecution being ambushed at trial by a spurious defence.

Criminal prosecutors are required to disclose, to the accused's representatives, before trial, all of the 'prosecution material' they have, including that which is not part of their case. This makes it imperative that all evidence (whether important or not) collected in an investigation is catalogued and preserved so that, at the appropriate time, the prosecuting authority can decide what has to be disclosed. It should be noted that many prosecutions fail because of technical problems with disclosure. It is a very important issue.

IN CIVIL CASES

In routine cases, the parties go through a process of 'discovery', when any evidence in their possession has to be disclosed to the other side. For example, the defendant might be compelled to disclose all of his assets, or documentation which establishes his responsibility for wrongful acts. The claimant also has to disclose any evidence which could conceivably assist the defendant, and this aspect has to be handled carefully, usually by lawyers.

Defendants in civil cases have no general right against self-incrimination although some will argue to the contrary on the basis that disclosure could result in criminal prosecution or interfere with their human rights. The case of *Rank Film Distributors* v. *Video Information Centre* 1992 is an example of how the protection against self-incrimination is increasingly being applied in civil cases. The point is particularly relevant when pre-emptive orders are being sought. Defendants may refuse to comply on the grounds that to do so could expose them to criminal liability. Thus the drafting of the pre-emptive order, in relation to future criminal proceedings, is vital.

When a Search and Seizure Order is executed, any material which the defendant argues is privileged should be retained by the supervising solicitor, who will refer the matter to the judge. In short, the self-incrimination argument should not be an issue. However, any case evidence recovered in civil proceedings is not normally admissible in criminal courts – but there are exceptions.

Information Privileged Against Disclosure

CRIMINAL PROSECUTIONS

There are circumstances in which information that could be relevant to an opposing party does not have to be disclosed. In criminal cases, this may include the name of a confidential informant, or other material which should be protected in the public interest or by *legal professional privilege* (see below). The procedures are complicated, and will be handled by lawyers at the appropriate time, but the rule is total openness with the court.

CIVIL CASES

Again, a fundamental principle is that material that could be relevant to the case is disclosed to the opposing party, usually during the discovery process. For this reason, investigators should catalogue all material collected during a case and make sure it is brought to the attention of lawyers.

LEGAL PROFESSIONAL PRIVILEGE

In both criminal and civil proceedings, certain material is classified (by legal advisers acting for one or more of the parties, and ultimately by the trial judge) as 'privileged' and does not have to be disclosed to the opposing party, including:

- all communications between a client (or his agent) and his solicitor (or his agent), in contemplation of proceedings, including requests for legal advice, reports and statements; this is usually known as *legal professional privilege* (or in the USA, client–attorney privilege), and it protects the client against adverse disclosure
- 'without prejudice' correspondence
- internal reports prepared by a special task force specifically created to investigate an important matter
- communications between employees and others who have a common business interest – for example, internal reports, staff appraisals and personal references are usually protected under the rule for common business interests; also, an accusation made about a suspected

crime to the police with a view to detecting an offender is privileged (in the UK, see *Kine* v. *Sewell* 1838).

For all practical purposes, privileged information does not exist, and protection is substantive rather than procedural, as was the case until a few years ago. Exceptions include cases where privilege is waived, privileged material is foolishly disclosed, where publication is excessive or malicious, or when otherwise privileged information is obtained by illegal means (see the cases of *Dubai Aluminium and Memory Corporation* v. *Sidhu* 1999, where the courts ruled that the work product of investigators was not privileged, because they had broken the law in obtaining it). But this does not necessarily mean that the evidence will be excluded, although it may be regarded as 'tainted' and lacking credibility. Breaches may also be used to discredit the investigation generally or to undermine an otherwise solid case. The rule is that investigators must not break the law.

Important Developments in the Law

KEY AREAS

In all countries the law is evolving and there are three aspects which require careful consideration, as they have an impact on both criminal and civil investigations:

- human rights
- interception of communications
- data protection and privacy.

To a high degree, these are related and driven by an intent to protect the rights of citizens against improper intrusion into their private lives by instruments of the State. This is all to the good.

However, the interpretation of the new laws and regulations – especially by inexperienced lawyers, some Human Remains Departments, mandarins and ill-informed investigators – goes well beyond their intent. For safety's sake (and to remove the possibility of legal action ever being taken against them), some take a pathetically weak line with the result that crooks escape.

THE EUROPEAN CONVENTION ON HUMAN RIGHTS

The role of the European Court

All States that have contracted to the Convention, with the exception of Ireland and Norway, have incorporated its principles into their laws, enabling their domestic courts to take full account of its provisions when considering a matter. If domestic remedies are not available (for example, because the complained of action is not 'lawful' under local laws, as in the *Halford* case discussed below) or have been exhausted, an individual may seek redress in the European Court in Strasbourg. The Strasbourg process is not a substitute for national justice, but is, in a sense, an extension of it, and a forum for final appeal. Maggie Thatcher was right: we should never have agreed to the Tunnel!

The Convention empowers the European Court of Human Rights to deal with individuals' petitions and inter-State disputes. The judges are independent, and elected by the

'To be honest, Mr Nice, we were hoping to see one of the other partners.'

Parliamentary Assembly. When the court finds that there has been a violation of a Convention right, and if the domestic law of the State concerned allows less than complete reparation to be made, it may award the victim *just satisfaction* (Article 50). This generally involves the reimbursement of costs and expenses, and – when appropriate – compensation.

In accordance with Article 53 of the Convention, the Contracting States undertake to abide by the decisions of the court. To date, States which have been ordered to make payments under Article 50 have consistently done so.

A finding by the court of a violation of the Convention has often led the respondent State, and sometimes even other Contracting States, to take general measures to comply. The Regulation of Investigatory Powers Act 2000 is an example of domestic laws being changed by European Court decisions.

There are six points to note with decisions by the European Court of Human Rights:

- It takes years to get a case dealt with by the court: fast it is not.
- The judges assigned, usually mob-handed, to any case have seldom agreed unanimously on anything: consistent it is not.
- The compensation imposed has been minimal.
- There are no criminal penalties for violations of human rights.
- It has avoided taking tricky decisions, such as to what extent (under Article 8(2)) people are entitled to privacy at work.

Finally, lawyers and smelly-socks engaged in the human rights area seem to have ignored all of the cases where the European Court has ruled in favour of law enforcement. A classic example is the case of *LÜDI* v. *Switzerland* (17/1991/269/340: see <http://hudoc.echr.coe.int/hudoc2doc/HEJUD/sift/369.txt>), where it was decided that people lost their rights to privacy when they engaged in a course of criminal conduct. The European Court may be a dead sheep, but it is not an ass.

Details of the Convention

There are 59 Articles in the Convention, but those of interest in the fraud and employment areas are as follows:

Article 6 – Right to a fair trial

1 In the determination of his civil rights and obligations or of any criminal charge against him, everyone is entitled to a fair and public hearing within a reasonable time by an independent and impartial tribunal established by law. Judgement shall be pronounced publicly, but the press and public may be excluded from all or part of the trial in the interests of morals, public order or national security in a democratic society, where the interests of juveniles or the protection of the private life of the parties so require, or to the extent strictly necessary in the opinion of the court in special circumstances where publicity would prejudice the interests of justice.

2 Everyone charged with a criminal offence shall be presumed innocent until proved guilty according to law.

3 Everyone charged with a criminal offence has the following minimum rights:
   a   to be informed promptly, in a language which he understands and in detail, of the nature and cause of the accusation against him

b   to have adequate time and facilities for the preparation of his defence

c   to defend himself in person or through legal assistance of his own choosing, or if he has not sufficient means to pay for legal assistance, to be given it free when the interests of justice so require

d   to examine or have examined witnesses against him and to obtain the attendance and examination of witnesses on his behalf under the same conditions as witnesses against him

e   to have the free assistance of an interpreter if he cannot understand or speak the language used in court.

Article 8 – Right to respect for private and family life

1   Everyone has the right to respect for his private and family life, his home and his correspondence.

2   There shall be no interference by a public authority with the exercise of this right, except such as is in accordance with the law and is necessary in a democratic society in the interests of national security, public safety or the economic well-being of the country, for the prevention of disorder or crime, for the protection of health or morals, or for the protection of the rights and freedoms of others.

Article 10 – Freedom of expression

1   Everyone has the right to freedom of expression. This right shall include freedom to hold opinions and to receive and impart information and ideas without interference by public authority and regardless of frontiers. This article shall not prevent States from requiring the licensing of broadcasting, television or cinema enterprises.

2   The exercise of these freedoms, since it carries with it duties and responsibilities, may be subject to such formalities, conditions, restrictions or penalties as are prescribed by law and are necessary in a democratic society, in the interests of national security, territorial integrity or public safety, for the prevention of disorder or crime, for the protection of health or morals, for the protection of the reputation or rights of others, for preventing the disclosure of information received in confidence, or for maintaining the authority and impartiality of the judiciary.

Article 13 – Right to an effective remedy

Everyone whose rights and freedoms as set forth in this Convention are violated shall have an effective remedy before a national authority, notwithstanding that the violation has been committed by persons acting in an official capacity.

These rights have all been incorporated in the Human Rights Act 1998.

The Importance of Article 8

This Article is crucial from a fraud investigation point of view. It consists of two sections. Article 8(1) deals with the right to respect a person's private and family life, his home and correspondence. The European Court has been consistent in its spinning – almost Dervish-like – ability to avoid giving a precise interpretation of the four elements of:

• private life
• family life

- home
- correspondence.

Most judgments have been concerned with the right to respect for private life, although some have involved incidental claims relating to the home, family or correspondence. For example, in a 1997 decision (*Niemeitz* v. *Germany*), the court seemed, under the particular facts of the case, to extend 'home' to include office premises. No general conclusions can be drawn from this, and if the Eurocrats intended that people were entitled to Article 8 rights in their business lives and offices, they would have said so. They could never argue that they kept the Convention brief to preserve ink and paper!

Article 8(2) exposes three important principles:

1 There must be a specific legal rule which authorizes action by a public authority which makes intrusion into the private lives of citizens 'lawful'. If there is no such rule, the action is by default 'unlawful'.

2 The individual must have adequate access to the law in question.

3 The law must be formulated with sufficient precision to enable the individual to foresee the circumstances in which the law might be applied.

The way these principles apply can be seen clearly from the case of Alison Halford.

THE HALFORD CASE

Alison Halford was a senior police officer in the Merseyside Constabulary. During an employment dispute, her managers tapped her office telephone, and after exhausting her remedies under English law, she took her case to the European Court of Human Rights, arguing a breach of her right to privacy in her private life under Article 8(2). The court found in her favour stating that the interception was 'unlawful'. This is a misleading term, and what it meant is that there was no applicable law under which a public authority could intercept communications on its own internal networks. Since there was no law under which such interception could be regulated, the result had to be 'unlawful'.

The full Halford judgment can be found on the Internet site <http://www.dhcour.coe.fr/eng/ JUDGMENTS/HALFORD.html> and it is not at all what you may have been led to believe. The allegations and decisions, in relation to Article 8 and Ms Halford's office

telephones, can be summarized as shown in Table 3.3.

It is obvious from the above that the court's decision was based on the very unusual facts of an exceptional case:

- The employer was a 'public authority'.
- The matter being investigated was not a crime.
- The interception was not proportionate to the matters in issue.
- The intercepted telephone was specifically designated for her private calls.
- She had been assured that she could use the telephone to seek advice in relation to her case alleging sexual discrimination.

The court went to some lengths *not* to draw general rules on the application of section 8(2), and rather than being an overwhelming victory for Ms Halford, the judgment was something of a damp squib. If it was not a damp squib for her, her lawyers were damned with faint praise, and their bills were hammered by the court.

Table 3.3   The decisions in relation to Article 8 of the *Halford* case

Alleged breach of	Provisions of the Article *Comments on the Halford judgment*	Finding of the court *Comments*
Article 8(1)	Everyone has the right to respect for his private and family life, his home and his correspondence. *Note that in paragraph 1 the court uses the word 'may' when dealing with the general position.* *In paragraph 42, the court is dealing with the specifics of the Halford case, in which:* • *One telephone had been specifically designated for her private use (paragraph 44).* • *She had been specifically assured she could use the telephones for the purposes of her sex discrimination case.* • *She was given no warning that her telephones might be intercepted.*	**Paragraph 1** Telephone calls from business premises *may* be covered by notions of 'private life' and 'correspondence' – the applicant had a reasonable expectation of privacy. Conclusion: Unanimously agreed. **Paragraph 42** The applicant argued, and the Commission agreed, that calls made on the telephones in Ms Halford's office at Merseyside Police Headquarters fell within the scope of 'private life' and 'correspondence', since the court in its case law had adopted a broad construction of these expressions. **Paragraph 44** For all of the above reasons, the court concludes that the telephone calls, made by Ms Halford fell within the scope of 'private life'.
Article 8(2)	There shall be no interference by a public authority with the exercise of this right, except such as in accordance with the law and is necessary in a democratic society in the interests of national security, public safety or the economic well being of the country, for the prevention of disorder or crime, for the protection of health or morals, or for the rights and freedoms of others.	**Paragraph 48** [The interception had] the primary aim of gathering material to assist in the defence of the sex-discrimination proceedings. This constituted an 'interference by a public authority'. **Paragraph 49** 'Interference by a public authority' must be in accordance with the law. Such interference was not in accordance with the law, since the domestic law did not provide any regulation of calls on telecommunications systems outside the public network.

Mainly as a result of the Halford case, panic set in. The British Government had to pass laws so that interception of private networks by public authorities could be made 'lawful'. Proclaimers of doom and gloom put forward the view that companies could no longer intercept internal communications systems for any purpose. OFTEL, the British telecoms regulator, put out 'guidelines' that were, by any measure, incredible. These stated that telephones could never be intercepted; that all employers had to provide separate communications facilities (for both voice and data) on which confidentiality was guaranteed, and so on and so on. Fortunately, the guidelines were ignored as being excessively mandarinesque. Their appearance does, however, highlight the tendency of bureaucrats to apply their own liberal aspirations to interpretations of the law.

There have been a number of other decisions by the European Court that are of interest in the fraud area. They mostly centre on Article 6 and the right to a fair trial, where the main stumbling block has been the failure by law enforcement agencies to produce undercover investigators and confidential informants as witnesses at criminal trials. Defendants have argued (sometimes successfully – but with minimal compensation) that by being unable to cross-examine confidential informants, their trials were not fair.

HUMAN RIGHTS ACT 1998

Background and scope

This Act came into effect in England on 2 October 2000, and incorporates most of the provisions of the European Convention on Human Rights. English court decisions will be influenced by Strasbourg, which is still the court of final appeal once all domestic remedies have been exhausted.

It is not widely appreciated that breaches of the human rights legislation are primarily directed at government agencies or 'public authorities' in their relationships with the private lives of citizens. The objective of the legislation is to strike a fair balance between the demands of the community at large and the protection of individual human rights. Any interference with these rights must be in accordance with the law (that is, 'lawful'), necessary and 'proportionate'.

This is all fair enough, but recent cases show how the laws are being interpreted and misinterpreted, especially by lower courts.

THE ELECTORAL ROLE

In November 2001, a retired Scottish accountant living in Yorkshire won a landmark case in the High Court. His grouse was that he had refused to register on the Electoral Roll because the local authority would not give an undertaking that details would not be sold to marketing companies or used for other than voting purposes. As a result, he complained that he had been deprived of the right to vote for both local and national politicians (can you think of anything more dastardly?). During the case, his lawyers argued that information on the electoral register should be used only for electoral purposes to which the subject consented or for other purposes which were justified in the public interest. The court has still to decide what compensation might be appropriate, but figures in the range of £1000 to £1500 have been mentioned. What is less clear is whether the claimant would benefit, or whether he would have to pay for being absolved of responsibility for electing politicians. Like most cases, the point is arguable either way.

SMOKING POT IS OKAY

An employee was dismissed for smoking cannabis on his employer's premises, when his employer had a 'zero tolerance' attitude towards drugs abuse. The employment tribunal upheld his claim of unfair dismissal because it 'infringed his Human Rights Act right to privacy'. The tribunal's approach 'rested on the perception that public opinion was tolerant towards the smoking of cannabis'.

SMOKING CIGARETTES IS NOT OKAY

A biscuit factory worker fired after he was caught smoking in a restricted area lost his unfair dismissal claim. Patrick Mitchell, 42, of Viewpark, Uddingston, accused Thomas Tunnock Ltd of Uddingston, Lanarkshire, of unfair dismissal after he was sacked for gross industrial misconduct from his £200-a-week job. He claimed he was addicted to smoking at the time and was under stress. But the employment tribunal didn't accept this as there was no medical evidence to support his claim. It also accepted that while smoking was a minor offence in certain circumstances, in the Tunnock's business context, smoking in non-designated areas justified dismissal without notice.

People could be forgiven for reaching the conclusion that the smelly-socks are personally supportive of smoking pot but not cigarettes, and therefore interpret the laws accordingly. This happens a lot in other areas. In another case, a senior employee won an unfair dismissal claim on the grounds that business calls made to his home were an invasion of his right to a private life.

Finally, in perhaps the saddest case of all, a man was fired simply because he smoked at home. Attilla the Hun, his employer, said, 'I think smoking is revolting and I won't have smokers anywhere near me: no way.' The employee had agreed not to smoke before reporting for work, but the employer would not budge. So much for his human rights!

If 'public authorities' break the law, there is an extensive range of remedies available, including judicial review, injunctive relief and damages. For other than public authorities, the penalties for infringement are limited to reinstating the position had the claimant's rights not been violated. There is no criminal penalty, and it should be remembered that there is a great deal of difference between someone making a complaint – often with the intention of frustrating an investigation – and succeeding with it.

Possible extensions into privacy areas

Companies and private citizens have never been convicted of any human rights violations, and arguably cannot be. However, the recent English cases involving Michael Douglas and Catherine Zeta Jones (actors!) and John Venables (the murderer of the toddler James Bulger) seem to have taken the law a step further and implied a right to privacy. This was not the intention of the law.

Vertical and horizontal interpretations

The scope and extent of human rights legislation is endlessly arguable (especially if the time spent doing so is on fees), and some lawyers say that there are two possible interpretations. The first is known as 'vertical' which means that violations can only be committed by 'public authorities', and thus the bucket of mud only spills downwards.

The second interpretation is known as 'horizontal', and this – fully supported by the sandal-wearers – means that private citizens and companies *can* interfere with the rights of others (that is, the laws do not just apply to public authorities). Under this interpretation, the bucket of mud flies in all directions and covers everyone who happens to be around. The 'horizontal' point has been raised in both criminal and civil cases, and has generally had little impact except in the lower courts and Industrial Tribunals. Interestingly, the Regulation of Investigatory Powers Act 2000 is based on a vertical interpretation of human rights.

There is no doubt that the Human Rights Act 1998 will be influential in supporting the dreaded horizontal interpretation, in that it:

- imposes a duty on public authorities to act in a way which is compatible with Convention rights
- requires all UK legislation, whenever enacted, to be interpreted by both the civil and criminal courts in a way which is compatible with Convention rights.

Thus it remains to be seen whether there will be any long-term, major impact on well-established laws and precedents in the fraud area. So far, it has been containable and relatively sensible, except in Employment Tribunals, where the smelly-socks seem to have lost the plot.

The bottom line of proportionality

The common theme in both the convention and the Human Rights Act 1998 is that the action taken to investigate crime must be *proportionate* to its seriousness. This is a sensible yardstick, and one which should be addressed by all potential victims as a matter of policy and in investigatory procedures (see page 106). Other than this, commercial victims of fraud need not be worried about human rights legislation.

REGULATION OF INVESTIGATORY POWERS ACT 2000 (RIPA)

Background and coverage

This Act was passed so that the UK would conform to the European Convention on Human Rights, primarily in the area of communications interception by public authorities on private networks, and to make cases such as Alison Halford's 'lawful'. But like kids confronted with a cookie jar, English politicians and mandarins could not resist the urge to take matters a few steps further and the Act was extended.

The introduction states: 'The main purpose of the act is to ensure that the relevant investigatory powers are used in accordance with human rights' and 'to create a new regime for the interception of communications … it goes beyond what is strictly required for human rights purposes and provides also for the changed nature of the communications industry since 1985'. RIPA repealed the Interception of Communications Act 1985.

There are six things to be noted about RIPA:

- It is one of the most badly drafted, convoluted Acts in the history of convoluted Acts.
- It is primarily directed at 'public authorities' and intrusions into the private lives of citizens.
- It is based on a vertical interpretation of human rights legislation (see page 48).
- It creates masses of confusion and exceptions.
- There were no transitional arrangements.
- It adds unnecessary, and arguably insecure, bureaucracy to the investigatory process with the creation of quangos. These include the Surveillance Commission, which is intended to monitor the application of the laws by the police, Customs & Excise and other public authorities, but which may supplant their authority.

However, the Act does not remove (at least yet) most of the investigatory powers needed by businesses to detect, investigate and recover from fraud. But victims do have to understand the fine print and have procedures in place to avoid violations of both the criminal and civil law. This is the key. A flowchart summarizing the important aspects of RIPA is reproduced in Appendix 6.

The coverage of the act can be summarized as shown in Table 3.4.

Table 3.4 Coverage of the Regulation of Investigatory Powers Act 2000 and Regulations

Law	Applicability		
	Public authorities acting as an agency of the State	Public authorities acting as a business. See Section 4(7)	Companies and firms (businesses)
Part 1, Chapter 1: Communications; interceptions of communications transmissions			
Imposes criminal penalties and authorization methods			
• Public networks	Home Office Warrant	Not applicable	Not applicable
• Private networks	Permission of the person having control etc. (see below)		
• Public postal service	Home Office Warrant	Not applicable	Not applicable
• Private postal service	Permission of the person having control etc. (see below)		
Part 1, Chapter 2: Acquisition and disclosure of communications data (for example, call logging)			
Sets out authorization methods, but no criminal penalties			
• Public networks	Rights to obtain	Not applicable	
• Private networks			
Part 2: Surveillance and covert human intelligence sources			
Sets out authorization methods, but no criminal penalties			
Informants' undercover pretexts	Authorization methods	Not applicable	
Part 3: Electronic data protected by encryption etc.			
Sets out authorization methods, but no criminal penalties			
Protection disclosure	Authorization methods Access rights	Not applicable	

For each of these areas, the Act will (but does not yet do so) ensure that the law clearly covers:

- the purpose for which the powers may be used
- which authorities can use the powers

- who should authorise each use of the power
- the use that can be made of the material gained
- independent judicial oversight
- a means of redress for the individual.

Various quangos have been established – such as the Surveillance Commission and the Interception of Communications Commission – to confirm 'lawful authority' monitoring and approval processes for public authorities. Also, Statutory Instruments, rules, guidelines and codes of practice have been written, again primarily for public authorities.

Communications interception

Communications transmissions

Section 1 of Part 1, Chapter 1 makes it a criminal offence – punishable by an unlimited fine and up to two years imprisonment – for any person intentionally and without lawful authority to intercept a 'communications transmission' on a private or public network. Section 1(3) creates a separate civil liability for interception of communications transmissions without lawful authority.

Definitions

A private communications system is defined as:

> any telecommunication system which, without itself being a public telecommunication system, is a system in relation to which the following conditions are satisfied:
>
> (a) it is attached, directly or indirectly and whether or not for the purposes of the communication in question, to a public telecommunication system; and
> (b) there is apparatus comprised in the system which is both located in the United Kingdom and used (with or without other apparatus) for making the attachment to the public telecommunication system.

Some lawyers have made the point that the word 'attached' is pivotal and thus argue that 'internal loops' or 'internal extensions' as well as 'radio extensions', are not part of the private system because they are not 'attached'. This is probably an unsustainable argument. However, an 'entirely self-standing system' (such as an intranet) is not to be regarded as a 'private communications system'. The safe line for businesses is to work on the basis that any voice or data communications system is covered by the Act and the regulations made thereunder.

The definitions of 'public telecommunications service', 'public telecommunications system', 'telecommunications service' and 'telecommunications system' are wonderfully owlish, but mean what they say. They are communications systems provided to a substantial section of the public, such as British Telecom and so on.

Section 2(2) states:

> a person intercepts a communication in the course of its transmission by means of a telecommunications system if, and only if, he:

(a) so modifies or interferes with the system or its operation
(b) so monitors transmissions made by means of the system
(c) so monitors transmissions made by wireless telegraphy to or from an apparatus comprised in the system

as to make some or all of the contents of the communication available, while being transmitted, to a person other than the sender or intended recipient of the communication.

Interception of public networks

As far as the interception of communications transmissions on public networks is concerned, lawful authority comes from a specific warrant issued by the Home Secretary to a shortlist of eligible government agencies, such as the police, Customs & Excise or the security services. Companies and individuals cannot apply for a Home Office warrant to intercept communications transmissions on public networks.

Interception on private networks

For a private communications system, removal of criminal liability under Section 1(2) is achieved under four main provisions:

- Section 1(6), when the person with the right to control the system gives permission
- Section 3(1), with the consent of both the sender and the recipient
- Section 3(2), with the consent of either the sender or the recipient and, for public authorities only, subject to the surveillance conditions in section 48(2)
- Section 5, under the authority of a warrant signed by the Home Secretary.

Most businesses (and the police when intercepting a private network) will rely on permission of the controller (Section 1(6)), which removes criminal liability. However, there is a second condition of authorization for 'lawful authority'.

Lawful authority to intercept communications on a private network will normally be derived from:

- a Section 5 warrant signed by the Home Secretary
- the consent of one or more of the parties to the communication
- compliance with the Telecommunications (Lawful Business Practice)(Interception of Communications) Regulations 2000 (the Regulations).

The Regulations came into effect on 24 October 2000, and are very important to businesses:

Section 2(a) of the Regulations states 'references to a business include references to the activities of a government department, or any public authority or of any person or office holder on whom functions are conferred by or under any enactment.' This implies that government departments are put on the same footing as businesses when investigating internal fraud relating to their statutory obligations.

Section 3 sets out the conditions for 'lawful interception' including 3(1)(a)(iii) 'for the purpose of preventing crime' and then subject to section 3(2) which has three main conditions:

(a) the interception in question is effected solely for the purpose of monitoring or (where appropriate) keeping a record of communications relevant to the systems controller's business

(b) the telecommunications system in question is provided for use wholly or partly in connection with that business

(c) the system controller has made all reasonable efforts to inform every person who may use the telecommunications system in question that communications transmitted by means thereof may be intercepted.

Unsurprisingly, the Regulations do not state what constitutes 'all reasonable efforts', to advise users that communications transmissions might be intercepted, but common sense suggests that a statement along the lines of that shown on page 101, as part of the company's policy on fraud would be sufficient.

But what happens if a business discovers a serious fraud, where interception of communications would be proportionate, but has not already advised potential users of that possibility? Would it be 'reasonable' to publish a statement about communications interception and thus put the crooks on specific notice? Experts argue that it would be 'reasonable' to do nothing until the current suspicions have been resolved, and then to issue a policy. The Home Office and police have relied on this interpretation in a number of recent cases involving interception of private systems, although the issue has yet to be tested in court.

Exceptions

It should be noted that the regulations apply to interception of communications transmissions. They do not apply to cases where:

- a room is subject to audio or video monitoring using a linear microphone or other device that is licensed under the Wireless and Telegraphy Act, for example by an adapted baby alarm, infra-red or microwave transmitter

- a linear microphone or other legal device is placed in a room or vehicle which incidentally picks up only one side of a communications transmission, even if the signal is transmitted to a receiver using telecommunications lines

- emanations from a computer are collected on a passive receiver; neither would such a device contravene the Computer Misuse Act 1990

- keystrokes entered into a computer terminal are captured by a buffering device and then transmitted by a legal transmitter to a receiver

- a voice mail system is accessed after messages have been read by the intended recipient.

However, the techniques that a victim will use in any investigation should be approved as part of a fraud policy, which sets out authorization and other procedures. This aspect is covered on pages 97 *et seq.*

Admissibility of intercept evidence

Section 17 of the Act repeats the principles of the Interception of Communications Act 1985 to the extent that transcripts of communications intercepted under the authority of a Home

Office warrant – and any matters relating to them – cannot normally be introduced in evidence in legal proceedings, although there are some exceptions.

There is nothing to prevent intercept evidence being introduced in either civil or criminal courts if it was obtained by consent or under the authority of the system controller.

Anomalies

If a private communications system is intercepted under the Regulations without reasonable efforts being made to inform employees and others potentially involved, the behaviour is technically unlawful. If it is unlawful, it fails the second part of the test of Section 1(2), and should therefore be a criminal offence. This conundrum is resolved by Section 1(6), which is definitive. Thus it is not illegal to intercept communications transmissions on a private network without prior warning to the potential users. It might, however, still be unlawful under Section 1(3), and give rise to a civil claim for damages. What, if anything, these might be will be determined on a case-by-case basis, but it should be emphasized that in practice neither the police nor the Home Office believe that a pre-warning is critical. A decision chart summarizing the important aspects of communications transmission is reproduced in Appendix 6.

Businesses and other sections of RIPA

No regulations have been issued for the business sector clarifying other sections of the Act covering the use of call logging data, surveillance, or human and semi-human intelligence sources. Further regulations covering these areas are likely to coincide with the creation of the Security Industry Board (to be established under the Private Industry Security Act 2001: see <http://www.hmso.gov.uk/acts/acts2001/20010012.htm>), and God alone knows what will happen then.

Public Authorities have been overwhelmed with paper on the rules covering directed, covert and intrusive surveillance, use of covert human intelligence sources, interference with property and officers working undercover. (see <http://www.homeoffice.gov.uk/ripa/ripact. htm>). The point to note is that everything is directed at public authorities and based on the principles of lawful authority and proportionality.

Thus, as matters now stand, business victims are able to access call logging data, use covert, directed, intrusive and other forms of surveillance and human intelligence sources without breaching RIPA. The only restrictions are that the disclosure of call logging data obtained from a public communications carrier must not contravene the Tele-communications Act 1984 (which it should not if the investigation of crime is concerned) and the Data Protection Act, of which more later. Surveillance must not contravene the laws on trespass or the Prevention from Harassment Act 1997. Also, companies should consider their position on access to encrypted data and keys (Part 3 of the Act). All of these matters should be covered in a fraud policy (see Chapter 5).

DATA PROTECTION ACT

Not a privacy act

This is another piece of legislation where liberal interpretation runs ahead of literal intent and oiks up and down the country are using its provisions as a cover for their own incompe-tence or to build empires. The first thing to remember is that the Act only applies to personal data processed on a computer or through a structured 'relevant' manual system. It is not a privacy Act, nor a 'let's be nice to crooks' Act, despite what the chattering classes might wish.

The Act is based on the following important principles for the processing of personal data. It must be:

- fairly and lawfully processed
- processed for limited purposes
- adequate, relevant and not excessive
- accurate
- kept no longer than is necessary
- processed in accordance with the data subject's rights
- not transferred outside Europe.

To comply with these very fair principles, controllers of computers and structured manual systems must register with, or notify, the Information Commission (formerly the artiste known as the 'Data Protection Registrar' or 'Data Protection Commissioner') and conform with various standards. It is an offence under Section 17 to process personal data and so on, without first making the appropriate registration. Under Section 22, the Commissioner is required to assess the notification, and it may be declined if it appears that processing will cause substantial damage, distress or otherwise significantly prejudice the rights and free-doms of the data subject. Otherwise, if the Commissioner is satisfied, the appropriate entry will be made in the register, which is accessible to the public.

Part IV of the Act makes substantial exemptions for specified purposes, including (under Section 29(1)) the prevention or detection of crime, the apprehension or prosecution of offenders, and the assessment or collection of taxes. The Commissioner has extensive powers to issue Enforcement Notices and to require the production of information.

Section 55(1) makes it a criminal offence for any person, knowingly or recklessly, without the consent of the data controller to obtain or disclose personal data, except (under Subsection (2)) if the person can show that:

- the obtaining, disclosing or procuring was necessary for the purpose of preventing or detecting crime or was otherwise authorized
- that he acted in the reasonable belief that he had the right in law to procure, disclose and so on
- that he acted in the reasonable belief that he would have had the consent of the data controller
- that in the particular circumstances the obtaining, disclosing and so on was justified in the public interest.

Sections 55(4) and (5) make it a criminal offence for anyone to sell, or offer to sell, illegally obtained data. Interestingly, Section 56 states that it is a criminal offence for a person to require a data subject to supply a record which relates to his criminal convictions or cautions in connection with recruitment, continued employment or the provision of services, 'unless it is in the public interest'. Section 56(4) clarifies the position and specifically states that requiring the production of certificates of criminal records, etc. (under Part V of the Police Act 1997) is 'not . . . justified as being in the public interest on the ground that it would assist in the prevention or detection of crime'. This is a good example of political duplicity. On one hand businesses are held liable if they recruit bad people, and on the other the law takes away a critical means of checking. However, there appears to be no reason why employers cannot require the production of such certificates from the Criminal Records Bureau, once it gets its act in gear.

A few recent decisions also illustrate how the law is being applied and the scope of data protection legislation being extended far beyond its principles.

NUMERICAL NONSENSE

Mandarins working for the Information Commission do not like British people being able to work out the identity and address of a subscriber from his telephone number. God knows why. In most other EU countries, whose laws are based on the same convention, the reverse telephone directory is part of the service. In France, not only can you reverse the number, the Website gives a street map showing adjacent subscribers, their telephone numbers, and also the photographs of the buildings concerned.

Our requests to the IC for clarification of its interpretation all went unanswered. The reason is obvious: they cannot justify it!

CLOSED-CIRCUIT TELEVISION

In November 2001, the Information Commissioner put out guidelines for the use of closed-circuit television in public places and the collection and processing of images. It is difficult to see how CCTV can be regarded as a computerized or structured manual system. Fortunately, exceptions apply when a specific crime is being investigated, although for general crime prevention purposes, warnings that recordings might be made must be displayed.

CANCER RESEARCH

The Head of the Institute of Cancer Research has complained that the Department of Health would not supply information about doctors who have patients who could benefit from the treatment.

DESTRUCTION OF EVIDENCE

In March 2001, the Divisional Court remitted a case for reconsideration in the Crown Court because, presumably under the Data Protection Act's retention provisions, the police had destroyed video evidence that might potentially have been relevant. The defendant argued that absence of the evidence deprived him of the right to a fair trial. The court agreed.

The fact is that even the most sensitive data can be collected, processed and retained providing the proper registration has been made and other standards, subject to data access conditions are met and disclosure is made only to registered third parties. For example, data supplied by employees on their job application forms, pension plans, salary, transaction records and just about anything else can be processed for crime prevention and investigation purposes, providing the appropriate registration is made.

Unjustified extensions of the law

Some chatterers have argued that pretext calls, undercover investigations and surveillance cannot be carried out at all because they contravene the concept of 'fairness' in collecting data. If collection is self-contained and not processed by a computer or structured manual system, there can be no contravention of the Data Protection Act. The fact that an organization is registered for computer and structured personal data does not mean that all data is covered. Despite the Data Protection Act, life goes on.

Examples of reality

Many banks, credit card companies and telecommunications carriers have Data Protection Act registrations that permit the release of sensitive personal data to the police, other public and private investigators and – providing they have compatible registrations – there is nothing to stop information passing freely between them. This is especially true when the investigation or prevention of crime is involved.

The bottom line

The Data Protection Act does not mean that businesses have to cower in the face of crooks or abandon their crime prevention and investigation rights. The art is to make sure their registration is accurate and comprehensive (see Policy Areas, pages 97 *et seq.*) and to appeal if they do not agree with the Information Commissioner.

OTHER STUFF

Throughout 2001, many of the large English law firms put out papers, held lunches, breakfasts, teas, suppers, soirées, love-ins, workshops and clinics on the Human Rights Act 1998, RIPA and other worrisome legislation. It was flavour of the year. The result has been to spread panic and dismay among the great unwashed in investigative communities, and to deter victims of fraud from retaining them, unless under the umbrella of the law firm concerned. This is clever marketing by the lawyers – and who can blame them?

The legislation, subject to forebodings of immediate doom, has included the provisions set out in Table 3.5.

A reason can always be found for doing nothing, and it is true that great care has to be taken in all investigations. The best protection is always to work with experienced litigation lawyers and professional investigators.

In addition, there are four recommendations for dealing with the endless stream of laws, rules and regulations:

• Live your life according to honest principles; do your best, work hard, and tell the truth. If you inadvertently break the law at least your conscience will be clear – and who knows, you might even share a cell with a politician or lawyer. Now that would be fun!

Table 3.5   Effects of legislation on investigatory procedures

Law of regulation _What the chattering classes say you cannot do_	What you can do _How to do it_
Computer Misuse Act 1990 _You cannot carry out a covert examination of an employee's computer._ _You cannot passively collect emanations from a computer._	There is no restriction on accessing the company's own equipment. A policy along the lines of pages 97 _et seq._ would allow companies to examine personal computers owned by the employee and used for business purposes. There is no restriction.
Copyright Act 1945 _You cannot photocopy trash without the owner's permission._	This may be a civil breach. The wronged party would have to show that he had been financially damaged.
Criminal Justice and Public Order Act 1994 and Vagrancy Act 1861 _You cannot enter onto enclosed premises to pick up trash._	This act only applies where entry onto premises is related to a criminal act. Trash collection (see page 59) should never be a crime.
Criminal Procedure and Investigations Act 1996 _You have to disclose intelligence to the opposing side. Therefore, it is best not to record it._	Disclosure will be determined by lawyers at the appropriate time. Confidential informants and privileged information can be protected.
Customs and Excise Management Act 1979 _You cannot impersonate an officer._	CORRECT. This is illegal (under Section 13), and impersonating any official should not be contemplated.
Data Protection Act 1998 _You cannot access call logging information._ _You cannot access personnel files._ _You cannot use personal data for automated fraud. detection purposes._ _You cannot use pretext investigations._	All incorrect. It is wise to make sure that registration under the Data Protection Act is comprehensive. There are exceptions when crime is being prevented or detected.
Freedom of Information Act 2000 _This will have a major impact on the access rights of people and companies to sensitive information._	The Act has been delayed or abandoned until 2004.
Human Rights Act 1998 _May be used as a reason for doing nothing._	The Act is not a charter for crooks and, properly interpreted, is fair and sensible.
Official Secrets Act 1911 and 1989 _You cannot obtain details of a person's convictions or other evidence from an official database._	You can, providing the information is not required in connection with employment or continued employment.
Police Act 1998 and the DPA _You cannot ask a person to produce a certificate of conviction during the recruitment process._	CORRECT. See above. You can ask under other circumstances. When the Criminal Records Bureau (see its Website <http://www.crb.gov.uk>) is operational, employers will have access to information that can be used to eliminate unsuitable candidates.
Police and Criminal Evidence Act 1984 _If managers and auditors do not administer a caution at the appropriate time, all interview evidence will be inadmissible._ _Auditors and others need to tape record interviews overtly and follow police procedures._	The need to caution is determined on a case-by-case basis, and only applies to criminal proceedings. Each company should determine who is 'charged with the investigation of crime', whether or not they should administer a caution, and the procedure for tape recording.

Continued

Table 3.5   Effects of legislation on investigatory procedures – *continued*

Law of regulation *What the chattering classes say you cannot do*	What you can do *How to do it*
Prevention of Corruption Act 1906 and 1916 **Public Bodies Corrupt Practices Act 1889** *You cannot pay for confidential information.*	CORRECT, as it is likely to amount to corruption.
Privacy Act *You cannot ask personal questions.*	There is no Privacy Act in the UK, although smelly-socks would argue that a combination of RIPA and the Data Protection Act achieves the same objectives. They do not.
Private Security Industry Act 2001 *You must be an accredited investigator.* *You must hold the appropriate licence.* *You must be a member of a professional organization.*	The Security Industry Board does not yet operate.
Protection from Harassment Act 1997 *You cannot carry out surveillance.*	The targets should never detect that they are under surveillance. Thus harassment should not be an issue.
Public Interest Disclosure Act 1999 *You must have a whistle-blowing procedure.*	Optional. See page 103.
Regulation of Investigatory Powers Act *You cannot tap your own computer and communications systems.* *You cannot use intercepted material in evidence.* *You cannot obtain call log data.* *You cannot search personal property on company premises.* *You cannot carry out surveillance (intrusive or otherwise).* *You cannot use undercover investigators or informants.* *You cannot use vehicle tracking equipment.*	You can, although public authorities must comply with codes of practice. Commercial organizations should have equivalent procedures, although this is not mandatory (see page 103).
Rehabilitation of Offenders Act 1974 *You cannot ask about a person's criminal convictions.*	You can. However, he is entitled not to disclose 'spent' convictions.
Telecommunications (Data Protection and Privacy) Regulations 1999 *You cannot intercept communications.*	You can, with appropriate authority.
Telecommunications (Lawful Business Practice) (Interception of Communications) Regulations *You cannot intercept communications.*	You can, with appropriate authority.
Telecommunications Act 1984 *You cannot obtain call log data (Section 45).* *Pretext calls are 'offensive' and contravene Section 43.* *Pretext calls are illegal because they are a 'nuisance'.*	There is an exception for the investigation of any criminal offence.

Continued

Table 3.5   Effects of legislation on investigatory procedures – *concluded*

Law of regulation *What the chattering classes say you cannot do*	What you can do *How to do it*
Theft Act 1978 et seq. *You cannot carry out pretext investigations.* *You cannot carry out trash searches.*	You can, under controlled conditions. See page 59. You can. See below.
Trespass (Civil) *You cannot enter onto enclosed premises to pick up trash.*	You can. If you are asked to leave, you must do so. There is an offence under Section 4 of the Vagrancy Act 1861 of being in enclosed premises for an unlawful purpose.
Wireless and Telegraphy Act 1948 *You cannot use bugging devices.*	You can, providing they are of an approved type and, when communications transmissions are being intercepted, comply with RIPA.
Wireless and Telegraphy Regulations 2001 *You cannot use bugging devices.* *You cannot intercept communications.* *You cannot fit a tracking device to a vehicle personally owned by a suspect.*	You can, especially when the prevention or detection of crime is concerned. There is no restriction providing only magnetic attachments are used and there is no damage to property. There is similarly no breach of RIPA or the Wireless and Telegraphy Acts.

- Make sure the most sensible risks and investigatory methods are covered in a fraud policy and procedures (see pages 97 *et seq.*).

- Question every interpretation. If you see the word 'guideline' in an official or quango publication, remember it is not mandatory, and may simply reflect the liberal aspirations of the author, rather than the literal interpretation of the law.

- Keep your eyes open for changes in the law and regulatory procedures.

Finally, although the law is full of dangers – and most give advantage to the fraudsters – there are always ways of solving even the most difficult case, within the law and in full compliance with the ethical standards of the organization concerned.

TRASH SEARCHES

One of the common ways in which investigators, journalists and even lawyers obtain evidence is by raking through the trash thrown out by suspects and others at their homes or offices. Although this is not the most odorous job, it can be very productive. In most countries, this trash-searching is legal and the resulting evidence is admissible.

To avoid the trainee dustman being charged with trash theft, he may have to prove that the material was returned to the place from which it was removed and that there was no intention to permanently deprive the owner of it. Copies may be retained and tendered in evidence, but a creative defence lawyer may argue that the crook's copyright has been breached, and take diversionary legal action on that basis. It is unlikely to succeed.

In practice, investigators should keep a record of trash searches, how and when they were conducted, and how and when the material was returned. This record will demonstrate that there was no intention to permanently deprive the owner of the trash.

'Mrs Scrubbs will now read the contents of our competitors' waste paper bins.'

Some lawyers caution that trash should not be removed from enclosed premises, such as a garden or driveway, because to do so would amount to criminal trespass and risk prosecution under the Vagrancy Act 1861. In fact, this is not so, as the offence involves entering onto enclosed premises with the intention of committing a criminal act. If trash is to be returned, there is no offence, and thus no criminal trespass.

The argument that trash-searching might violate the 'fair collection' provisions of the Data Protection Act does not apply where the collection is for the purpose of preventing or detecting crime or where the data is not entered into a computer or structured manual system.

BANKING RECORDS

Introduction

In many investigations, details of the criminal's bank records, the telephone calls he has made and other sensitive data may be of great value as intelligence. This can be used to obtain production and other orders so that admissible evidence may be obtained. The law in the UK is typical internationally and illustrates that usually even the most sensitive information can be obtained and used quite legally.

Basic position

In principle, banks have a civil law contractual obligation of confidentiality to their clients, and if they break it, may be liable for any resulting damage. Bank employees have a duty to their employers not to disclose sensitive information to third parties – although, not surprisingly, bankers often freely exchange information between themselves, and 'bankers' references' are tools of the trade. References and information exchanges between bankers are expected rather than condemned. Unlike official secrets, there is no statutory protection of banking information.

Most banks are registered under the Data Protection Act to process personal data, and many have specific provisions covering the disclosure of information to the police, their own investigation and security departments, to private investigators, regulators and others. If their registration is defective, they (and the person receiving personal data) could be in violation of Section 55 of the Data Protection Act unless the disclosure is for the detection or prevention of crime, in which case there is no restriction.

When security departments employed by different banks work together on joint investigations, they and any investigators or lawyers retained by them exchange information freely without anyone – except the crooks – taking offence.

Banks also freely disclose sensitive information to the regulators, and under money laundering regulations, to the police. The point is that there is nothing sacred about bank information, although there is a feeling that for third parties to obtain it – without the permission of the client – is malodorous or worse.

Voluntary disclosure by banks

Courts have decided (*Tournier* v. *National Provincial and Union Bank of England* (1924)) that bankers are not liable for any breach of confidentiality where:

• the customer has provided his express or implied consent

- disclosure is under the compulsion of law
- there is a duty to the public to disclose (typically where State security is involved or where the public duty overrides the obligations to the customer)
- the interests of the bank require disclosure (where, for example, a bank sues a customer for a bad debt).

In the Canadian case of the *Canadian Imperial Bank of Commerce* v. *Sadrudin Alibhia Sayani and Others*, the Court of Appeal went further and stated that a bank has no liability when it acts in order to prevent the deception of itself or of a third party. In fact, it could be argued that a bank would be liable if it did nothing while it knew a third party was being cheated.

A leading English lawyer commenting on the Canadian case stated:

> this essentially confirms that the bank has no liability for breach of confidentiality where it acts in order to prevent the deception of a third party. This Court of Appeal case confirms what I always understood the position to be under English law, which is that a bank may disclose information relating to customers or potential customers where it is necessary to avoid third parties being misled. The fact that in this case the circumstances related simply to misrepresentation, and not fraud, is a major step forward.

Thus banks can provide information when it is in their interest – or in the interest of a party who might be deceived – to do so. Even if disclosure is of personal data to parties not included in its registration under the Data Protection Act, there is no offence if the purpose is the prevention or detection of crime.

Pretext calls against the bank

An investigator may pose as the customer and approach a bank on a pretext, possibly asking for copies of an account to be forwarded to an accommodation address. Such pretexts expose the investigator to the risks of criminal prosecution for obtaining property by deception if a tangible object, such as a document, disk or piece of paper, is obtained as a result. An offence of attempting to obtain may also arise, however.

'Information' is not defined as 'property', and cannot be stolen. The practice of simply obtaining information or knowledge, however gross the deception might be, is not a breach of the criminal law (see the case of the *Director of Public Prosecutions* v. *Withers* 1974). The test under the Theft Act is whether or not a tangible item was obtained as a result of the pretext. However, pretext calls could result in breaches of the Data Protection Act 1998, unless the objective is the prevention or detection of crime. Again, the exclusion applies.

A very interesting point arises in countries where breaches of bank secrecy expose employees to a criminal charge, and there is no exception for the detection and prevention of crime. Obviously, if a bank employee knowingly contravenes the law, he is unlikely to have a defence. Equally, the third party inducing him to break the law may also be guilty under the banking laws, for conspiracy or under any law making attempts to commit crime illegal.

But if the bank employee is deceived by a pretext call, his disclosure lacks guilty knowledge and he has not committed an offence. Since no offence has been committed by the employee, the third party is most likely to be absolved of both an attempt and conspiracy. It is an esoteric point, which investigators would be most strongly advised not to test.

Pretexts against the suspect

The suspect may be approached on a pretext, for example that a brilliant investment opportunity is available to him. Once hooked (and fortunately, most crooks are excessively greedy), the suspect may be asked to prove his financial standing and to produce 'information' (but not physical statements) relating to his bank and investment accounts. Surprisingly, this technique works more often than it fails. The resulting evidence is admissible. However, care has to be taken that the undercover investigator does not pose as any form of government official, as such pretences would contravene Customs & Excise, immigration, police and other legal strictures on 'impersonation'.

Bribery of bank officials

Criminal offences will be committed if a bank employee receives a personal benefit for disclosing sensitive information (whether personal or not), and the person paying him will be equally liable. If the employee removes a physical item – such as a statement – or takes a photocopy and passes it to a third party, both could be prosecuted for theft. No professional investigator would ever pay to obtain such information.

Trash searches

If sensitive banking information is collected from the trash outside a bank (and there is usually a limitless supply of it) or from outside the home of the suspect or a bank employee, there is no contravention of the criminal law, if the originals are returned. The investigator may go a step further and telephone the bank, posing as the customer, and ask for duplicate statements to be sent to his home so that when they are thrown out in the trash they can be copied and returned. This is dangerous territory and should not be entered.

Overseas banks and trusts

Many offshore financial centres (see pages 191 *et seq.*) have tough laws on banking secrecy, and specific legal advice should be obtained before any enquiries are made to obtain confidential information from them.

The bottom line

Investigators are most strongly advised *not* to try to obtain sensitive information directly from banks or bankers without specific endorsement by litigation lawyers. Working through a common interest with the bank or pretexts against the suspect are another matter, but should still be legally blessed.

CREDIT AND DEBIT CARDS

The rules and possibilities for obtaining credit card transaction and account details parallel those for banks.

TELEPHONE CALL RECORDS

Most providers of telephone services are allowed, under their Data Protection Act registrations, to pass call data to third parties, including the police and external investigators, for the prevention and detection of crime. Such disclosures do not contravene the Telecommunications Act 1984 nor the Regulation of Investigatory Powers Act 2000 if the investigator has equivalent conditions of registration. However, with the forthcoming imple-mentation of the Private Security Industry Act, the position could change – as they say: 'Watch this space.'

NAMES AND ADDRESSES OF TELEPHONE SUBSCRIBERS

Providers of telecommunications services are required to maintain an up-to-date directory of subscribers which is available to the public based on an alphabetical search of the name and on the address. In addition, in most civilized countries the telecommunications providers supply reverse searching facilities so that the name and address of a subscriber can be traced from a number.

In the UK, reverse searching is not possible (see page 55), although the information can often be found through a pretext, through an Internet search (<http://www.192.com>) or through a CD called *Info Disk* (<http://www.icdpublishing.com>). Both are excellent, and give world-wide coverage.

INTERNET SITES, NEWSGROUPS, CHAT AND E-MAILS

The content of e-mail messages and the Websites visited by the suspect can provide a wealth of information. If a suspect's e-mail address or Internet chat account is known, then a pretext approach can often yield results (particularly when supposedly undertaken by an attractive 20-something female against a male target!). It is more difficult to attract a suspect to join a particular thread of discussion in a newsgroup or lure him to visit a particular Internet site without a little legal jiggery-pokery and imagination.

A court order can be obtained at the appropriate stage of an investigation to examine the content of a suspect's computer or their ISP's records. Computer forensic techniques are then employed – see page 86. Under no circumstances should an investigator ever engage in remote computer 'hacking' or any other violation of the Computer Misuse Acts.

OFFICIAL SECRETS AND POLICE RECORDS

Although the all-embracing Section 2 of the Official Secrets Act 1911 has been repealed, many of its provisions have been replaced by the Data Protection Act, and the circumstances in which government bodies can disclose information are very limited.

Thus for any professional investigator, vehicle licensing, police and other governmental records are absolutely taboo, and under no circumstances, short of a court order, should they be sought. Even the mildest attempt to obtain them can result in criminal prosecution under the Data Protection Act – and deservedly so,

However, at the appropriate time, suspects can be asked to obtain a certificate from the Criminal Records Bureau under Part IV of the Police Act 1997. The result is admissible in both civil and criminal proceedings. Similarly, details of a vehicle's ownership may be obtained by a pretext or by speaking to the garage from which it was purchased. The source of the vehicle is usually obvious from window stickers and number plates.

UTILITY COMPANIES

Water, gas and electricity providers usually have extensive databases that contain intelligence vital to fraud investigations. Providing the Data Registrations are properly made, information may be passed to police and private investigators without breaches of either the civil or criminal laws.

THE BOTTOM LINE

The bottom line is that victims of fraud – who are investigating or preventing crime – can often obtain most sensitive information quite legally, and use it in both civil and criminal proceedings.

The Dangers of Partners in Crime

In 2000, the British Government announced an 'initiative' under which certain fraud cases would be delegated by the police to private firms which had – supposedly – been designated as 'accredited investigators'. The initiative anticipated the Private Security Industry Act, but was ill-considered, contravened European laws on competition, and was generally a disaster. The Home Office liked it. The only upside was that the initiative would have resulted in fees for the big accounting firms and other members of the Confederation of British Industry, to which the scheme was limited. Ultimately, the victims of fraud would have to pay the bills of the accounting firms retained by the police.

THE GRANNY PARALLEL

This is much like reporting to the police that your Granny has been kidnapped, only to be told: 'Go and see PriceWaterhouseCoopers, they will do the investigation for you, and when they have found the people responsible – and hope- fully your Granny – we will process the criminal charges. And by the way, PWC's fees will be around £100 000 which you will have to pay, but you don't have to retain them if you don't want Granny back.'

The big problem was that the so-called 'accredited investigators' (and none were) would be acting as agents of the government, and thus could fall under the definition of 'public authorities', with all that it entails. The point was never argued, because no cases under the 'initiative' came to trial. But if they had, there is little doubt that the human rights issues would have been dominant, and the private firms – acting as surrogate public authorities – held to the appropriate standards, with the risks of evidence being excluded in both civil and criminal proceedings.

The lesson for commercial victims of fraud is to take care that chosen investigators are not classified as 'public authorities', for if they are, the techniques they can use on their clients' behalf – whether civil or criminal – may be severely limited.

'Oh no! We knew Hannibal had elephants, we just didn't realize he was capable
of launching them!'

Intelligence and Evidence

INTELLIGENCE

A phrase often heard in investigations is: 'We know he did it, but we don't have any evidence.' This is rarely correct. In many investigations, information (or intelligence, which is essentially the same thing and consists of knowledge, suspicions, deductions and extrapolations made there from) is uncovered suggesting that X did Y or something else happened. Often, intelligence is dismissed, but it is critical, and turning it into 'evidence' calls for a combination of legal and investigative skills.

Table 3.6   Types of evidence

Types of evidence *Examples*	How it is presented in court	How it is collated by the investigator
Oral evidence *What the suspect said when he was interviewed*	Given on oath from the witness box by a person with first-hand knowledge of the facts at issue	In statements (including his own), Proofs of Evidence, Affidavits or transcripts of tape recordings
Documentary evidence *False purchase invoices*	Produced by a witness as part of his oral evidence. Items which are produced to a court by a witness are normally called 'exhibits'	Originals, copies and schedules prepared by the witnesses
Photocopies of original exhibits *Photocopies of sales invoices*	Produced by a witness as part of his oral evidence, providing the court is satisfied that the originals are no longer available	Copies, extracts and schedules prepared by a witness
Copies of overseas bank accounts and other records	Produced by an employee from the bank concerned as part of his oral evidence or by another witness under the Criminal Evidence Acts	Certified copies and schedules prepared by the witness
Real evidence *Stolen goods and weapons*	Produced by a witness as part of his oral evidence	Produced in court or illustrated by photographs
Tape and video recordings *Of interviews with the suspect or telephone calls made by him*	Produced by a witness as part of his oral evidence	The original recording and a transcript may be produced in court
Expert evidence *Opinion by a computer technician*	Expert evidence is one of the main exceptions to the hearsay rule. The expert may give evidence under oath of his opinion concerning some or all of the facts in issue	Proof of Evidence or statement
Computerized evidence *Disks, tapes, printouts, etc.*	Produced by a witness as part of his oral evidence; the witness must be able to establish the exhibit was produced in the normal course of business on a computer of proven reliability	Proof of Evidence or statement; original or copies of computer media

EVIDENCE

Evidence is simply facts, relating to a matter in issue, which are admissible in court.

Ultimately, the judge in the case concerned will decide what is admissible and what it not. There is nothing magic or difficult about evidence.

There are a number of categories of evidence, and these are set out in Table 3.6.

REAL EVIDENCE

Real evidence is a physical item that is relevant to the facts in issue; for example, a gun in a murder case, a fraudulent invoice, or a screwdriver used in a burglary. Real evidence is produced as an *exhibit* by a witness who has first-hand knowledge of its relevance.

THE NEED TO ESTABLISH CONTINUITY

Witnesses must be able to establish continuity, or the 'chain' between the time an exhibit came into their possession and its production in court. For example, an investigator will need to show how, when, where and by whom a document was recovered, and how it was handled from that time to its production in court. This makes it imperative that accurate records are maintained. Equally important, the witness must satisfy the court about the integrity of the exhibit, confirming that it has not been altered in any way.

INTERVIEW EVIDENCE

It is very important that people suspected of fraud are not forced or tricked into making confessions, and that interview techniques can be defended without embarrassment in court. Under no circumstances should the investigator make threats or promises to induce a person to confess.

In England, people who work as professional investigators must administer a 'caution' as soon as there is evidence that causes them to suspect that the person being interviewed is responsible for a crime. The effect of the caution is that the person is not obliged to say anything unless he wishes to do so, and that anything he says may be given in evidence. He must also be warned that an adverse inference may be drawn if he fails to explain anything on which his defence will rely.

In the UK, the Police and Criminal Evidence Act (PACE) sets out the rules for police officers and others 'charged with the investigation of criminal offences', whatever this term means. If a caution is not given at the appropriate time, all statements made by the suspect, both before and after, are unlikely to be admissible.

It should be noted, however, that the requirement to administer a caution only applies to criminal prosecutions and to professional investigators. Nevertheless, each company should consider its approach and set out its position on cautioning in a fraud policy (see pages 97 *et seq*.). The optimum solution is to have auditors and investigators who might be called on to investigate crime trained in interview techniques in general, and in the administration of cautions and tape recording of interviews. Cautioning is not a big deal, and most suspects will answer questions – untruthfully – whether they are cautioned or not.

HEARSAY EVIDENCE

Evidence in criminal cases must usually be given – under oath – by a witness who has first-hand knowledge of the facts in issue. For example, if A who is accused of a crime makes an admission to B who repeats it to C:

- B can give evidence against A, stating what A told him.
- C cannot give evidence against A, because he was not present at the conversation between A and B. Thus his evidence is 'hearsay'.

In some civil cases, hearsay evidence will be admitted at the discretion of the judge.

Equivalent rules apply to documentary and other evidence. For example, a clerk who prepared a purchase order can go into the witness box, produce it as an exhibit, and can be cross-examined by the opposing side about its contents. Any evidence from the clerk's manager (who has no firsthand knowledge of the document) may be excluded under the 'hearsay' rules.

There are some important exceptions to the hearsay rule. Some witnesses who are recognized by the court as experts are able to express an opinion. For example, a document-examiner may express his opinion that a certain person's handwriting is on a document. Computer evidence may be exhibited by a witness who has no firsthand knowledge of the transactions concerned, but who is able to prove to the court that the records concerned were produced in the ordinary course of business by a system of proven reliability.

ENTRAPMENT AND AGENTS PROVOCATEURS

Lawyers will sometimes argue that their clients have been entrapped into committing a crime by an unscrupulous investigator or confidential informant. Again, the allegation is easily made, but far more difficult to sustain. Entrapment means cajoling someone into committing a crime they would not otherwise commit. If the crime – or a continuum of dishonest activity – is ongoing and an investigator or informant infiltrates it, this is not entrapment.

In some cases – and the brutal murder of Rachel Nickell on Wimbledon Common is a tragic example – investigators may approach the suspect on a pretext to gain his trust in the hope of discovering real evidence, such as the knife used or some feature of the crime known only to the perpetrator. The trial judge in Rachel's case was unjustly scathing over the approach used by the police, and excluded damning evidence on grounds that were clear to him, but less clear to anyone else. This case aside, investigators can infiltrate criminal groups, with the resulting evidence being admissible.

However, whatever the circumstances, undercover investigations, infiltration and pretexts must be handled with care and under advice of experienced litigation lawyers. If the undercover investigator or confidential informant is not prepared to give evidence in a criminal trial, that fact should be made clear to the prosecuting authorities at the outset, as the defendant's inability to cross-examine him may result in a breach of the fair trial principle under the European Convention of Human Rights.

LIBEL AND SLANDER

People who are the subject of investigation sometimes threaten to take action because they claim that they have been libelled or slandered. In most cases, these threats should be viewed as being no more than a ploy to throw the investigation off course.

Libel is an untrue defamatory statement in a permanent form – usually in writing. Slander is oral libel, and is governed by similar rules. It is obvious that anything which is true cannot be libel or slander.

An accusation made directly to a suspect that the interviewer believes him responsible for dishonesty is not slanderous. Similarly, an unproved, or even incorrect, allegation to a potential witness will not normally be actionable because it is privileged under the common business interest rule (see page 39). However, an unproved and untrue defamatory state-ment, for example that someone is a thief, made in public or to a person who does not have a common business interest may be actionable.

In proceedings for libel or slander, the claimant must establish that the words used about him were *untrue*, defamatory and lowered his estimation in the minds of right-thinking people (for example, not readers of *The Sun*). Interestingly, in the extremely nauseating fight between Neil Hamilton and Mohamed Fayed, it was argued that neither could be defamed, as their reputations were already in tatters. This is an interesting concept, but not relevant to fraud.

In any case, the claimant has to prove that the statement was made to at least one person, other than the defendant's wife, and that it caused him some quantifiable damage. There is a vast difference between threatening to take action for alleged defamation and succeeding. Besides that, during the discovery and legal processes which result from the libel action, the claimant may be compelled to produce records that destroy his case and provide evidence of other transgressions. Threatening action for libel is easy; seeing it through to success can be a very unwise move for the crook.

There are a number of defences to actions for libel and slander:

- **Justification** – The burden of proof is on the defendant to show that the statement was substantially true. For example, in the British case of the *Observer* v. *Redgrave*, the general article was substantiated, although some words could not be justified. The court deter-mined that libel had not been committed. So if a defendant can prove that the allegations were substantially true, he will not be penalized.

- **Legal Professional Privilege** – Communication between a lawyer and his client is absolutely privileged (see page 39).

Thus it is only in exceptional circumstances that the victim of fraud, or someone working on his behalf, could be successfully prosecuted for slander or libel. However, all investigators must act fairly and respect the rights of those with whom they deal.

TAPE RECORDING AND NOTES

Laws on the legality of tape recording conversations without the consent of all of the parties concerned vary from country to country. In the USA, covert tape recording is legal in some states and illegal in others. In England, recordings can be made secretly by any party to a conversation, and the resulting tapes are admissible in civil and criminal proceedings.

STATEMENTS AND PROOFS OF EVIDENCE

Statements made by suspects and witnesses are vital in fraud cases, and are used by counsel to lead the witness through his evidence. If he fails to 'come up to proof', his statement can be used to cross-examine him as a hostile witness. In civil cases, statements may be read by the lawyers concerned without the need to call the witness.

All formal statements (whether the witness is called or not) have to be disclosed to the opposing party but unsigned Proofs of Evidence (obtained in contemplation of legal proceedings and possibly including the same material as in a statement) are normally protected against disclosure by legal professional privilege. Thus in the early stage of most investigations, Proofs of Evidence are preferable to formal statements. Ultimately, lawyers will determine whether disclosure is necessary.

Under the Criminal Justice Act and the Magistrate's Court Act 1980, witnesses may make a statement on a special form which certifies that it is true and correct, and on the understanding that if it is untrue, they could be exposed to criminal prosecution for perjury. Such statements are very useful, but should only be used by experienced investigators. An example of the form is given in Appendix 5.

DOCUMENTARY EVIDENCE

General provisions

Documents which are relevant to the facts in issue may be produced in court (as 'Exhibits') by a witness giving evidence under oath. In most countries, the originals are considered the best evidence but, when these are not available, copies may be admitted. In some developing and transitional countries, the original documents are vital, and if they cannot be produced, the evidence is lost for ever. Unsurprisingly, there are a lot of document-eating dogs and spontaneous combustions in such jurisdictions.

There is no generally available authority given to a fraud victim to demand access to, or to search for, documents in the possession of third parties. This is the starting point, but there are some exceptions.

Co-operation

Often, third parties, such as customers and suppliers, will co-operate voluntarily in a fraud investigation and produce records in the hope that business relations with the corporate victim will not suffer. The victim's position is obviously enhanced if in its Standard Terms and Conditions of Business it has rights to audit the records of suppliers, distributors, agents and others with whom it has a commercial relationship. This point is addressed on page 127.

Civil action for discovery

Where the co-operation of third parties or defendants is unlikely to be forthcoming, lawyers should be consulted with a view to taking a civil action, to obtain pre-emptive orders for important evidence in the possession of innocent third parties as well as the suspects.

Citizens' arrest

In the United Kingdom, under Section 24(4)–(7) of the Police and Criminal Evidence Act 1984, 'any person may arrest anyone without a warrant', providing:

- He is in the act of committing an arrestable offence (this includes all thefts and frauds).
- He has reasonable grounds for suspecting him to be committing such an offence.
- Where an arrestable offence has been committed, he may arrest anyone who is guilty of the offence or anyone whom he has reasonable grounds for suspecting to be guilty of it.

This is an important power, available to all citizens, especially if a person is caught while trying to remove or destroy evidence. All that is necessary is to tell the person he is being arrested and to take him to a police station or call for police assistance as soon as possible. Reasonable force can be used (see Section 3 of the Criminal Law Act 1967), but great care must be taken in all cases, especially when the villain is larger than the investigator and is with his mum or dog.

Searches on the employer's premises

Employers are entitled to search anything, but not any person, on their premises. This means that desks, briefcases, cupboards or computers used by a suspect and owned by the victim may be searched. This has become a potentially controversial area (because of human rights legislation), but the dangers can be minimized by setting out the employer's rights in a fraud policy (see pages 97 *et seq.*).

Searches of third-party premises

The owner of any premises, or a manager in charge of them, may give permission to search. Permission may be revoked, in which case the documents or other evidence concerned must be returned without delay, although copies may be retained.

The consent of third parties must not be obtained by deceit or trickery, otherwise the investigator could be accused of the serious criminal offence of obtaining property by deception under the Theft Act 1968 *et seq.*

COMPUTER EVIDENCE

Legality

Particular attention should be paid to the acquisition and preservation of computer evidence. Again, the investigator must comply with a raft of new legislation. Computers owned by the company can be accessed overtly or covertly without the user's permission when crime is being investigated. However, it would be illegal to access a laptop computer, personal digital assistant or mobile telephone memory owned by an individual, even when it is on company premises, without his permission. If he has used diskettes paid for by the company, even on his personal computer, there is a strong argument that they can be copied and examined without his authority.

The Regulation of Investigatory Powers Act 2000 gives government investigators the right to demand the production of encryption keys. There is no equivalent in the business world. Thus businesses should address this issue in their fraud policy (see page 97).

Evidence required

Wherever possible, original media, such as disks, diskettes, tapes and so on, should be obtained. There are two main reasons for this:

- **Admissibility** – The courts in most countries have ruled that to be held admissible, computer evidence must have been produced in the normal course of business and on a machine of proven reliability. Copies taken for other than normal processing requirements or special reports might be inadmissible.

- **Integrity** – It is possible that original computer media may contain data in image or digital form which will not be read by a copy program. For example, deleted files usually remain on the original disk until their space is overwritten by new data, but are not read by normal copying and back-up utilities. Thus computers should only be examined by qualified experts, so that full and accurate images are obtained.

Conclusion

The laws are complex and evolving. It is essential that investigations comply with the highest legal and ethical standards, while standing a realistic chance of exposing crooks. Balance (or proportionality) is critical. It can be turned to the advantage of victims if potential victims address the more controversial and difficult issues in a fraud policy and investigatory procedures (see page 97).

'Ye Gods! That's it? You nicked the whole pension fund for that??'

4 Essential Aspects of Investigations

The Problems and Principles

DISHONESTY GENERATES EMOTION

Investigations can be contentious and controversial, and – of necessity – are sometimes conducted in uncharted aspects of the law. Each case is different, suspects and witnesses react inconsistently, and there is the ever-present danger that one mistake will jeopardize everything and cause adverse publicity and long-lasting problems. The first golden rule for the investigator is:

If a mistake has been made, admit it. Never lie.

In many cases, criminals counter-attack and make threats that cool the victim's enthusiasm for pursuing his rights. Fraud investigations are never easy, they take time and cost money, but everything should be recoverable. Management should be made to understand this point.

Perhaps the biggest problem is aligning management's expectations. Many are used to watching television detective programmes where even the most complex case is solved within an hour, including commercial breaks. In real life, investigations are much more difficult.

ESSENTIAL COMPONENTS OF SUCCESSFUL INVESTIGATIONS

There are three vital components of most successful investigations:

- effective, independent management control, based on clear objectives and policies
- skilled resources
- effective processes that result in the *First Step* being devastating for the crooks.

These are discussed later in this part and the essential features incorporated in Part 2 (pages 113 *et seq.*) under the appropriate investigation stages.

OVERRIDING PRINCIPLES

An overriding principle of all cases is that investigators must always act honestly, within the law, and in anticipation that their results and the methods used to obtain them will be subject to the closest scrutiny in court by skilled lawyers with the benefit of hindsight.

Never do anything that you could not defend honestly in court.

The second overriding principle is that suspicions must be investigated thoroughly, sometimes using techniques which, although legal and ethically sound, can be controversial. Criminals seldom volunteer evidence of their guilt unless an investigation puts them under pressure to do so, and they usually counter-attack.

If you don't like smells, don't hunt skunk.

Essential Requirements of Investigations

There are three important elements that must be established in most fraud investigations.

PROOF OF LOSS

Proof of loss or intended loss is vital, and may be established by, for example:

Table 4.1   Proof of loss

How proof is established	Examples
Admissions by the suspect or his accomplices about the amount they have stolen	The admissions may be presented to a court by the person who interviewed the suspect, or by the suspects themselves.
Documentary evidence schedules	• sales by a receiver of stolen goods or sales in excess of his legitimate purchases • analysis of bank statements • analysis of stock or other losses
By surveillance	The results of surveillance or observation may be summarized on schedules produced by a witness.
Expert testimony	An expert may give an opinion on the amount lost or defrauded.

The method of proof and computations must be fair and capable of scrutiny, but the victim is entitled to investigate fully, to maximize his recoveries. It should be noted that calculations of inventory losses cannot be used for quantifying fidelity insurance claims unless other evidence links the figures to specific dishonest behaviour by an insured employee. For example, if an employee admits he has been stealing for twenty years at an average of £20 000 per annum, £400 000 of stock losses can be included in the claim.

PROOF OF GUILTY KNOWLEDGE

Proof of responsibility for the alleged act and guilty knowledge (or *mens rea*) are essential ingredients in all criminal and most civil cases.

Criminal intent may be proved by:

• admissions and confessions by the fraudster or by the co-accused

- failure to volunteer the truth when initially questioned, or inconsistent and demonstrably untrue answers
- inference, being the outcome of a deliberate act or repeated transgressions
- circumstances surrounding the crime, and deviations from accepted procedures
- falsified, destroyed records, deception or false excuses
- physical evidence, photographs and films
- opinion of expert witness.

Usually, the best method of establishing guilty knowledge is from admissions made by the suspects during interviews or from the statements of witnesses. Success in this area depends on effective interviewing. (See Chapter 10, page 149)

PROOF OF PERSONAL GAIN

Proving that the fraudster gained from his dishonesty is useful whatever the objectives of an investigation. Some fidelity insurance policies require proof that an insured person acted with 'manifest intent' to cause the victim to sustain a loss, usually with the object of personal gain for himself or of providing a benefit for someone else.

Proof of personal gain may result from:

- admissions made by the suspects
- analysis of the suspect's bank accounts, cash books and other records
- analysis of bank accounts of suppliers, customers and third parties showing payments to the perpetrator or to a party nominated by him
- analysis of records kept by the perpetrator
- statements of witnesses, especially expert testimony
- observation records
- extrapolations of known facts.

Any combination of the above may also constitute proof. There is an important word in most fraud cases and all insurance claims: 'causation'. This means that it is vital to show that the loss was *caused* by the fraudster's intent, and was not merely consequential. In reality this is not a difficult point, but it should be noted that the cause of a multi-million pound loss could have been prompted by a small gain to the perpetrator. The insurance claim is then for the full amount of the loss.

Methods of Investigation

SUMMARY OF MAIN METHODS AND TECHNIQUES

Each case must be planned using professional, legal, ethical and co-ordinated methods. Some steps can be carried out without any danger of alerting the suspects, and others cannot. The timing of investigative steps and consideration of whether they might forewarn the suspects is critical (see Table 4.2).

Table 4.2   Methods of investigation

Method (See pages 80 to 95 for details)	Timing in relation to the First Step	Establishes proof of		
		Loss	Intent	Responsibility
1	**2**	**3**	**4**	**5**
Investigation control	Throughout			
Database checks	Before	Unlikely	Possibly	Yes
Covert searches	Before	Yes	Yes	Yes
Intelligence analysis	Throughout	Possible	Possible	Possible
Analysis of documents	Before	Yes	Yes	Yes
Schedules	Before	Yes	Possibly	Yes
Analysis of computers	Before	Possibly	Yes	Yes
Fraud profile analysis	After	Yes	Possibly	Possibly
Observation and surveillance	Before	Possibly	Yes	Yes
Audio surveillance	Before	Yes	Yes	Yes
Contrived opportunities	Before	Yes	Yes	Yes
Pretexts and undercover	Before	Yes	Yes	Yes
Confidential informants	Before	Yes	Yes	Yes
Site visits	Before	Possibly	Unlikely	Possibly
Asset location and tracing	Before	Possibly	Possibly	Yes
Pre-emptive legal actions	First Step	Yes	Yes	Yes
Interviews with suspects	During	Yes	Yes	Yes
Interviews with witnesses	During	Yes	Yes	Yes
Forensic and expert evidence	After	Yes	Possibly	Possibly
External audits	After	Yes	Yes	Yes

Column 2 on Table 4.2 shows whether the technique can be used before the First Step is taken without alerting the suspects. Columns 3–5 show the type of evidence that each technique should produce.

IMPORTANT PRINCIPLES

Many inexperienced investigators fail because they do not recognize the central issues that must be proven, or the theory of the case. The general rules of investigation are as follows:

- Always have a clear theory of the worst case, and revise it as the investigation proceeds (see page 123) . Work on the basis that everything that happened was deliberately planned, and that there is a reason for everything. Pay particular attention to things that should have happened, but didn't.
- Pay particular attention to information that does not fit the fraud theory, and always keep an open mind.
- Do not let emotion or bias affect the theory or investigations plan.
- Never overlook the obvious, and check everything.

Table 4.3   Investigation control

Method	Detail
PLANNING	
Using only legal techniques and compliance with the law	• Written investigatory procedures (see page 103) • Ensure that the victim's registration under the Data Protection Act is accurate and does not impede the exchange of information with other organizations
Aligning top management expectations	• Timing • Cost • Action plan • Adverse consequences
Setting objectives and case registration	• Decide on the optimum outcome especially whether criminal or civil litigation is a potential outcome • Obtain top management approval • Register the case internally to show it concerns the prevention or investigation of crime (thus assisting with Data Protection Act requirements)
Fraud theory and investigations plan	• See page 123
PROCESSES	
Managing the investigation professionally	• The investigation should be under the control of a senior line manager with the appropriate authority and budget and totally independent of the area in which the fraud is suspected • He should have access to professional legal and investigative resources • He should seek to cost-justify the investigation at various stages
Controlling the budget	• Should focus on cost-effectiveness rather than pure cost
Co-ordination and documentary standards	• A secure network should be established for members of the project team • Sensitive files – especially on laptop computers – should be encrypted • Standard document formats, templates and naming conventions should be used by all team members • All documents should show their date of creation and modification and their version numbers. This is especially important for spreadsheets
Establishing the privileged nature of findings	• The investigations team should address all reports to its legal advisers • All documentation should be marked 'privileged and confidential, with a view to legal proceedings'
Controlling and securing the evidence	• The evidence should be catalogued and secured • The continuity of all evidence should be established • The integrity of evidence should be preserved
Working quickly and accounting for time	• The investigation should be completed as quickly as possible • All people working on the investigation should keep diaries and submit timesheets • All people working on the investigation should communicate regularly with each other • Hold regular update and brainstorming sessions

Continued

Table 4.3   Investigation control – *concluded*

Method	Detail
Documenting results	• Reports, statements or file notes should be prepared for every completed action
Reviewing results and deciding on further action	• The investigation team should review results at least once a week and decide on further actions • Planned actions should be approved by the team's lawyer and controlled through a data base management system
Combining selected legal actions and field investigations	• Manage disparate disciplines • Avoid political posturing
Counter-intelligence	• Assume the suspects are watching you • Maintain the tightest levels of security
Maintaining professional standards and discipline	• Members of the team should be fully briefed • They should understand the theory of the worst case • They should work to the Investigations Plan • They should understand the law • They should not comment on the case to people who do not have the need to know • They should not take actions which have not been approved, unless there are exceptional circumstances

- Use a combination of investigative techniques.
- If you hit a brick wall, find a way around it, and never give up. The last person left standing wins.

Investigations are 90 per cent hard work, 15 per cent luck, 25 per cent intuition and 9.75 per cent being able to add up (this is just to make sure you are still awake . . .).

The best investigators pursue every angle, and never give up.

INVESTIGATION CONTROL

This may not be a self-standing technique, but overall control of a large investigation is vital. Control should be maintained by the means outlined in Table 4.3.

The critical factors of control are adequate professional resources and defined, planned processes, based on an evolving fraud theory and investigations plan. The investigation must be driven by these, and *not* by an emotional wish to limit recovery costs (see the 'Deadly Sins' on page 13).

DATABASE CHECKS

Checking the backgrounds of fraud perpetrators and their associates through public databases, credit bureaux, voters' lists and other sources can pay dividends, and should be completed at the earliest stage in an investigation, and repeated from time to time thereafter. Some recommended public information sources are set out in Table 4.4.

In addition, the Internet should be searched thoroughly for all references to the suspects

Table 4.4   Main sources of information

Database: Subscription service *Free services are shown in italics*	Information available
UK Companies House <http://www.companies-house.gov.uk>	Registration details of all UK companies Directorships and shareholdings Annual accounts and returns Disqualified directors Filing history
Experian and Equifax www.experian.com www.equifax.com	Register of UK electors Credit information (by name and address) Address affiliations
Reuters Business Briefing <http://www.business.reuters.com>	Global press reports for the past 10 years Powerful search facilities
Lexis Nexis <http://www.lexis-nexis.com>	Legislation and case law Global company information Global broadsheet and tabloid coverage
ICC Information Ltd <http://www.icc.com>	Directors and companies (UK and Ireland) Company accounts Microfiche and document imaging
Corporate annual reports online <http://www.carol.co.uk>	Annual reports on line
Corporate Information <http://www.corporateinformation.com>	Listed stock exchange information (global)
Lawtel <http://www.lawtel.co.uk>	Legislation and case law
Financial Times <http://www.ft.com>	Global business coverage
Internet Domain Reverse <http://www.domaincheck.com>	Identifies all known Internet domain names
Yellow Pages Hard-copy *Yellow Pages* <http://www.yellowpages.com> <http://www.yell.com>	

and their associates. Over the years, three search engines have proven most successful in digging out important data. These are:

- **Web Ferret** – <http://www.Ferretsoft.com>
- **Info Ferret** – <http://www.Ferretsoft.com>
- **Copernic Professional** – <http://www.Copernic.com>.

The programs can be downloaded on a trial basis. They are cheap, and very flexible.

KEY POINTS

• •

DO	DON'T
Remember that access to public data and subscription databases is without restriction.	Alert the suspects.
Check everybody, every address, every company and every telephone number.	Overlook anything.
In larger investigations, repeat the process from time to time.	Throw away the results of checks.
Maintain an up-to-date index of all people and companies involved in the case.	Keep any computer or structured manual system without Data Protection Act notification.

COVERT SEARCHES

Work areas

At the earliest stage of an investigation, consider carrying out detailed searches of office and other premises used by the suspects, provided that this will not alert them.

KEY POINTS

• •

DO	DON'T
Make sure the suspects (or their colleagues) are not alerted.	Search personal items such as briefcases or laptops unless the company has the appropriate policies in place.
Video the area before the search, and put everything back in place.	Leave clues that premises have been searched.
Take photocopies, videos or digital photographs of anything that could be relevant.	Enter a person's home without permission.
Copy telephone and fax memories.	
Pay particular attention to the items listed on pages 128 *et seq.*	

Trash searches

Consider having the trash outside the suspects' office or home collected and analysed (see page 59).

KEY POINTS

● ●

DO	**DON'T**
Use professional, experienced operatives for the collection and return (it is not easy!).	Try to do the work yourself.
Make sure the suspects are not alerted.	Keep original material. It must be returned.
Return the trash to the place from which it was removed after copying. Keep detailed records.	Enter onto enclosed premises. Keep original material.
Analyse the results carefully. Update the fraud theory and investigations plan.	Bribe clearners to remove the trash.

INTELLIGENCE ANALYSIS

Depending on the nature of the case, it may be useful to have intelligence on telephone calls made by the suspect and his associates, as well as credit card and other information. Again, it is critical that the suspects are not alerted, and that collection is legal (see Chapter 3).

KEY POINTS

● ●

DO	**DON'T**
Think about all of the sources that might be available. Develop these as part of a fraud contingency plan.	Overlook potential sources of intelligence.
Make sure all parties comply with the Data Protection Act, and record that the dominant purpose is the prevention and detection of crime.	Contravene the Data Protection Act, and don't pay for information.
Analyse the results carefully. Update the fraud theory and investigations plan.	Dismiss any intelligence as being unimportant.

ANALYSIS OF DOCUMENTS

The analysis of documents is very important. The checklists in Appendix 1 sets out the basic processes for analysing documentary evidence.

KEY POINTS

● ●

DO	DON'T
Consider pre-emptive legal action to obtain vital documentation.	Alert the suspects until after the First Step.
Obtain every document that could be relevant, and catalogue it so that the chain of evidence can be established and proper disclosures made at the appropriate time.	Discard any information that could be subject to disclosure in civil or criminal actions.
Always obtain all relevant expense statements, diaries and internal telephone call log records. If possible, obtain call logs from appropriate telecommunications companies.	Overlook this critical intelligence.
Analyse the results carefully. Update the fraud theory and investigations plan.	Ignore the analysis procedures explained in Appendix 1.

SCHEDULES

Standard

Schedules are the lifeblood of successful investigations, and every entry should be traceable to source documentation or evidence. The most important schedules are listed in Table 4.5.

Table 4.5   Important schedules

Type of schedule	Coverage and purpose
Chronology of events or time bar embedding a summary of correspondence	Sets out all of the details, in date and time order, of the fraud concerned. Analysis of call log data and correspondence should be included in this schedule.
Computation of losses	A detailed calculation of losses, working from detailed records to a single-page summary schedule.
Summary of key evidence	This may be used for interviews with witnesses and suspects, and drawn on for the management overview of the investigating report.
Telephone call log analysis	A detailed spreadsheet analysis in *Microsoft Excel* of all internal and external calls, e-mails and faxes that could be relevant to the case.
Details of people involved	A *Microsoft Word* table showing names, addresses, telephone numbers and so on of all suspects and witnesses. This schedule should be updated as the investigation proceeds.

Microsoft Excel is an extremely powerful program, and should be used (in preference to *Microsoft Word*) for all schedules where dates, times and calculations are involved. Its advantages are:

- ability to handle and calculate dates and days between events
- excellent import, export and data cleansing functions
- ability to handle large data sets and make mathematical and logical calculations
- in-built audit trails
- the 'pivot table' function for summarizing large data sets
- powerful sorting and filtering functions.

At least one member of the project team should be an *Excel* specialist. Other useful programs for preparing charts and diagrams are *Microsoft Visio* and *Mind Manager* (see <http://www.mindjet.com>).

KEY POINTS

● ●

DO	DON'T
Use schedules – at every opportunity.	Present complex schedules to management or juries.
Make sure they are auditable and accurate.	Make schedules or charts greater than A3 size.
Use the most appropriate software.	Confuse intelligence with evidence.
Use standard templates showing the version number and last saved date.	Have different versions in use by different members of the investigations team.
Keep schedules up to date as the investigation proceeds.	Rely on out-of-date versions.

I² Charts

I² Limited (see <http://www.i2group.com>) produces excellent software for preparing link diagrams. Some of the variations are shown in Table 4.6.

Table 4.6   Types of I² charts

Type of I² chart	Contents and purposes
Link analysis	Showing the connection between people, organizations, etc.
Network analysis	Produces links from large data sets such as telephone call records, Internet traffic or transactions
Sequence of events	Showing how events unfold over time, and establishing cause and effect
Transaction pattern analysis	Detailed analysis of specific transactions

I² charts should be used extensively in major investigations. They should be kept up to date, and used to refine the fraud theory and investigations plan. An example of an I² chart is given in Appendix 7.

ANALYSIS OF COMPUTERS

All personal computers, diskettes and disk drives to which the suspect may have had access should be examined carefully, ideally by a forensic scientist, rather than by a conventional technician. Examinations may be undertaken covertly before the First Step, or carried out openly afterwards.

Table 4.7 gives some recommendations for hardware and software.

Table 4.7   Computer forensic hardware and software

Type of hardware or software	Use
Current high-end desktop PC with large SCSI hard drives and at least 256 mb RAM. The Award BIOS is particularly friendly to the computer forensics expert	Processing the forensic copies back at the laboratory
Current high-end laptop PC with SCSI and Network Carbus cards	For field acquisitions – either in conjunction with *FastBloc* or through network card or parallel port
Guidance Software's *FastBloc*	High-speed forensic copying of IDE hard drives in the field – with guaranteed 'write-blocking'
Sony DDS external SCSI tape drive, and a selection of SCSI cards	Used in the target desktop with a bootable DOS floppy disk and software such as *SafeBack* which prevents writing to the target medium; no need for a laptop for field acquisition
Guidance Software's *EnCase*	The premier integrated *Windows* computer forensic application; the best all-round performer recognized by courts world-wide
NTI technology forensic software suite	Very capable DOS-based applications preferred by some, again, recognized by courts world-wide
The DIBS range of forensic hardware and software	Excellent range of tools
Access data's password recovery tools	Excellent for recovering encrypted documents; some encryption (such as PGP) is unbreakable when used correctly, so password recovery is essential
JAH's read-only SIM card reader	For interrogating GSM phone SIM cards; denies the user the ability to write to the SIM card, thereby preserving forensic integrity
Readers for Iomega ZIP 250, ZIP 100, SmartMedia, Compact Flash, LS-120, Sony Memory Stick, PCMCIA memory cards etc.	There are a multitude of storage media which may need to be examined – with new formats emerging regularly
Netherlands Forensic Institue's *ZERT*	Retrieval of passwords from personal organizers
Netherlands Forensic Institute's *Cards4Labs*	Reading data from smart cards and SIMs
Netherlands Forensic Institute's *TULP*	Reading data from mobile phones via cable or infra-red

One member of the project team should be a specialist computer forensic technician. Under no circumstances should unqualified people interfere with computer equipment that could contain evidential material.

KEY POINTS

• •

DO	DON'T
Covertly examine the suspect's computers, e-mails, etc. as soon as possible, and ideally before the First Step.	Access any computer owned by the suspect unless the appropriate policy is in place (see page 100).
Maintain total confidentiality.	Interfere with any data or programs on the target machines.
Use experienced technicians and professional equipment.	Overlook floppy disks and other forms of off line storage.
Retain at least one image exactly in the state in which it was found.	Overlook data in the *Windows* swap file.
Examine the data thoroughly using appropriate search software.	Ignore deleted files.

FRAUD PROFILE ANALYSIS

In all cases, the investigator should consider carrying out a *fraud profile analysis* of all of the processes and transactions to which the suspect has access. This may involve the use of fraud-detection software (such as *ACL* or *IDEA*) to analyse large data sets, master and transaction files. The objective is to develop the 'worst-case' fraud theory.

KEY POINTS: NOT FOR PUBLIC AUTHORITIES

• •

DO	DON'T
Analyse every process and transaction to which the suspect has had access.	Overlook other potential frauds by the suspect.
Use automated tools to analyse large data sets.	Alert him to the investigation.
Try to develop the 'worst-case' fraud theory.	Limit the investigation only to the suspicions known at the start.

OBSERVATION AND SURVEILLANCE

Observation or surveillance (watching and following the suspects) can be an important aid to the detection and investigation of fraud:

- to monitor activities at the suspected scene of fraud or conversion
- to identify receivers of stolen goods and associates
- to trace assets.

Observation may be from a fixed position, or may involve following people, boats, bicycles or vehicles. In both cases, photographs, film or video recordings may be taken and produced in evidence.

Despite what television detective films imply, surveillance is a specialist skill, calling for great care and planning. Fraud victims are strongly advised to obtain professional assistance, and not to attempt any surveillance without it.

In difficult cases, consideration should be given to using GPS/GMS tracking equipment. This is legal in the UK, and provides a detailed printout and mapping of movements of target vehicles (see <http://www.maxima-group.com>).

This equipment is very effective, even when suspects are 'surveillance-aware'. It can be rented or purchased.

KEY POINTS

DO	DON'T
Introduce policies and procedures for authorizing all forms of surveillance on private addresses and people. Although this is not mandatory at the moment, it is prudent to anticipate the law, and to ensure in both civil and criminal proceedings that the chances of evidence being challenged is minimized. Record that approval in a permanent form, showing that the dominant purpose was the prevention or detection of crime.	Carry out unplanned or casual surveillance: it is bound to fail and alert the suspects.
Consider the possibilities for surveillance at any time in an investigation, and particularly before the First Step.	Expect surveillance operations to be cheap or fast.
Use qualified and experienced operatives.	Alert the suspects.
Consider using GPS/GMS tracking equipment for vehicles, boats, etc.	

AUDIO SURVEILLANCE

General

Equipment must comply with the law (see page 59) and be professionally installed and monitored. All tapes and transcripts must be retained and made available for disclosure at the appropriate time.

Communications interception

The laws and procedures under which commercial and governmental victims can intercept communications transmissions were explained on pages 48 *et seq*. The technique should be considered in all cases, subject to the test of proportionality.

KEY POINTS

• •

DO	DON'T
Introduce policies and procedures for authorizing all forms of surveillance and communications interception. Although this is not mandatory at the moment, it is prudent to anticipate the law, and to ensure in both civil and criminal proceedings that the chances of evidence being challenged is minimized. Record that approval in a permanent form, showing that the dominant purpose was the prevention or detection of crime.	Intercept communications transmissions without appropriate authority.
Consider intercepting private telecommunications and computer networks, subject to the above, at or before the First Step.	Interfere with public communications networks.
Use professional equipment only on the private network.	Alert the suspects.
Use mass storage devices, so that repeated access is not necessary to retrieve intercepted data.	Disclose intercepted material to anyone who does not have an immediate need to know.
Have all intercepted communications reviewed by someone familiar with the case.	Ignore any information: every word is important.
Maintain all intercepted data securely and catalogue it so that continuity can be established and disclosures made to the opposing party at the appropriate time.	Throw away apparently unwanted material until instructed to do so by legal advisers.
Update the fraud theory and investigations plan.	Waste time preparing transcripts of irrelevant material.
Filter out unwanted personal material and anything that might be subject to legal professional privilege.	Fail to report the results of any interception to the appropriate legal advisers.
Consider using audio clips in reports.	

Room audio

Conversations taking place in offices and in or on other business premises may be monitored and the results produced in evidence. Monitoring should start at the earliest possible point in an investigation, and always before the First Step. It may continue throughout the investigation, but should cease as soon as possible.

KEY POINTS: NOT FOR PUBLIC AUTHORITIES

DO	DON'T
Use only equipment which complies with the Wireless and Telegraphy Act (hard-wired microphones, lasers, microwave, etc.).	Use radio transmission devices that contravene the Wireless and Telegraphy Acts.
Maintain all intercepted data securely, and catalogue it so that continuity can be established and disclosures made to the opposing party at the appropriate time.	Disclose information to anyone that does not have a need to know.
Have all intercepted communications reviewed in detail by someone familiar with the case.	Alert the suspects.
Update the fraud theory and investigations plan.	Prepare transcripts of irrelevant material.

CONTRIVED OPPORTUNITIES

It is permissible in most countries to provide criminals with a tempting opportunity to repeat their fraudulent behaviour, but such techniques must be carefully controlled and proportionate. For example, if the theft of incoming cheques is suspected, one or two cheques, not recorded as receivables, may be mailed to the company. These can be traced, and the accounts through which conversion takes place identified.

KEY POINTS

DO	DON'T
Consider setting traps before the First Step, under controlled conditions.	Cajole people into crimes they would not otherwise commit, or alert the suspect.
Monitor the results carefully, to track previous crimes.	Rely on the contrived opportunity as the only evidence of malpractice.

UNDERCOVER INVESTIGATIONS AND CONFIDENTIAL INFORMANTS

During larger investigations, there may be many occasions when a particular piece of information which cannot be obtained by conventional means is vital. Thus consideration should be given to covert, infiltration or undercover techniques.

'Whatever we do is investigative journalism; anything by anyone else is called dirty tricks.'

FALSE HEADHUNTERS

It appeared that the main competitors of Company X had access to its most confidential commercial information. Investigators, posing as headhunters, approached the senior vice-president of the competitor to discuss an imaginary new job for which he might be a candidate. Not surprisingly, he was interested. A few days after their first meeting, the headhunters telephoned him to say they could take his interest no further. He was disappointed, and asked why. They said: 'We have the impression that you are a straight shooter and honest. Our client is not too honest and believes in stealing other people's information, evading tax and other things . . .'. The vice-president interrupted and said: 'God, I don't mind that. I do it all the time!'

The pretext meetings continued and culminated with the vice-president explaining on tape and video exactly how Company X's secrets had been stolen, and how he would do the same for any new employer.

In due course, he was told the true nature of the meetings and, although not happy, he signed an affidavit which was used by Company X's lawyers to recover over £10 million.

In the UK and most other jurisdictions, parties to civil actions must appear before the court with clean hands, and any pretext investigation should be handled with care

In many cases there are people who can supply critical information. The problem is finding them, and convincing them to help. There are also people – often criminals themselves – who will assist for a personal reward or for some other reason. These are labelled *confidential informants*, and they must be handled very carefully because they may feign co-operation to conceal their own dishonesty. Sometimes the biggest crook is the confidential informant.

KEY POINTS

• •

DO

Introduce policies and procedures for authorizing the use of confidential informants and undercover investigators. Although this is not mandatory at the moment, it is prudent to anticipate the law, and to ensure in both civil and criminal proceedings, that the chances of evidence being challenged is minimized. Record that approval in a permanent form, showing that the dominant purpose was the prevention or detection of crime.

Use only trained and professional operators for specific, targeted enquiries.

Confirm from the outset that the confidential informant or undercover operative is prepared to give evidence.

DON'T

Rely on the honesty of confidential informants. Remember that their co-operation may be to deceive you.

Rely on everything you are told.

If the confidential informant is not prepared to give evidence, issues under Article 6 of the Human Rights Convention could result in the trial being deemed 'unfair'.

SITE VISITS AND INSPECTIONS

Many frauds succeed because victims have never checked the physical integrity of the supposed facts on which they have relied. For example, many banks have found out after the event that the address of the multinational conglomerate to which they advanced funds was a camper in a parking lot. Thus a covert visit to the premises used by suspects or their associates should be considered in all cases at the start of the investigation, and regularly thereafter.

ASSET LOCATION AND TRACING

This is an essential action in many investigations, but normally comes towards the closing stages. Important considerations are set out on pages 191 *et seq.*, but the most important principle to note is that hidden assets never appear on public records and, to find them, innovative methods must be used in conjunction with focused legal actions.

KEY POINTS

DO	DON'T
Consider how assets might be recovered at the earliest stage in the investigation. Start planning from the outset.	Expect hidden assets to appear on the public record.
Consider taking pre-emptive legal action as part of the First Step, to freeze assets and require disclosure.	Use pretext calls against banks.
Consider retaining specialist consultants.	Expect fast results.
Use only legally admissible and ethical techniques.	Expect to be the only claimant, especially in a large case.

PRE-EMPTIVE LEGAL ACTIONS

Orders of the types discussed on pages 35–37 are critical and should be viewed as an investigative technique and woven in to the investigations plan.

KEY POINTS

DO	DON'T
Consider pre-emptive legal action at the start of the investigation, and possibly as part of the First Step, and at all points thereafter.	Expect legal actions to be cheap. However, if the victim is successful, costs can be recovered.
Retain lawyers of the highest quality.	Use inexperienced lawyers.
Make totally honest disclosures to the court.	Mislead the court, especially in *ex parte* applications.
If evidence is discovered, analyse it carefully.	Work on the basis that the work is over once the legal order has been served.

INTERVIEWS

Interviews with suspects and witnesses are critical, in terms of their timing and objectives. The essential considerations are discussed later and supported by the checklist in Appendix 4. Also, Maxima's Website (<http://www.maxima-group.com>) has a detailed book on interviewing which can be downloaded.

KEY POINTS: NOT FOR PUBLIC AUTHORITIES

● ●

DO	DON'T
Have a policy in place for conducting investigative interviews, and to determine whether people charged with the investigation of crime should or should not caution suspects (see page 68).	Ever conduct an interview without first setting its objectives and structure.
Have an overall interview plan: timing is everything.	Try to develop initial suspicions by means of unplanned interviews.
Make sure interviews are probing, yet fair.	Threaten or make promises to interviewees.
Make sure proper records are maintained.	Use inexperienced employees to conduct important interviews. This includes lawyers and investigators.

FORENSIC AND EXPERT EVIDENCE

In some cases, particularly those involving computers, it may be necessary to employ a specialist adviser, and to use his testimony on an expert witness basis. People accepted by a court as experts may express an opinion (see Table 4.8).

Table 4.8   Expert witnesses

Professional background of the expert	Examples of evidence which may be given
Accountant	Opinion on accounts or an accounting system
Doctor	Reasons for death
Computer technician	Validity of a program or data
Handwriting expert	Authorship of a document, or the printer on which a document was prepared; he may also state whether he believes a signature is valid or not
Audio expert	To enhance poor-quality tape recordings
Fingerprint expert	To prove authorship of a document
Video expert	To enhance poor-quality video recordings

The areas in which technical support may be necessary will vary from case to case, but should always be on the advice of lawyers.

EXTERNAL AUDITS

Every attempt should be made to audit the records of third parties, especially companies with which the suspects are associated. In some cases, the right to audit will be derived from the victim's Terms and Conditions of Business, or more often by negotiation or persuasion.

BLOOD, SWEAT AND TEARS

All of the above techniques are brought together by an unquantifiable magic which centres on pure hard work and digging into the most minute detail. Good fraud investigators never sleep, and never give up.

The harder you work, the luckier you become.

Conclusion

A few fraud investigators seem to 'make things happen', while the majority simply go through the motions, with little to show at the end. The art, for fraud victims, is to retain the former. A checklist that will help in making the best selection is given in Appendix 3.

'Bloody investigators! They're all the same.'

5 Essential Planning and Policy Areas

Background

Investigations are made much easier when the problems have been solved in advance through specified policies and procedures. Planning involves three main aspects:

- resources
- policy
- investigative procedures or contingency plans.

A detailed draft policy, protocol and contingency plan are available in electronic format on Maxima's Website (<http://www.maxima-group.com>), and may, subject to acknowledgement of copyright, be adapted by readers. This chapter highlights the most important aspects of policy and procedures.

Resources

INVESTIGATORS

Investigations fail because the people put in charge of them are unqualified, inexperienced, naïve, lazy or plain dumb. In fact, the most common reason why investigations fail is because the victim turned to poor advisers, or had inadequate internal resources.

Thus the starting point of any fraud contingency plan is to make sure there are skilled resources available in all areas of the world in which problems could arise. Ideally, these resources should come from within the organization – primarily because they are cheaper. The company may decide to recruit specialist personnel or train those it already has, providing they have aptitude and attitude. The fact that a person worked at some time in the past for the police or Customs & Excise or security services does not mean that he is qualified to investigate fraud.

If you plan to recruit a fraud specialist, in addition to the normal screening and interviews, ask him to give his advice on a current or past case in writing, setting out his 'fraud theory', method of approach, timetable and likely costs. Allow 24 hours for a written response. It will soon be obvious whether he is a competent fraud investigator or not.

Alternatively, the company may decide to use external specialists and, if this is the case, the time to select, screen and build relationships is *now*, before the disaster happens. Victims should never use their external auditors to investigate fraud, because to do so results in a serious conflict of interest where there will only be one loser. Do not believe the stuff about 'Chinese Walls' or watertight compartments. The victim needs skilled, totally independent investigators who are committed to his cause. A checklist for selecting the most suitable external investigators is given in Appendix 3.

LAWYERS

By now, you will have realized that good legal advice is essential. If you pick the wrong lawyers, you have absolutely no chance of success. The lawyers and investigators should have a track record of working together, and should, ideally, come as a package. The last thing you want are turf battles between retained lawyers and investigators in which your company is caught in the crossfire. This happens a lot!

Policy Areas

INTRODUCTION

A fraud policy and associated investigatory procedures ensure that problems, arising in the heat of battle, are resolved quickly and effectively. They also ensure that recent and other legislation does not impede investigative and recovery options unnecessarily.

GENERAL PRINCIPLES

The company should set out its overall approach to fraud, possibly along the following lines.

STATEMENT OF VALUES

The values that govern all aspects of [your company's] operations are set out in staff handbooks, training programmes and elsewhere, and include the following:

- The company intends to maintain its reputation as an exemplary corporate citizen, and to support its position as a respected member of the international business community.

- Its ethical values will always take priority over short-term financial gain, and all employees are expected to take decisions based on principle.

- As far as practicable, every process, procedure or task and every asset will be under the control of a designated employee who is regarded as its 'owner'. Owners have the authority to apply appropriate safeguards and will bear responsibility if they fail.

- The company will make every effort to control all aspects of its business in accordance with the law and commercial best practice. Wherever possible, the controls which employees are expected to maintain will be specified in writing, and they will be given every possible assistance in maintaining them.

PRINCIPLES IN RELATION TO FRAUD

Employees are not expected to guarantee that fraud will never take place in operations under their control. They are, however, expected to react effectively when suspicions are aroused, and dishonesty will not be tolerated.

The company will support employees and others wrongly accused of impropriety, and will investigate, based on a presumption of innocence.

All employees (and others granted equivalent rights) are required to report suspected dishonesty and control weaknesses to [Name and contact numbers] without delay.

The responsibility for investigation will be taken out of the management line and into the hands of the Audit and Legal departments as quickly as possible.

Employees who report suspected dishonesty in good faith will be protected, and any person who attempts to impede or sanction them will be subject to immediate dismissal.

The company will investigate thoroughly to establish the facts, prosecute and take other appropriate action against any person or organization it suspects of dishonesty.

The company will not stand passively by when it sees other people or organizations being defrauded. It will report suspicions without delay, and make every reasonable effort to assist the victim.

The company will provide assistance to law enforcement and other regulatory authorities in their fight against crime.

Every employee should be made aware of, and agree to comply with, the above principles, and if they fail to do so without a reasonable excuse, they should be subject to disciplinary action. The principles should be promoted at every opportunity.

HUMAN RIGHTS AND DATA PROTECTION

All company forms should be reviewed for compliance with data protection and human rights legislation. Wherever possible, appropriate instructions and warnings should be given, in bold type on the face of the form. Rather than trying to hide the provisions, forms and related procedures should be designed to deter deception and to provide the legal basis for using potentially controversial investigatory procedures, for example as in the following statement:

> The information you provide on this form may be used for crime prevention and detection purposes. If you object to such use, please tick here, giving your reasons.

The company should also take a very open and public position on its approach to human rights.

HUMAN RIGHTS AND DATA PROTECTION

● ●

Company Standards

The company will comply with all relevant legislation, but will assert its rights to protect the interests of honest employees and investors.

Rights to Privacy

Employees and others are permitted to use company premises, telephones, computer systems, communications networks, postal, courier and other facilities on the specific understanding that there is no guaranteed right of privacy.

Any item on company premises or in any vehicle or craft owned by the company is subject to search for security purposes.

Personal information provided by employees and others may be used for data matching and other fraud prevention or investigation purposes, and may be released to other organisations involved in the investigation of crime and public authorities.

Use of Privately Owned Computers, etc.

Employees are allowed to use personal computers on company premises to download, process and upload data and programs, on the basis that they will secure such data or programs and will permit inspection by the company at any time.

Registration of Encryption Keys

Employees using encryption or other security packages on company or their own computers for company work, must register the keys or other devices with the IT manager and permit inspection at any time. If the key or other security feature has not been previously registered, the employee will immediately make it available on request by [state name and contact details]. Failure to comply will result in disciplinary action.

Appropriate statements, along the above lines, should be promoted as widely as possible throughout the organization.

Processes

INTRODUCTION

A number of processes should be specified under the above policies.

DATA PROTECTION REGISTRATION

The company's Data Protection Act registration should be amended to allow it to receive, store and process confidential information, and to exchange data with banks, credit card companies and communications providers for the prevention and detection of suspected crime. It should ensure that organizations with which it might want to share data have equivalent registrations. Great care should be taken to ensure that all aspects are addressed, including the use of closed-circuit television, e-mail, mailboxes, and other forms of computer and structured manual systems.

WARNINGS PRIOR TO EMPLOYMENT

Job application forms, job descriptions, and staff handbooks should – subject to specific legal advice and drafting – include statements along the following lines.

IMPORTANT EMPLOYMENT CONDITIONS

● ●

False and Misleading Applications
The applicant accepts that errors or omissions will result in his application being rejected or employment terminated without compensation, and understands that providing false information to obtain employment is an offence under the Theft Act 1968. He warrants that all information provided on this form and in connection with his application for employment is true and correct.

References
The applicant authorises the company to contact referees (but not including his present employer, until after appointment) and releases the company from any liability in this regard.

Use of Personal Data
The applicant accepts that any data provided on the form or at any time during his employment may be used at any time for the purpose of preventing and detecting fraud, and may be released to other organizations involved and public authorities.

Compliance with Security Procedures
The applicant agrees to comply with the company's procedures on security and on the conduct of investigations (copies of which have been provided to him).

Conflicts of Interest
Neither the applicant nor his close family members have any interests that could conflict with his employment, and he undertakes to keep the company advised of any material changes in his circumstances including:

- change of address or significant changes in his domestic or financial circumstances
- potential conflicts of interest that may arise during his employment including:
  - appearances in court
  - county court or other financial judgments made against him
  - treatment or counselling for drugs or alcohol-related illnesses.

Rights to Privacy
Employees and others are permitted to use company premises, telephones, computer systems, communications networks, postal, courier and other facilities on the specific understanding that there is no guaranteed right of privacy.

Any item on company premises or in any vehicle or craft owned by the company is subject to search for security purposes at any time. Personal information provided by employees and others may be used for data matching and other fraud prevention and investigation purposes.

Use of Privately Owned Computers etc.
Employees are allowed to use personal computers on company premises to download, process and upload data and programs, on the basis that they will secure such data or programs and will permit inspection by the company at any time.

Registration of Encryption Keys
Employees using encryption or other security packages on company or their own computers for company work must register the keys or other devices with the IT manager, and permit inspection at any time. If the key or other security feature has not been previously registered, the employee will immediately make it available on request by [state name and contact details]. Failure to comply will result in disciplinary action.

Co-operation in Investigations
He will assist the company in investigations, and will answer questions truthfully.

The applicant should be required to sign his agreement to the above terms.

'Right! Who did it?'

ANNUAL APPRAISALS

The company should consider introducing a security and control element into the annual staff appraisal process, possibly including Letters of Representation or an annual declaration of compliance with security and other procedures.

STAFF HANDBOOKS AND TRAINING

The position on human rights and so on for existing employees should be clarified and brought up to date in staff handbooks, management meetings and training courses.

RISK ANALYSIS

A process for conducting annual *control self-assessment reviews* should be introduced. Consideration should be given to issuing booklets, CDs and intranet training on fraud awareness (see page 6).

GENERAL INVESTIGATORY PROCEDURES

The company should introduce a procedure for reporting and investigating incidents which extends to employees, customers suppliers and other third parties. It should also set up a hotline through which suspicions can be reported, anonymously if necessary. Details of the procedures should be reproduced on purchase orders and other relevant documents.

The terms of the Public Interest Disclosure Act should be included in staff handbooks and drawn to the attention of all employees, suppliers, customers and contractors.

REPORTING OF INCIDENTS

• •

1. Objectives of the Reporting Procedure
The objectives of the reporting procedures are to ensure that suspicions of alleged dishonesty or control weaknesses are placed into independent hands as quickly as possible, and investigated thoroughly thereafter.

2. Hotline
The company recognizes that there may be circumstances where an employee who suspects dishonesty has a good reason for not wishing to reveal his identity. It has therefore provided a HOTLINE and PO Box number to which suspicions can be reported anonymously.

3. Routine Procedure
Every employee is expected to remain alert to the possibility that fraud will occur. When concerns are first aroused, the employee must:

• treat his suspicions, including anonymous letters and telephone calls, with the utmost care and must not discuss them with anyone who does not have *both* an immediate and obvious need to know

• report suspicions without delay, directly to [name and contact details]. No employee will be criticized for not first informing his immediate supervisor. In fact, any manager who impedes or censures an employee for reporting directly to [name and contact details] will be subject to disciplinary action

- Secure all information or evidence on which suspicions are based, providing this will not alert the people under suspicion

- NOT take disciplinary, investigative or any other action against the person or persons suspected until the matter has been fully investigated.

Thereafter, the employee will be guided by the Auditor or by his designated representatives.

Any employee who fails to comply with this paragraph will be subject to disciplinary action.

4. Other Matters to be Reported

4.1 Introduction
The company has a right to know of any circumstances which fundamentally change the basis on which a person was employed or which could have an adverse impact on its business or reputation.

4.2 Potential Conflicts of Interest
Employees who are contemplating engagement, or who are already engaged, in any commercial activity – either in their own names or through a nominee – which has the potential to conflict with their obligations to the company should report the facts to the Auditor and Legal Adviser [or some other nominated function] without delay. Failure to comply with this procedure will result in disciplinary action.

4.3 Employees Charged with a Criminal Offence or Insolvency
Any employee who is charged with a criminal offence involving potential exposure to a term of imprisonment, in a private or business capacity, or who may be subject to an action for insolvency or bankruptcy must report the facts, without delay and in total confidence, to [name and contact details]. Failure to comply will result in disciplinary action.

4.4 Employees Required to Give Evidence in Court
Employees required to attend court in a private or commercial matter involving an allegation of dishonesty – whether as a complainant, defendant or witness - which could have an adverse impact on the company's reputation must report the facts, without delay, to the Auditor and Legal Adviser [or some other nominated function]. Any employee who disregards this paragraph will be subject to disciplinary action.

4.5 Improper Approaches and Solicitation
Employees who are approached – either directly or through a nominee – to act in any way which could be to the company's disadvantage or who are offered a bribe or personal inducement, must report the facts, without delay, to the Auditor and Legal Adviser [or some other nominated function]. Any employee who disregards this paragraph will be subject to disciplinary action.

4.6 Medical and Drugs
Employees must report any treatment or counselling in relation to drugs or alcohol abuse.

5. Protection of Employees

5.1 Introduction
It is fundamental to this Policy that employees should have total confidence in the company and the Board's unconditional undertaking that internal reports will be dealt with, and that, where they act in good faith, they will be appropriately protected. Any employee who at any time in his career with the company believes otherwise should discuss the matter with the Auditor.

5.2 Public Interest Disclosure Act
The company will comply fully with the Public Interest Disclosure Act 1998 in the UK, and with equivalent legislation in other parts of the world. This legislation, which is concerned with what is known as 'whistleblowing', sets out the circumstances in which employees will be protected against internal disciplinary action if, in good faith, they report suspicions of fraud *directly* to external bodies. It should be noted that

neither the legislation nor the company will protect any employee who makes malicious, slanderous or libellous allegations whether they are made internally or externally. All employees are strongly advised to report matters internally in the first instance.

6. Conduct of Investigations

6.1 Overall Requirement

All employees are required to co-operate with investigations conducted by the company, and to secure and volunteer all records and other information that may be relevant. Any employee who fails to comply with this paragraph will be subject to disciplinary action.

6.2 Responsibilities of Line Management

Under no circumstances will an employee working in, or responsible for, an area in which fraud is suspected have any control over an investigation, unless specifically invited, in writing, by [name and contact details] to provide assistance. Any improper interference in an investigation by any employee will result in disciplinary action.

Similarly, employees are prohibited from retaining the services of external investigators or others providing similar services without the specific approval of the Auditor. Any employee who disregards this instruction will be subject to disciplinary action.

6.3 Presumption of Innocence

The rights of employees and others suspected of fraud, whether against the company or not, will be respected, based on a presumption of innocence. It is important to note that innocent people usually assert the right of explanation, while offenders claim the privilege of silence. Thus failure by an employee to assist in an investigation will be considered a breach of contract. The company will terminate the services of any employee who refuses to answer questions on the grounds of self-incrimination.

6.4 Rights to Representation

At fact-finding or investigative interviews, employees suspected of dishonesty will not normally be entitled to representation by a colleague, Legal Adviser or union official. The [name and contact details] will normally make exceptions in the case of employees under the age of 17, or for those with mental disabilities.

However, where:

• criminal prosecution is a likely outcome of an interview

• *and* as soon as the Auditor and Legal Adviser [or some other nominated function] believe that evidence affording 'reasonable grounds' of guilt has emerged,

the employee will be told that he need not say anything further and may seek assistance from a colleague or legal representative.

6.5 Access to Records of Interviews

Interviews with people suspected of dishonesty may, at the Auditor's discretion, be tape-recorded, with or (where permitted by law) without their permission, to ensure that an accurate record is obtained.

Providing, in the opinion of the Auditor, this does not impede an investigation, the person suspected of dishonesty will be provided with notes or transcripts of his interview and a copy of any tape recording, notes or written statement.

A person suspected of fraud will not be entitled to copies of notes of interviews with other people, statements or investigation reports until such time as they are required to be officially disclosed to legal representatives.

Procedures along the above lines should be issued to all employees, part-time and temporary staff. They set out the ground rules, and help clear the legalities in specific cases.

INTERNAL INVESTIGATORY PROCEDURES

The company's procedures for conducting investigations should be in writing, and based on specific legal advice. The procedures are necessary to achieve adequate control and to demonstrate, after the event, that proper authorization was obtained and that all processes and techniques were in compliance with the law. Aspects to be addressed are set out in Table 5.1.

Table 5.1   Clearance of investigatory procedures

The aspects to be covered	Objectives and comments
Authorities Who is responsible for conducting investigations?	The designated person or department should be professionally trained.
What are his authorities and his reporting lines?	These must be stated clearly, so that they cannot be challenged effectively during the heat of an investigation. Ideally, authority to conduct investigations should be given at the highest levels on a universal, rather than case-by-case basis.
What is his authority to retain external lawyers and investigators?	Selection should be from a pre-qualified list of individuals (rather than firms). Working relationships should be established before the event.
What is his authority to control budgets for external support?	The person given authority to conduct investigations should be provided with both annual and special budgets. Line management should not be able to intervene.
What is his authority to report matters to regulators, police, external auditors and insurers?	Ideally, all disclosures to third parties should be through the company's legal advisers.
What authority is necessary to commence pre-emptive legal actions?	This should normally be in conjunction with the legal adviser.
What authority is needed to suspend and dismiss employees, terminate contracts with third parties, and what are the processes for doing so?	The authority and procedures should be agreed by legal and human relations representatives.
Legality: consider data protection registration: of any computer or structured manual systems used in or for managing the investigation, if they they have not already been registered	Registration details should be reviewed at least annually, and amended if necessary.
The computer and structured manual systems records investigators are entitled to rely upon and access	Special notification may be necessary for large-scale cases where separate databases are created.
The external organizations with which personal data may be shared and the access rights to internal databases and personnel files	These should be covered fully in the basic Data Protection Protection Act registration, so that information can flow freely.

Continued

Table 5.1   Clearance of investigatory procedures – *concluded*

The aspects to be covered	Objectives and comments
Processes: define The way new cases are registered.	There must be a formal process for recording new cases. The record must state the purpose of the investigation. If it is other than for the prevention and investigation of crime, many of the techniques described below would be illegal or 'unlawful'. it is also important to record the size of the case, as this will act as a measure of 'proportionality'.
The procedure for issuing cautions to employees and others against whom there is evidence of crime (see page 68)	Ideally, all people charged with the investigation of crime should be trained in the administration of cautions. This only applies when the objective is criminal prosecution.
The processes for recording investigative interviews	For example, whether to tape record interviews overtly, covertly or not at all.
The general investigative techniques that are authorized	These should include most of the techniques shown below. It should be accepted that sometimes robust and controversial methods must be used to expose fraud.
The method of authorizing potentially controversial techniques in specific cases: • Collection of call logging data • E-mail interception • Forensic examination of company computers • Forensic examination of privately owned laptop computers • Human intelligence sources • Interception of post • Interviews with suspects and witnesses • Mail interception • Other forms of eavesdropping • Pretext investigations • Rights of audit to third party records • Searches of work areas • Surveillance • Telephone interception • Trash searches • Undercover investigations • Use of closed-circuit television • Vehicle tracking devices	See the RIPA question on authority explained on pages 48 et seq. These should be based on the concept of 'proportionality'. The process for authorizing sensitive techniques should be defined. When the purpose is the investigation of crime by 'businesses', all of the techniques are legal and the results can be introduced in evidence. Public Authorities must align their procedures to RIPA and the Codes of Practice (see <http://www.homeoffice.gov.uk/ripa/codelett.htm>).
Records retention procedures for completed investigations	This may be necessary to comply with the records retention aspects of the Data Protection Act.
The results of the person or department charged with the responsibility of investigating frauds should be independently reviewed, at least once a year. Special attention should be paid to the control of controversial investigatory techniques.	This review might be carried out by independent lawyers, or by the Audit Committee.

DISCIPLINARY PROCEDURES AND EXIT INTERVIEWS

The company's disciplinary procedures should be reviewed, so that they are compatible with investigation processes. Specifically, failure to co-operate in an investigation should be a dismissible offence. Policy and procedures MUST differentiate between investigatory and disciplinary procedures:

DISCIPLINARY INTERVIEWS

• •

When, in the opinion of the Auditor and Legal Adviser, the facts of a case have been fully established, the employee will be invited to attend a disciplinary interview at which he will be entitled to representation by a colleague, Legal Adviser or union official. At such interviews, the evidence will be produced and the person invited to provide an explanation. Thereafter, he will be subject to the company's normal disciplinary procedures.

SUSPENSION

• •

Employees suspected of dishonesty or wrongful acts may be suspended – with or without compensation – while investigations are being completed. If, on completion of the investigation, the employee resigns or is dismissed, compensation for any period of suspension will be deducted from his normal entitlement on termination of employment.

All employees and temporary staff should be asked to attend an exit interview and invited to comment on the company's control procedures. They should be asked specifically to report problems of a security nature.

RIGHTS OF AUDIT

The company's terms and conditions of business and purchase contracts should be amended to include rights of audit and co-operation of third parties in investigations. Failure to co-operate should be regarded as a breach of contract, and action taken accordingly.

FIDELITY INSURANCE

The company's fidelity insurance policies should be reviewed generally, and the subrogation clauses amended so that the carrier's rights to sue the company's directors and officers are removed. Also the clauses on 'prior dishonesty' should be limited to commercial dishonesty of the nature insured. Special care should be taken over the definition of 'employee' and 'director', and to ensure that part-time and temporary staff are insured.

PREPARATION FOR ASSET TRACING

Credit officers, salesmen and relationship managers should be trained, and processes developed, so that information is systematically collected on *debtors* which will enable assets to be located if they subsequently default.

EXTENDED ROLE OF THE AUDIT COMMITTEE

In larger organizations, the *audit committee* should be empowered to carry out what is akin to a judicial review of the company's compliance with the Regulation of Investigatory Powers Act and human rights legislation.

Conclusion

The reaction of some lawyers and human resources specialists to the above recommendations may be: 'It can't be done.' It *can*, and *should* be if you don't want to fall foul of the law, but wish to investigate thoroughly so that you get your money back. The time to plan and clear investigatory policies and procedures is *now*, and not in the heat of the moment.

'The man from the Mafia . . . he say YYYYEEEEEEESSSS!!!!'

'Ignore him. He's an auditor.'

Introduction

Part 2 sets out action plans for conducting an investigation into a large-scale fraud.

Table I.1 The eleven stages of major investigations

Stage		Description	Principles	%
1	2	3	4	5
TAKE YOUR TIME	A	Dealing with initial suspicions	Do not rush Keep matters confidential Do not decide on the outcome of the case until the facts have been established	5
	B	Setting objectives	Normally these are to • Establish the facts • Press for criminal prosecution • Recover funds • Prevent future losses • Create a deterrent to others	5
	C	Planning and preparing to strike	Consider the mechanics of the worst case and a FRAUD THEORY Develop an investigations plan Consider the evidence necessary Secure critical evidence, if you can Appoint an investigations team Plan in the finest detail	10
MOVE QUICKLY	D	THE FIRST STEP	Make this an ambush	20
	E	Interviews	Plan carefully	60
	F	Follow-up	Complete this stage as quickly as possible	
	G	Preparing investigation reports	Prepare carefully and obtain the protection of privilege	
	H	Insurance recoveries	Expect a hard fight	
	I	ASSET TRACING		
	J	Giving evidence		
	K	Clearing up	Closing the case	

Column 1 in Table I.1 shows that time should be taken in planning the First Step, which must be an ambush. Column 5 shows the percentage of resources used in each stage of a major fraud investigation.

The following sections explain each stage by way of a general introduction of principles, followed by recommended action steps with background and comments. To avoid ambiguity, the actions steps are written as direct instructions. This will help when you need to refer to them.

IT IS ESSENTIAL THAT THE FIRST STEP IS AN AMBUSH!

6 Stage A: Initial Suspicions and Information

Background

Suspicion can be aroused in many ways, as shown in Table 6.1.

Table 6.1   Initial suspicions

Event arousing suspicion	Likely credibility and recommended action
Anonymous oral or written information	Most anonymous information has a degree of truth attached to it and should never be disregarded without a detailed investigation. In the closing stages of the subsequent investigation, the person against whom allegations have been made should be asked for his explanation or advised that the letter has been received and his name subsequently cleared. **Under no circumstances should anonymous letters remain on file unactioned.**
Audit findings	Usually audit findings are less than conclusive and lack hard evidence. The victim should proceed on the basis that the suspicions are true. On the balance of probabilities this is the safest course.
Apparent error	Great care should be taken and enquiries to obtain more details should be conducted. When this cannot be done without alerting the possible crooks, the investigation should move forward on the basis that the findings are indicative of fraud, rather than error. This is the safe course.
Excessive spending by an employee in a position of trust	This should be treated as a definite symptom of fraud.
Specific information from an identified source	This should be treated as a definite symptom of fraud.
Instinct	In more cases than not, the instincts of honest managers and employees should be treated seriously and detailed enquiries made to resolve them.

In the first few hours after suspicion has been aroused, victims rush in blindly and make mistakes from which they never recover. Through disbelief, they try to seek confirmation, hoping that their suspicions are unfounded, or press too hard or too soon and alert criminals too early. The result is that the initiative is lost, evidence destroyed, funds disbursed, and, in some cases, the culprits are forewarned and disappear.

But the biggest mistake is relying on poor advisers.

Your primary objective is to plan, so that in due course the suspects are caught by surprise as part of the First Step. This must be an overwhelming ambush!

Principles

♦ Do nothing that might alert the suspects to your interest in them, and do not discuss the case with anyone who does not have an immediate need to know.

♦ Do not rush to take disciplinary or other action until the facts are known. The victim has a right to investigate thoroughly, and an obligation to establish the facts before asking the suspects for their explanation.

♦ Anticipate that everything you do, or do not do, will be examined in the courts or by the press, and possibly in years ahead by people who have the advantage of judgement by hindsight. Do not be impeded by the fear of criticism, but always act within the law, take positive action, and do your best. If you believe the case is beyond your resources, retain specialist support.

♦ Do not rush into unplanned or casual enquiries in the hope that further information might be developed or the suspicions confirmed or disproved. The chance of these being successful is slight, and may alert the criminals to the fact that their dishonesty has been discovered. This will make the investigation much more difficult.

♦ Assume that the perpetrators are watching for the first signs that their dishonesty has been detected, and that they will make every effort to frustrate the investigation and prepare a counter-attack.

Maintain Total Confidentiality

Do not discuss the suspicions with anyone who does not have an immediate need to know.

It may be repugnant, but you must assume that at least one level of management above the suspect could be involved, and that even honest line managers may resist an investigation (see 'Deadly Sins' page 14).

TAKING THE SAFE COURSE

An undercover investigation in a multinational company revealed that unexplained losses were due to an entire country's sales force systematically defrauding its customers. Periodically, salesmen were the subjects of complaints by suspicious customers. The result would be promotion for the individuals concerned, so that they were kept away from hostilities in the field. Coincidentally, the complainants received the impression that the salesmen had been disciplined because they no longer saw them. Supervisors and intermediate managers demanded their share in a weekly division of the spoils, so the fraud had to be perpetuated to enable those involved to keep their jobs. If any new recruits showed signs of honest reluctance to participate, they failed their probation. There was no evidence that the subsidiary's top management were involved in the fraud, but they knew something was wrong.

Their reluctance to investigate was caused by fear of adverse publicity and its effect on their careers. They were replaced, and the investigation was commenced. It *did* finish their careers, but only because they were too weak to initiate it.

Do Not Rush to Report Externally

Do not report the case to the police or anyone else unless it is vital to take urgent preventive action. If you have to report a suspicion to a regulatory agency, you must do so through the appropriate channels (hopefully, as set out in your fraud policy) at the appropriate time. As a general principle, do nothing until you have confirmed your understanding of the case and decided upon your company's objectives.

Do Not Rush to Advise External Auditors

Do not rush to retain, or even advise, your external auditors, or to inform insurers.

Remember that evidence may subsequently justify an action being taken against external auditors for negligence or worse. Even more importantly, if a claim is made under fidelity insurance, the insurer may sue the external auditors in *your company's name* under the subrogation clauses. There may be a serious conflict of interest in retaining your own auditors to assist with an investigation. In effect, you may be asking them to build up a case against their audit practice for negligence.

Under most fidelity insurance policies, notice has to be given within a reasonable period (normally 'as soon as practicable') after discovery of a loss. Discovery means that evidence is available which would cause a reasonable person to charge another with dishonesty. This is a high standard. Mere suspicion, or the fact that a loss might occur, is not regarded as 'discovery' within the terms of most policies. There is no advantage in advising the insurer too early, and there are many possible disadvantages. In any event, notification of insurers must be through the appropriate channels, and in the appropriate form.

Assume the Suspicions are True

The safe course is to assume that the suspicions are true or even worse than you currently believe. However, consider the source of the information on which the suspicions are based. Is it reliable? Does the informant have a personal or malicious motive? Have similar and unfounded allegations been made in the past? Are audit or other findings correct? Is there another explanation for the suspicions? Take a cynically balanced view, but err in favour of believing the suspicions.

Do not rush to confirm the suspicions or take any other overt action unless:

- You can be absolutely sure any action you take will not alert the suspects before you are ready to make a pre-emptive strike as the First Step.
- Immediate action is necessary to stop the disbursement of funds or the loss of some other asset. *Clearly, if you take action to block funds, the suspects will be alerted, so be prepared to move ahead quickly.*
- Immediate action is necessary to secure vital evidence.

In all other cases, take your time. Take all cases seriously. *If you cannot confirm the suspicions without alerting the suspects, assume the worst and proceed on that basis.* This is the safest course.

'I guess none of you have been involved in a fraud investigation before.'

A BAD CASE OF LEAKAGE

One auditor was worried that his findings seemed to implicate a sales manager in conflicting interests. To verify his suspicions, he checked whether the customer master file had been printed recently, and contrary to normal practice. He found that it had been – by the sales manager. The following day, the entire sales force received an e-mail from their manager explaining changes in the allocation of accounts which he had decided upon after studying the customer master file.

He had evidently miskeyed, because the e-mail was received by everyone, not just the sales department. However, the auditor was pleased that he had sought confirmation of his suspicions, which he could see were unjustified. Six months later, the sales manager had joined a competitor and was systematically targeting his former customers. Eventually, it emerged that he had programmed the computer to warn him if the customer master file were interrogated. The e-mail was untrue, and its wide distribution was no accident.

The subsequent investigation proved that he had stolen proprietary information. Court injunctions were obtained to stop him and his new employer using it. However, much damage could have been prevented if the auditor had been less anxious to confirm his suspicions.

Establish the Facts Before Deciding on Their Resolution

Resist any attempt to take a firm decision on the resolution of the case until the facts have been established. Under no circumstances start disciplinary action until the investigations have been completed.

DECIDING ON ACTION IN THE ABSENCE OF THE FACTS

A director of human resources argued strongly that the police should not be called when clear signs of fraud were discovered in a computer department. He suggested that a witch-hunt would be bad for the morale of employees who were under extreme pressure to complete a large conversion project. Three employees were interviewed by personnel officers and issued with written warnings. Two years later, over $3 million went missing. This time the police were called, and two of the three men were prosecuted and imprisoned. However, the company's claim under its fidelity policies was, quite properly, denied on the grounds that the men's previous dishonesty disqualified them from cover.

There is a clear distinction between finding the facts, and the management decisions that have to be taken as a result. Deciding on the outcome of suspicions without knowing the facts is similar to signing a blank cheque. If line managers try to prevent a full investigation, the matter should be reported to the Board without delay. Alternatively, the manager opposing the investigation should be asked to put his instructions in writing. Then file it and go off and play golf. This is a good example of pinning responsibility to authority.

'Are you sure he's a vegetarian?'

7 *Stage B: Setting Objectives*

Principles

♦ Make every effort to find the truth before deciding how a case should be resolved.
♦ Get your money back, punish the guilty, clear the innocent, establish a deterrent and get back to work. Take time to plan, and make sure the First Step is effective, then complete the case as quickly as you can.
♦ Take the toughest line possible: aim for criminal prosecution, civil action, dismissal and recovery under fidelity insurance.

Align Management's Expectations

Ensure that senior managers fully understand the case, and the time and cost that may be involved.

Agree the Objectives

Ideally, objectives for all cases should have been determined as part of the company's fraud policy (see Chapter 5). If this is not the case, discuss the suspicions with the appropriate levels of management, and agree the objectives and the ideal outcome of the investigation.

Without a positive decision on the desired outcome, any investigation is likely to lurch from one crisis to another and fail to reach a successful conclusion – after all, if you don't know where you're aiming, how will you know when you get there? On occasions, criminal prosecution and civil litigation may not be viable options – for example, when law enforcement officials and the legal system are corrupt in the jurisdiction concerned. In such cases, the objectives may be limited to dismissing a dishonest employee or terminating a business contract. However, the principle of taking the toughest line possible still applies, and the investigation should still be conducted to the highest possible standard so that it can be demonstrated – after the event, if necessary – that the company acted with the utmost propriety.

The objectives will, to some extent, depend on the assets the suspects might have available and the extent of your insurance coverage. These should both be considered at this stage. It may be prudent to consult investigators and lawyers at this stage.

8 *Stage C: Planning*

Principles

♦ Plan to seize the initiative away from the criminals at the First Step.
♦ Take no unplanned or unco-ordinated action. Plan ahead, and don't rush unless immediate action is necessary to prevent funds being disbursed or to stop vital evidence being destroyed.

Develop a Fraud Theory

Consider the exact mechanics of the suspected fraud, and write down everything that is known about it. Start creating a chronology of events, and add detail to it as you move forward. Prepare an investigations plan (see page 142) which focuses on developing evidence to prove or disprove the theory. Keep an open mind on both the theory and the investigations plan.

Initially, you may have only flimsy information about the suspected fraud. In fact, at the early stages only a fraction of the true extent of the dishonesty will be known. You should consider and **write down** in as much detail as possible:

* How, precisely, does it appear the fraud was committed?
* What records – both written and computerized – might have been falsified, and where may important evidence be found?
* Who appears to be involved in the fraud or its cover-up? Try to identify at least one person or company against whom the evidence is strongest. This will provide an anchor for the investigation and, in most cases, a logical starting point.
* Were similar patterns or suspicions discovered in the past? If so, how were these resolved?
* Who are the people or companies who have received a benefit? Identification of receivers of stolen goods is often vitally important, especially in planning the First Step. A good principle is: 'Always follow the money.'

It is also important to identify any deviations from normal accounting or other practices, and to explain what may appear to be coincidences or unrelated errors, patterns or exceptions. Often, these are good clues to the way a fraud has been or still is being committed, and can be important points when suspects are interviewed. Remember, in fraud investigations there is no such thing as a coincidence, and there is always a reason for everything the criminal did or failed to do.

AN EXAMPLE OF CONCEALMENT

One manager suspected that materials for manufacturing were being diverted for use as spare parts. He based his suspicion on the fact that production yield had been consistently lower than anticipated over a period of months, while the rejection rate had remained normal. Internal Audit was asked to investigate. However, the auditors were unable to agree with the manager's interpretation: there was no evidence to suggest that materials were not being correctly taken into the production process. Also, the consumption of packaging had not reduced in line with the production yield. These findings showed that the manager's theory was wrong. A new theory eventually led to proving that finished product, equivalent to the output of an entire night shift per week, was being stolen.

The fraud theory is much like a jigsaw puzzle, and at the start you will only have a few pieces and may find it difficult to see the complete picture. As you get more pieces, fit them into the puzzle. If they don't fit, your theory is wrong, so revise it. Keep an open mind. Pieces that don't appear to fit the theory are often the clues to discovering compelling evidence: don't disregard them.

Extend the Theory to the Worst Case

Consider what other dishonesty the suspects might have committed, and who else could be involved. Examine other operations and processes to which the suspects have access. Could similar problems exist at other locations? Write down details of the worst case, and the potential losses that could be involved.

You should always aim to prove, and make recoveries based on, the worst case.

Proof of any – even minor - dishonest conduct helps swing the initiative in your favour, and is particularly important when suspects are interviewed.

THE EXPENSES WHAT DID IT

A senior marketing manager was suspected of large-scale fraud, although evidence was neither clear nor convincing. However, the investigators discovered that for the previous five years, he had falsified his expense statements. When they interviewed him, they made it clear that whatever happened, he would be dismissed and prosecuted for the expenses fraud. Against this background, the manager believed he had nothing to lose by admitting the more serious offences, and he did so and offered to make full repayment. Although he was still prosecuted, the victim company supported his pleas in mitigation.

Again, the theory is like completing a jigsaw puzzle. If a piece does not fit, the theory is wrong. Of course, the piece may fit elsewhere, or could be part of a completely different puzzle, so always keep an open mind.

Planning the First Step if the Fraud is Continuing

Is the fraud still continuing or likely to be repeated? If so, where and when could the First Step be taken to catch the suspects in an act for which they cannot provide a plausible excuse? For example:

- while handling stolen goods or converting funds
- while accessing premises or computer systems without authority
- while involved in an obvious breach of procedures or deviation from honest practice
- through pre-emptive legal actions.

It is much easier for the victim to seize the initiative if the fraud is continuing or might be repeated.

Planning When the Fraud is Not Continuing

If the fraud is not continuing, how and when can the First Step be planned with the maximum element of surprise?

In some cases, it may be difficult to identify an ideal weak point or special moment at which the First Step should be taken, but generally it should be at a time when:

- suspects can be kept apart and are unable to collaborate over their explanations: this is very important
- important records, computer and communication systems can be secured

and as early as possible in the morning to give time for the first wave of enquiries to be completed before the end of the day. *Again, consider pre-emptive legal actions.*

Consider Setting Traps

Is it possible to set traps or take other covert action to detect the suspects in a dishonest act which cannot be excused, or to trace assets or accomplices? Always check that techniques are legal. Ideally, everything should have been cleared as part of a fraud policy and protocol.

The possibilities include:

- **Test purchases** – to identify the origin of goods handled by a receiver, to identify counterfeits, or to establish prices.

- **Interception and covert recording of company telephone lines** – but first understand the legal position set out on pages 48 *et seq.*

- **Installing covert telephone logging equipment** – to record the details of calls made and received. This equipment is generally available and can be set to record the numbers dialled, the date, time and duration of outgoing calls. On some digital exchanges similar details can be captured for incoming calls. Also, make sure that old call logging records are preserved

- **Installing covert monitors on data lines** – hackers have been able to disable PSS call logging equipment as a means of concealing their activities. Equipment which is hardware-driven and cannot be disabled is available to monitor, copy and keep a covert record of all traffic on data lines.

- **Installing covert monitors on fax lines** – in normal circumstances, the victim might have great difficulty in establishing what fax messages were received and sent, and their sequence. A small computer can be attached covertly to fax lines to copy in full text all incoming or outgoing traffic.

- **Intercepting company mail** (including e-mail) – again subject to the legal issues explained in Chapter 5.

- **Installing video or audio monitors** – in offices, warehouses or computer centres, or on equipment which the suspects may use in carrying out the fraud.

- **Installing remote monitors on computer equipment** – to produce accurate logs. Microwave or infra-red transmitters may be fitted covertly to monitor the keystrokes on a console, data displayed on a terminal, or output from a printer. Similar equipment may be installed to monitor traffic on a local area network. Also, personal computers can be covertly frozen using a program such as *Vaccine*, which applies a cryptographic checksum to files through which alteration can be detected.

- **Installing covert tachographs or tracker devices on company vehicles** – this equipment can reconstruct, to an accuracy of one or two minutes, the exact routes taken by any vehicle.

- **Keeping observation** – on a receiver's premises. From a criminal's point of view, conversion is the most exposed element. Identification and surveillance of a receiver's premises usually produces good results.

- **Using pretext or undercover investigations** – there may be occasions when a particular piece of information is vital. Conventional investigative techniques may not be able to provide the answers. Thus consideration should be given to the ways in which important evidence or intelligence might be obtained by covert or undercover methods. But retain specialists for this work, and confirm its legality.

- **Searching the suspect's work area or office** – before doing this, take a Polaroid photograph or video recording, to help you make sure everything is put back in its original place.

- **Searching or freezing the suspect's PC** – and covertly copying his diskettes. Do not use standard software to take a secret copy of a hard disk as this may destroy the evidential value of what you find. It is much better to retain the services of a professional computer forensic technician. Consider carefully what rights you have to access the suspect's personal computer (see page 101).

These possibilities should be considered and, where appropriate, included in the Investigations Plan (see page 142).

Consider the Adverse Consequences

What are the adverse consequences of pursuing the investigation? Some of the possibilities include:

- blackmail – for example, the criminals may threaten to reveal misdeeds by others unless action against them is stopped
- counter-suits against the company by shareholders and others
- tax or other legal problems
- violence against the company, employees or witnesses.

Potential problems should be considered in advance. It is always a disaster to start an investigation and then to find, in the face of adversity or bad publicity (which in any case is very rare), that management backs down. The rule should always be to take the hardest line possible. Publicity, which may seem important inside the company at the time, is rarely of any long-term public interest. Judges rarely allow mud-slinging for its own sake in court and very few fraud cases hit the headlines. And if your company has broken the law (usually because of the fraudster's acts), it is much better to admit it rather than to succumb to blackmail.

Consider the Evidence Potentially Available

Consider what evidence might be available to prove the worst case, including that listed in Table 8.1.

Consider the way such information might be obtained before or when taking the First Step.

Identify Potential Witnesses

What evidence might be required from witnesses, and how might they be persuaded or compelled to help? For example:

- by asking for their co-operation
- in lieu of civil or criminal actions being brought against them
- in lieu of dismissal or termination of a business relationship
- in lieu of payment of arrears or damages
- in response to a summons or witness order.

Also consider the possibility of taking pre-emptive legal actions (Search and Seizure Orders, etc.) against both suspects and witnesses (see page 34), and consider their personal security and safety.

It is often difficult to decide early in an investigation whether a person or company should be treated as a witness or as a suspect. Thus exceptional care should be taken before making any agreement with a witness that relieves him or her of civil or criminal liability or the repayment of losses.

Table 8.1   Potential sources of information

Potential sources of intelligence and evidence	Purpose/significance	How and when obtained
Access logs to premises	For the diary of events For comparison with expense statements	*Internal* Planning Stage
Accounts held at retail stores	Signs of overspending Check that private purchases have not been paid for by the company	*Seizure Orders* First Step
Accounts payable *All invoices approved by the suspect*	Check against the suspect's expense statements To identify personal purchases charged to the company	*Internal* Planning Stage
Address books (*written and computerized*)	Identify main/regular contacts Trace bank accounts and other assets	*Covert search* Planning Stage
Aircraft log books (*private jets*)	Free travel provided to the suspect and others Identify travelling companions	*Discovery* Follow-up
Airline club mileage statements	Signs of overspending Check against expenses Check against travel agency invoices	*Covert search* Planning Stage
Application forms (*any completed by the suspect for any purpose*)	Log information Note inconsistencies	*Internal* Planning Stage
Asset lists for the suspect's personal assets	Schedules to insurance policies Identify expensive items and especially jewellery	*Seizure Orders* *Discovery* Follow-up
Asset registers	Identify assets under the control of the suspect, especially computer equipment	*Internal* Planning Stage
Audio tapes	Recover and check all tapes Recover deleted conversations	*Covert search* Planning Stage
Authority manuals	To prove the suspect's knowledge Explain all highlighting and notes	*Internal* Planning Stage
Bank accounts used by the suspect	For evidence of over-spending and conversion	*Trash search* *Covert search* Planning Stage
Boarding passes (*aircraft*)	Check against expense statements Check class of travel	*Trash search* *Covert search* Planning Stage
Boats and light aircraft registers	For assets owned by the suspect	*Public records* Planning Stage
Bookmakers' records and slips	For signs of over-spending Track dates of large losses	*Trash search* *Covert search* Planning stage
Books on office bookshelves	Establish the suspect's knowledge Trace purchase of expensive books	*Covert search* Planning Stage

Continued

Table 8.1   Potential sources of information – *continued*

Potential sources of intelligence and evidence	Purpose/significance	How and when obtained
Briefcases	Check contents Remove company property	*Covert search* Planning Stage
Call logs (*internal*)	*See* Telephone call logs	*Internal* Planning Stage
Call logs (*external and home*)		*DPAct exchange* *Crime* *Investigation* Planning Stage
Cancelled cheques (*on the accounts of the company*)	For signs of false conversion Track missing cheques	*Internal* Planning Stage
Car park receipts	For the diary of events Check against expenses	*Trash search* Planning Stage
Casino records	As for bookmakers' records and slips	*Trash search*
Certificates, academic and other	Check their authenticity To identify associates	*Internal* *Personnel files* Planning Stage
Cheque stubs	As cancelled cheques	*Internal* Planning Stage
Christmas card list	Identify close associates Check names against accounts payable and receivable	*Covert search* Planning Stage
Club and other memberships	For the diary of events For signs of over-spending Check how memberships was paid To identify associates	*Covert search* *Trash search* *Surveillance* Planning Stage
Company registration records	Directorships of the suspect and his family	*Public record* Planning Stage
Computers: mainframes and networks to which the suspect had access	Check all files and programs Check logs against diary of events and expense claims Check all electronic mail messages	*Internal* Planning Stage
Computers: personal	*See* PCs	
Contract files	Check all contracts negotiated by the suspect	
Correspondence files (*live and archived*)	Proof of dishonesty For the diary of events	
Courier billing records	For the diary of events For signs of conversion	
Credit agencies	Debt record Financial position	*Public record* Planning Stage
Credit cards	For signs of over-spending To track assets and bank accounts To confirm expense statements	*Trash search* *Covert search* Planning Stage

Continued

Table 8.1   Potential sources of information – *continued*

Potential sources of intelligence and evidence	Purpose/significance	How and when obtained
Crime reports made privately by the suspect	To track assets	
Desk drawers	To recover diaries, etc.	*Covert search* Planning Stage
Diaries and personal organizers	For the diary of events To identify close associates Compare against expense statements	*Covert search* Planning Stage
Dictation tapes	Check all tapes	
Disks and diskettes	For evidence of fraud Unlicensed software	
Electronic mail	Reconstruct all mail	
Electoral Roll	People sharing the suspect's address Check all names for directorships	*Public record* Planning Stage
Expense statements	For the diary of events Analyse for evidence of expenses fraud	*Internal* Planning Stage
Fax billing records	To identify associates For the diary of events	*Internal* Planning Stage
Fax machines and memories	Print autodialler lists and memory	
Gift vouchers given and received	For signs of conversion and corruption	*Covert search* Planning Stage
Goods outwards passes	Identify goods removed from company premises by the suspect Compare against the diary of events	*Internal* Planning Stage
Household bills	For signs of over-spending Identify expensive items (such as furniture and pictures) for which there are no purchase invoices	*Trash search* Planning Stage
Identification cards	Track club and other memberships Identify associates	*Internal* *Cover search* Planning Stage
Insurance policies held privately by the suspect	For compiling an asset list Trace expensive items to source Track discounted deals given by company insurers	*Trash search* *DPA exchange* Planning Stage
Internet	Search for all references to the suspect	*Public record* Planning Stage
Keys	Withdraw company keys Identify all other keys, especially for cars and safety deposit boxes	*Covert search* Planning Stage
Laptop computers	Examine forensically	*Covert search* Planning Stage

Continued

Table 8.1   Potential sources of information – *continued*

Potential sources of intelligence and evidence	Purpose/significance	How and when obtained
Leave slips	Showing vacation addresses *Possibly owned by a third party with whom the employee has dealings*	*Internal* Planning Stage
Legal invoices	For intelligence purposes To trace hidden assets and conflicts of interest For identifying criminal convictions	*Internal* *Accounts payable* Planning Stage
Manuals used by the suspect	Check all notes and highlighting For proof of knowledge	*Internal* Planning Stage
Microfilms (and reproduction records)	For proving theft of confidential information	*Internal* Planning Stage
Mobile telephone	Address book Last numbers dialled	*Office search* Planning Stage
Notepads	Explain everything Consider an ESDA examination	*Covert search* *Trash search* Planning Stage
Overtime records	For the diary of events Check against expenses	*Internal* Planning Stage
Papers and billing records	For the diary of events Identify close associates	*Internal* Planning Stage
Parking tickets	For the diary of events To identify close associates Check vehicle registration numbers	*Trash search* *Covert search* Planning Stage
Passports	For the diary of events Check against expenses Check personal data	*Covert search* *Discovery* Any stage
Paying-in books on the suspect's accounts	Identify cash deposits Check against the diary of events	*Covert search* Planning Stage
Personal computers	Vital in all respects Check everything	*Covert search* Planning Stage
Personnel files	Check against all application forms Confirm personal details Identify close associates Identify and check out the employers of close family members Note wife's maiden name and check out her directorships	*Internal* Planning Stage
Petty cash records	For the diary of events Track personal purchases booked to the company For signs of other fraud	*Internal* Planning Stage

Continued

Table 8.1   Potential sources of information – *continued*

Potential sources of intelligence and evidence	Purpose/significance	How and when obtained
Photocopy billing records	To identify theft of customer lists, etc.	*Internal* Planning Stage
Photographs	To identify expensive assets (boats, etc.) To identify close associates Compare with the diary of events	*Covert search* Planning Stage
Planning permissions	For spending on the employee's home For signs of bribery	*Public records* Planning Stage
Press databases and other public records	Check the suspect's name against these Especially Reuters Business briefing	*Public records* Planning Stage
Purchasing invoices	See Accounts payable for items approved by the suspect	*Internal* Planning Stage
References from past employers	Check authenticity Consider the liability of the referee for providing inaccurate references	*Personnel files* Planning Stage
References for other people provided by the suspect	To identify close associates Check the companies concerned against Accounts payable and receivable lists	*Personnel files* Planning Stage
Safe deposit keys and receipts	To identify hidden assets To track stolen funds	*Covert search* Planning Stage
Scrap disposal records	Check the legitimacy of approvals by the suspect for the disposal of company assets	*Internal* Planning Stage
Share dealing and stockbroker records	For signs of overspending To trace assets	*Public records* *Covert search* Planning Stage
Shorthand notebooks	Reconstruct all correspondence	*Covert search* Planning Stage
Shredder used by the suspect	Reconstruct contents	*Covert search* *Trash search* Planning Stage
Tachometer records in company vehicles used by the suspect	For the diary of events Identify and explain missing records	*Internal* Planning Stage
Tape recorders used by the suspect	Reconstruct all correspondence and conversations	*Covert search* Planning Stage
Tax returns submitted by the subject	For comparison against asset lists For signs of fraud and illegal income	*Discovery* Follow-up
Tax billing records	For the diary of events Check against expense statements	*Covert search* *Expenses* Planning Stage
		Continued

Table 8.1   Potential sources of information – *concluded*

Potential sources of intelligence and evidence	Purpose/significance	How and when obtained
Telephone answering machines	Reconstruct all messages	*Covert search* Planning Stage
Telephone call logs	Schedule Add to the diary of events To identify regular contacts	*Internal* Planning Stage
Telephone directories	Confirm telephone numbers and address	*Public record* Planning Stage
Telephone memories	Print out autodial lists To identify regular contacts	*Covert search* Planning Stage
Telephones: portable	Check as above	↓
Telex memories and billing records	*See* Fax	*Internal* Planning Stage
Training manuals	*See* Manuals	*Internal* Planning Stage
Trash (search)	Everything!	*Search* Planning Stage
Travel agents' invoices	Check against expense statements For the diary of events	*Internal* Planning Stage
Vehicle maintenance records	For signs of fraud For the diary of events	*Internal* Planning Stage
Video archives	Public places	*Internal* Planning Stage
Visitors' books	To identify close associates For the diary of events	*Internal* Planning Stage
Voice mail	For the diary of events Associates	*Internal* Planning Stage
Wall charts and display boards	For evidence of fraud	*Covert search* Planning Stage
Waste bins	Recover all discarded documents	*Trash search* Planning Stage
Wills and trust documents	To identify hidden assets	*Covert search* Planning Stage

Firstly, deals of the sort mentioned on page 127 can lead to problems in court and secondly, the fidelity insurance company may claim that its rights to recovery under the subrogation clauses have been compromised. This argument can be used as a reason for refusing to settle a claim. In all cases experienced litigation lawyers should be consulted before any deal with witnesses or potential suspects is contemplated. Final decisions on this point can be left until later.

List the Ways in Which Recoveries Might be Made

List the best methods of making full financial recovery for all the losses, interest and costs:

- from the perpetrators – including freezing their salaries and pension benefits
- from third parties – including suppliers and customers
- from professional advisers – such as bankers, accountants and lawyers
- from the suspect's previous employer – if it provided misleading references on his honesty or suitability.

Providing such action does not alert the suspects, encourage line managers to delay payments to any suppliers concerned and press for collection of outstanding debts from customers, so that at the time the First Step is taken you are in an ideal position to apply financial leverage to obtain co-operation.

Consider civil orders to freeze assets.

Consider Recovering Under Fidelity Insurance

Consider the possibilities of making recoveries under fidelity and other insurances. It will not be possible to make a final decision until the investigation has been more or less completed. However, the possibilities of claiming should be considered at an early stage.

Prepare a Search Plan

Determine what premises and vehicles and so on must be searched as part of the First Step, and when, why and by whom. For example:

- office and work areas used by the suspects
- company vehicles
- lockers
- remote stores and warehouses
- homes of the suspects, *but only with their permission or on a court order*
- offices of third party suspects, *but only with permission or under a court order*.

These actions should be incorporated into the Investigations Plan, and their legality should be checked, if not already covered in policies and procedures.

Consider Stopping Outgoing Cheques

Consider stopping the clearance of outgoing cheques and payment instructions, or the instigation of a policy of obtaining special clearance of incoming cheques and so on, so that at the time the First Step is taken, you are in a position to exert financial leverage on the suspects, and especially on customers and suppliers who may be involved.

Table 8.2   Background on suspects (see page 136)

Source of the information	Description of the information	Purpose
Personnel files[1]	Date and place of birth Photograph Passport and driving licence numbers	Positive identification
	Name of next of kin Wife's maiden name Surname of married daughters Name of spouse's employer Details of other family members and their employers	Check against supplier and customer master files
	Details of previous employers, including the names of referees	Recovery possibilities for false references
	Bank and mortgage accounts Credit card numbers Salary record	
	Holiday addresses	Possibly provided by vendors or customers
	Handwriting samples Educational qualifications Conflict of interest declarations Previous disciplinary warnings Car registration details	To establish guilty knowledge
Accounting records controlled or approved by the suspect	Accounts payable and receivable Cancelled cheques	Background audit Evidence for interview
Job descriptions and authority manuals	Authority levels	To establish responsibilities and authorities
Expense statements	All expenses for three years	Diary of events Other dishonesty
Electronic mail and correspondence files	All correspondence	Diary of events Evidence for interview
Company telephone call logs	Calls made	Diary of events Dishonest contacts
External call logs	Calls made and received	Subject to appropriate DPA registrations
Asset registers	PCs used by the suspect	To enable detailed analysis
Public records and press reports	Debt judgments Other	General background
Previous statements on the case	Interview notes Statements	Interview preparation To detect conflicting evidence
Covert inspection of the suspect's home	Estimate of price Building works Cash spending	To detect signs of conversion

Note: [1]Laws on what information can be held in personnel files vary from country to country, but in the UK can be legitimately accessed for the investigation and prevention of crime.

Prepare a Dossier on the Suspects' Backgrounds

Prepare a dossier on the background of each suspect person reviewing and extracting information from the sources shown in Table 8.2.

Sometimes the dreaded Human Resources Department will argue – based on a misinterpretation of the Data Protection Act – that they cannot disclose information from personnel files. They are totally wrong, and such data can be disclosed for the purpose of preventing and detecting crime.

Prepare a Dossier on Suspect Companies

Prepare a full dossier on the background of each suspect company, extracting details from:

- official files, showing names of directors, shareholdings, annual accounts and so on
- credit agencies, such as Dunn and Bradstreet
- bank references
- trade directories
- telephone books and *Yellow Pages*
- indices of national and local newspapers and trade journals
- press reports, and especially *Reuters Business Briefing*.

Again, make absolutely sure that checking does not alert the suspects.

Decide on an Interview Timetable

Determine how, where, when and by whom each suspect will be seen and interviewed as part of the First Step.

Plan Each Important Interview

Interviews with suspects and important witnesses must be planned in the finest detail. (See Stage E for detailed considerations, and Appendix 4.)

Decide Who Will Advise the Police, and When

If prosecution is an objective, determine how, when and by whom the case will be reported to the police, and who will be responsible for liaising with them throughout the investigation. Ideally, the initial report or complaint should be made by the lawyer and the investigator from the project team.

Also consider whether the case should be reported under the money laundering regulations.

Cases should be reported, in a personal meeting, to the fraud squad or commercial crime section responsible for the area in which the fraud occurred. The objectives of the investigation should be explained and the method of pursuing parallel enquiries agreed. Sometimes the police are opposed to suspects and witnesses being interviewed by anyone other than their own officers, on the grounds that the admissibility of evidence could be compromised. Although there is some sense in this restriction, there are other circumstances where the company must conduct its own interviews in connection with civil litigation or insurance recoveries.

Decide on the Resources Needed

Decide on the resources necessary to complete the investigation quickly and professionally, if this has not already been determined as part of policy.

In the early stages of an investigation it is easy to underestimate the complexity of the case and the resources needed. The main areas of difficulty include:

- external investigations involving independent customers, suppliers, and third parties, including ex-employees
- cases involving organized crime
- surveillance including tailing vehicles and people and tracing the receivers of stolen goods
- multi-jurisdictional investigations
- interviewing witnesses and suspects
- asset tracing
- frauds involving the technical manipulation of computer and communications systems.

In some cases the victim company will have a common interest with other companies or trade associations or one or more government departments which often employ professional investigators. Experience shows that mounting joint investigations never works. Although co-operation may reduce your costs, it will drive you to utter frustration. So don't even think about it!

Decide Who Will Manage the Investigation

Determine who will be put in charge of the investigation. Ideally, this should be an experienced commercial manager at or near to Board level, but not from the business line in which the fraud is suspected. *It is absolutely essential that the managers responsible for the area in which the dishonesty took place do not have control over the investigation* or the budget for legal and investigative costs.

Also, experience shows that it is a grave mistake to have an investigation directed by lawyers, police, investigators, personnel managers, accountants, or auditors. The project team structure shown on page 139 has proven to be the most efficient method of completing complex investigations.

A letter of authority should be requested from the Board for all members of the investigation team.

Retaining External Investigators

In large cases, whether or not a Special Task Force is formed (see page 139) the services of external investigators should be considered. Ideally, you should already have selected and screened these as part of your fraud contingency plan. If you have not already done this, the checklist in Appendix 3 will help you make the right choice.

When external investigators are retained, the precise nature of the assignment should be agreed in writing together with a fee budget. Written instructions should make it clear that the investigation will be conducted in strict accordance with the law.

Initially the scope of work should not be set too narrowly. It is better to allow an external Investigator to review the case in total and to recommend those aspects he believes worthy of attention. However, in all cases, letters of engagement and confidentiality agreements should be signed.

It is important to set a reasonable initial budget and call for regular progress reports, so that extensions can be considered and approved depending on the progress being made.

Do not allow investigators to advise on the law.

Consider Retaining Lawyers

In important cases, whether you plan to form a Special Task Force or not, you would be well advised to retain case-hardened, blood-sucking litigation lawyers. Again, relationships should have been established with qualified lawyers as part of your fraud contingency plan. If not take great care. The fact that a lawyer works for a big firm does not mean he is a blood-sucker!

Invite a small number of firms to come and see you and listen to their ideas. Listen carefully, and consider whether they know their stuff. Are they problem-creators or problem-solvers? Do they have a 'can do' attitude, or is everything as bleak as a camel's armpit?

Obtain the lawyers' confirmation of the objectives of the investigation and plan. Agree a fee budget. Consider what civil action might assist in the discovery of evidence, especially as part of the First Step.

It is vital that the lawyers relied on for advice in major investigations are experienced litigators. This is not meant to detract from the value of in-house counsel or practitioners in general. If unqualified or inexperienced litigators are used, the most likely outcome is that a weak line will be followed, which will fail. Tough litigators are essential.

The lawyer should sign a letter of engagement and a confidentiality agreement.

Do not let lawyers believe they can investigate.

Consider Forming a Special Task Force

COMPOSITION

Consider establishing a Project Team or Special Task Force which has sufficient skills and experience to complete the investigation quickly and professionally. The structure of the team should be as shown in Figure 8.1.

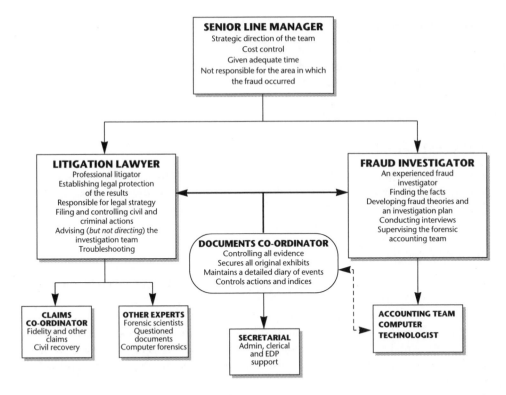

Figure 8.1   The Project Team or Special Task Force

DOCUMENTS CO-ORDINATOR

A documents co-ordinator should ensure that all evidence is catalogued, showing where and when it was found, and by whom, so that the chain of evidence can be proven. He should maintain a detailed diary of the investigation, showing the dates on which interviews were conducted and when important evidence was acquired. The object is to ensure that there is a complete record of every enquiry made. This can be important if the case goes to court or if payment is contested by insurers.

He should specify and maintain report and spreadsheet templates, maintain a secure network for team members, and control back-up and contingency plans. He should also be responsible for internal security and counter-surveillance. The documents co-ordinator is a very important person.

The documents co-ordinator should maintain a file of *all* documents, statements and reports. He should be the anchor man in the investigation. Action sheets should be prepared for all outstanding enquiries. Documents handed to the police or other third parties should be listed and approved by the team's lawyers before being released against a signed receipt.

Other members of the project team should work from copy documents, only borrowing originals when absolutely necessary, for forensic analysis, for example. They should hand copies of schedules, file notes, statements, reports and other work to the documents co-ordinator for cross-referencing and filing. **It is absolutely essential that a full set of all documentation is retained by the documents co-ordinator.**

ACCOUNTANT AND COMPUTER TECHNOLOGIST

The accountant and computer technologist should review records, accounts and computer files, looking for symptoms of concealment and deviations from normal procedures and for other actions listed in the Investigations Plan. Results and suggestions for further work should be recorded on Action Sheets.

FRAUD INVESTIGATOR

The investigator should uncover intelligence and follow up information. He should be given the prime responsibility for interviewing suspects and witnesses, and for other tasks of an investigative nature. He must not control the case!

LITIGATION LAWYER

The lawyer should review the evidence as it unfolds, and guide other members of the team on the legality of investigative techniques.

The lawyer should not be put in charge of the investigation, nor should he become involved in interviews with witnesses and suspects. There are three reasons for this. Firstly, lawyers are not trained as investigators, and some tend to be ineffectual in investigations in the field or when they are deprived of the authority of office. Secondly, they must provide an independent balance for the team.

Thirdly, if they take part in interviews, they may be called to testify, and this can have serious consequences for the way the case is presented in court.

The lawyer should control the filing of civil and criminal complaints, and screen all correspondence with the fidelity insurer and loss adjusters. All contacts with the press should be handled through the lawyer.

SUPERVISING SOLICITORS

If the First Step involves executing a Search and Seizure Order, the team's lawyers will need to appoint an independent supervising solicitor. it is essential that the person chosen is an experienced litigator.

CLAIMS CO-ORDINATOR

If the loss appears to be covered by insurance, a senior manager – and preferably not the person normally responsible for insurance matters – should be appointed as claims co-ordinator. He should be made the company's focal point for all matters connected with the *claim*.

OTHER EXPERTS

Consider retaining other experts, such as computer technicians or forensic scientists, when necessary. It is essential that the investigation team is provided with all of the resources needed.

CONTROLLING POLITICS AND MORALE

The senior manager should pay close attention to internal politics and team morale. Tension between lawyers and investigators is not uncommon and, after all, this is why they were put on the Earth. They are usually strong characters who don't give in easily, which is why you retained them. If warnings don't improve the relationship, the senior manager should fire the lawyers. (*This is a joke to make sure you haven't dozed off.*)

Consider Improving Controls

Determine what additional security controls, possibly increased to a very high level for a short period, will be introduced as part of the First Step – for example:

- installing access and exit controls, for goods, people and vehicles
- searching vehicles coming in and going out of premises
- changing locks and keys, especially those to which the suspects have access
- changing computer passwords and other access privileges
- increasing supervision on areas used by the suspects.

But whatever you do, *do not alert the suspects that they are under suspicion.*

Consider Setting up a Control Room

For major cases, obtain a secure control room and suitable equipment for the team:

- 24-hour secured access
- secure filing, including a large fireproof safe
- good photocopying facilities
- direct telephone lines, fitted with tape recorders

- shredders
- tape recorders and note books for team members
- portable telephones
- portable photocopiers
- clear plastic envelopes for protecting documentary exhibits
- exhibit labels
- authority letters and identification for team members
- vehicles to remove goods and records
- secure warehousing for seized goods and documents.

In smaller cases, it may not be necessary to designate a control room, but whatever premises are used by the investigations and legal team, they must be secure. Good crooks usually counter-attack.

Finalize the Investigations Plan

Based on the above considerations, finalize an investigations plan (possibly using *Microsoft Project*) showing what action has to be taken, by whom, and the timescale involved. The plan should be aligned with the Fraud Theory, and kept under review as the investigation progresses. The legality of the techniques planned should be subject to a final review by the victim's lawyers.

Set up a Budget for Costs

Set up a budget for legal, accountancy and investigation costs. This may seem an unimportant point, but it is not!

Major investigations are expensive. The art is to make sure that all losses, interest and costs are recovered from the perpetrators, insurers or third parties. The accounting process is described on page 188.

Brief Members of the Investigations Team

Immediately before the First Step, hold a detailed briefing for members of the project team. Make sure each member of the team (and, if possible, the supervising solicitors):

- understands the theory of the fraud and the elements in the worst case that have to be proved
- has clear instructions, and knows what is expected of him, such as:
  - marking and preservation of evidence
  - suspects to be interviewed
  - other actions to be taken
  - interview plans
  - contact list of everyone involved in the investigation

- reporting results to the control room as actions are completed (this means that every team should have a mobile telephone and contact list; it is wise to program the numbers into telephone memories the night before the First Step is due to be taken)
- understands the fallback plans and legal requirements
- has a contingency plan if witnesses and suspects cannot be found.

Good control over the First Step is critical if the investigation is not to drift off course. It must be an overwhelming ambush. It is essential that the supervising solicitor has a contingency plan if immediate entry to the defendant's premises is denied, and that there are sufficient resources available to deal with multiple defendants.

Final Briefing of Senior Managers and PR

Brief senior management on the final plans. Warn them not to speak to the press. Consider preparing a press release. Make sure their expectations are aligned to the possible outcomes, and set up reporting deadlines.

The Night Before

In many large cases, the First Step will be taken through simultaneous investigative and legal actions, possibly at various places throughout the world. This may mean that teams have to be in place the night before. There are four critical points:

- Make sure all members of the team are fully briefed and are in place on time; although lawyers are lovable, they are always late.

- Make sure all teams get to bed early the night before: investigators are also lovable, but stay too long in bars, telling war stories. The very worst thing is to execute the First Step with a hangover.

- Make sure the control room is manned and that communications work.

- If pre-emptive orders (Search and Seizure) are being obtained, make sure that the claimant's solicitors and supervising solicitors are fully briefed and have plans in place to ensure that critical evidence cannot be destroyed during the period when the defendant is permitted to seek legal advice.

Finally, make sure you know where the defendants are, and have a contingency plan to find them if, at the critical hour, they are not where they were expected to be. It is always a good sign when an investigation goes immediately off course. The victim will quickly discover how good its planning has been.

9 *Stage D: The First Step*

Principle

- Make the First Step an ambush . . .
- . . . from which the crooks never recover.

Take the First Step

Take the first steps through simultaneous visits, *pre-emptive legal actions* and interviews:

- catch the criminals in the act
- interview suspects and witnesses
- obtain all of the listed evidence
- recover property belonging to the company
- complete all of the other items scheduled in the Investigations Plan.

Make sure all of the documentary evidence is secured, chains of evidence are established, and that interviews with suspects and witnesses are completed and the results reported. Remember: *you might not get a second chance!*

Take Appropriate Civil and Criminal Actions

Consider taking further civil actions to discover evidence and freeze assets. Immediately any witness or suspect fails to agree to release important evidence, consider civil action for discovery.

Press criminal charges, if these are the objectives. Involve the police in every possible jurisdiction, and give police officers every assistance.

Negotiate or start litigation to trace and recover funds. Ideally, all negotiations should be directed towards recovering losses and costs of the type not covered by insurance. Always make sure settlement agreements are drafted by lawyers and secured on assets or bank guarantees. History is littered with unsecured settlement agreements which foundered.

Do not release anyone from liability without first consulting lawyers. To do so may lead to the fidelity insurer claiming that its subrogation rights have been compromised, thus enabling it to deny or mitigate its liability.

Do not release evidence to third parties, such as other companies which are victims of the same fraud, unless you do so through lawyers and with a specific, tangible objective. Do not agree to any employee giving evidence, or making any statement or affidavit on their behalf unless it is in response to a subpoena or other court order and cleared by lawyers. To do otherwise may result in your own legal action being compromised.

Prepare detailed file notes or reports (copied to the Documents Coordinator) on every significant meeting, interview or action in the investigation. Keep all original notes, and remember these may have to be produced to the defence at the appropriate time.

Maintain the Control Room

The senior manager in charge of the investigation, the documents co-ordinator and the lawyer should remain in the control room at least until the first wave of enquiries have been completed.

Report Progress

All members of the project team should report their progress to the control room and, if possible, should attend a full debriefing at the end of the first day and regularly thereafter. If you cannot brainstorm, at least braindrizzle! Evidence should be logged by the documents co-ordinator.

It is especially important that notes of interviews with suspects are prepared and tapes transcribed as soon as possible and at a time when the facts are fresh. Original tapes should be copied: the originals should be secured by the documents co-ordinator. It is vital that all team members document and report the results of all enquiries.

Analyse the Results

Analyse the results of the First Step, and plan further action for the short, medium and long term. Establish a list of new and follow-up actions, and allocate tasks on action sheets. Make sure the continuity of evidence is preserved. Revise the Fraud Theory and Investigations Plan, and complete all actions as quickly as possible. Once you have seized the initiative, keep it.

It is critically important that documents obtained as a result of discovery or legal actions are analysed. In far too many cases, once the orders have been executed, everyone relaxes, and this is a grave mistake. Work on the documentation and seek further orders if it is not complete. This is the stage for really hard work.

Report to Insurers

Depending on the results of the First Step, give formal notice to the fidelity insurance company.

Once notice has been given, the time allowed for filing a Proof of Loss is limited. Although it is usually possible to negotiate extensions, the timetable should be monitored carefully. The most important point to remember is that there is a time limit of two years after giving the preliminary notice. After this, the rights to sue the fidelity insurance company for non-payment expire. The task of monitoring the filing deadlines should be given to the lawyer or claims co-ordinator.

Advise Others Who Could be Involved

Advise subsidiary and associate companies of the investigation if this has not already been done. This is very important in cases of computer hacking and similar problems which could affect other company installations. Also advise employees, and keep them informed, as far as practicable, as the investigation continues. The lawyer should prepare press releases, and handle all enquiries and media interviews.

Throw Resources at the Case

Continue with all aspects of the investigation as quickly as possible. Go for overwhelming proof, and take the toughest line possible.

Computers as lie detectors

10 *Stage E: Interviews*

Principles

- Effective interviews with witnesses and suspects are vital.
- The objective is to find the truth and to uncover admissible evidence.
- Interviews may be conducted at any time during an investigation, but for convenience are set out as a separate stage.

Important Background

THE RECOMMENDED SYSTEM

The system for finding the truth in interviews recommended in this book has evolved over more than thirty years, and is now used extensively throughout the world by many regulatory agencies and enforcement bodies, banks and financial institutions. It has been consistently successful in finding the truth.

Some people argue that a crook could read the techniques and plan his answers accordingly. This is not the case, simply because when faced with a professional interviewer and incriminating evidence, it is impossible for the liar to completely submerge his memory while acting out all of the reactions of an innocent person. On the contrary, knowledge of the techniques and their significance is more likely to increase stress and to expose the liar.

ESTABLISHING RELATIONSHIPS AND RAPPORT

It is essential that the interviewer establishes rapport with the subject while remaining emotionally detached and in total control. This is one reason why line managers – under whose supervision a fraud took place – should be excluded from interviews: they are too emotionally involved.

In personal relationships (see the work on *Transactional Analysis* by Eric Berne), people adopt one of three roles – Parent, Adult or Child – depending to a large extent upon their perception of the other person's position (see Figure 10.1).

The roles shown on the above chart are as follows (see Table 10.1):

Table 10.1   Roles in Transactional Analysis

Ego state	Role model example
Parent: Critical	Father or mother who disciplines a child
Parent: Nurturing	Father or mother who nurtures and comforts a child
Adult	The (hopefully) normal ego state at work
Child: Adaptive	Straightforward, emotional and willing to comply
Child: Rebellious	Straightforward, awkward and looking for trouble

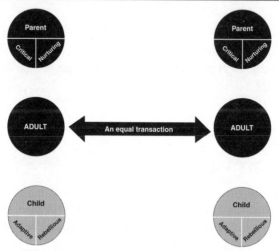

Figure 10.1   Transactional Analysis

When one party to a conversation (or a transaction) tries to force upon the other a role he does not wish to play, conflict usually arises. It is referred to as a crossed transaction, which generates an emotional reaction and usually increases stress. An equal transaction arises where the roles are acceptable to both parties (see Table 10.2).

Table 10.2   Equal and crossed transactions

Role adopted by the interviewer	Role adopted by the subject	Comment
Adult	Adult	This is the relationship of most conversations in business.
Critical parent	Adaptive child	This is the relationship in Phase 2 in which the interviewer stresses the inevitability that the truth will be established.
Nurturing parent	Adaptive child	This is the relationship in Phase 3 in which the interviewer establishes empathy and helps the subject resolve the problem.
Child	Child	May be a relationship that emerges in Phase 4, but must be very carefully handled.

Obvious problems arise where the subject perceives his role as that of a critical parent, and sees the interviewer as an adaptive child! In such cases, shock tactics may be necessary to change the relationship, and this is easily done once the interviewer understands the dynamics of his relationship with the subject.

Confessions are usually only obtained when the interviewer has manoeuvred himself into the position of a nurturing parent and the subject accepts the role of an adaptive child. There are exceptions, but this is the proper transaction level at which full confessions are made.

CHOOSING THE BEST INTERVIEWER FOR THE SPECIFIC CASE

It is unrealistic to expect a junior auditor to interview a hard-nosed senior vice-president who is suspected of having his hand in the till. It is equally wrong to expect results from any interview where massive cultural, social, economic or corporate hierarchical gaps exist between the position of a subject and an inexperienced interviewer because one or the other will be overwhelmed in an unbalanced transaction. It is also unlikely that rapport will be established.

Experienced interviewers automatically raise or lower their approach, depending on the standing of the subject being interviewed. This skill can be developed with practice.

The factors governing the selection of the most effective interviewer in any particular case are:

- the position, age, sex, status and character of the subject
- the skills, age, sex, status and experience of the potential interviewer, and his professional detachment from the subject
- the nature and complexity of the fraud suspected.

Under normal circumstances, a suspect should never be interviewed by more than two people at a time, and then the second person should stay out of the subject's direct line of sight and should remain silent unless the leading interviewer invites him to speak. As far as possible, the relationship should be one-to-one.

KNOW THE FACTS

The interviewer should know the facts of the case – backwards, forwards, sideways and inside out. He should have every detail at his fingertips, the clearest theory of how the fraud took place, and the likely worst case. He should be in a position to explain every piece of evidence, every rough note, jotting or comment in a witness statement or affidavit.

CHOOSING GOOD QUESTIONS

It is impossible to say which techniques will succeed most easily in a particular case, although the odds can be increased by careful planning and practice.

It is essential that the interviewer selects and uses techniques with which he feels comfortable and which suit his personality. Most people do not like shouting or getting involved in controversy or arguments, and those who do should never be allowed to conduct interviews. A quiet, professional but relentless approach is far more effective.

There are a number of ways in which questions can be asked.

Open questions require the subject to give a detailed reply – for example:

- 'Tell me everything you know about . . .'
- 'What did you do next?'
- 'How could this have been done?'

Open questions are useful in interviews with witnesses, since they allow them to explain, in detail, exactly what they did, saw or heard. They may be used with subjects to extract detail, but they can result in answers that stray off the point. If this happens, the interviewer can change to leading questions or bring the subject back to a relevant point. Open questions slow down the pace and take the pressure off the interviewer, and often off the subject.

Closed and leading questions usually call for 'yes' or 'no' replies or suggest the answer required – for example:

> . . . and then you threw the papers in the shredder?

They are useful in pinning subjects down, but they do not usually provide any free-flowing replies. Sometimes, if the matter results in criminal proceedings, the suggestion will be made that admissions were put into the mouth of the accused.

Negative and complex questions such as 'You didn't take the money, did you?', can only bring one answer. Negative questions provide negative answers and should be avoided. Normally, questions should be *simply constructed*, so that there can be no misunderstanding.

Complex questions usually disorient the subject, but they can lead to disagreement concerning which answer applied to what question.

Positive confrontation is vital. It is crucial that the interviewer tells the subject what he believes to the truth to be, and repeats accusatory statements throughout the interview – for example, 'It is obvious to me from this document, Mr Smith, that . . .' or 'I have to say, Bill, that things don't look good for you. I believe you took the money . . .'.

In a closed interview, such statements are not libellous. They are important for two reasons. The first is that they emphasize the fact that the truth will emerge, and therefore increase stress. Second, they are an important test of guilt or innocence.

Sometimes, this approach will result in an innocent person being wrongly accused, and may require the interviewer to apologize at the end of the interview, but these cases are rare, and very seldom does any long-term damage result.

Summary statements are very important, and can be used to get the interview back on track – for example:

> 'So far you have told me, Mr Smith, that you have . . . now I want to go on to . . .'.

When supported by the production of incriminating evidence or schedules, they reinforce the notion in the mind of the subject that detection is inevitable.

Blocking questions which are usually asked early in an interview, are intended to close off a later untrue explanation of innocence – for example, where a person is suspected of taking bribes, he might be asked in a low-key way at the start of the interview:

Do you understand the company's policy on ethics?
Do you know of any employee who has taken a gift, money or anything else from a supplier?
Have you ever taken anything from a supplier?
Have you ever been offered anything by a supplier?

In this way, the subject can be pinned down so that when, for example, a subject has categorically denied ever taking anything from a supplier, a photograph of him taking a bag of cash is shown to him, and he cannot explain that it was an innocent gift. Equally, honest answers to blocking questions can clear innocent subjects.

Dealing with lies

Generally, the subject should not be allowed to escape with a lie. There are two reasons for this. The first is that it builds his confidence. The second is that it makes it more difficult for him to admit the truth later on, simply because he now has two problems to admit: the original offence, and the fact that he lied to the interviewer. Never, ever, tell the subject that he is 'a liar': *attack the false statement, not the person.*

The options for dealing with lies include those shown in Table 10.3.

Table 10.3   Dealing with lies

Ways in which the interviewer should deal with lies	Comments
Look away, up or down, put your hand over your mouth, smile, or brush non-existent dust off your arm while the person is giving the false explanation.	This is a body language statement that you do not believe him.
Interrupt the statement and say, 'Come on, Bill . . .'.	If he defers to this interruption, the chances are he is guilty, and will confess.
Point out that the subject must have misunderstood the question, and ask it again.	This is a low-key approach, but achieves the objective of not allowing the person to escape with a lie.
Say, 'That was not true, Mr Smith. I am going to ask the question again, and please be very careful how you answer it . . .'.	This raises the stakes. It will cause a liar to think carefully. An innocent person may object.
Joke about the answer: 'Oh yes, and pigs fly . . . now come on, Bill, what about . . .'.	This approach depends on the status of the subject and his relationship with the interviewer. Don't try it on the Chairman!
Pull out your notebook and say something along the lines: 'That is absolutely incredible, Mr Smith . . . I just cannot believe it's true. Please go over what you said again . . .'.	This raises the stakes. it will cause a liar to think carefully. An innocent person may object.
In extreme cases, draw the liar out into giving more and more detail; let him come to realize that his story is ridiculous.	This approach should normally be used when all other ideas have failed. The interviewer must force the liar into layers of incredible detail, and, at appropriate points, revert to some or all of the techniques described above.

In most cases, the interviewer should immediately follow up any of the above approaches with a direct statement or question which implies the subject's guilt.

DEALING WITH COUNTER-ATTACKS

This is one of the most difficult areas for the inexperienced interviewer, whose reaction is to panic when the subject counter-attacks with statements such as:

> 'I am going to sue you.'
> 'My lawyer will be in touch.'

If possible, the interviewer should pretend he has not heard the statement, and carry on with the next question, regardless. If this does not work, the interviewer must stay cool and say something along the lines: 'I am not interested in that, Mr Jones, now what about . . .'.

If this approach fails, the interviewer should say: 'Let's leave that until later. I am trying to find the truth. Please tell me why . . .'.

It is vital that the interviewer does not get into an argument. To the very common response 'Are you calling me a liar?', the interviewer should say, 'It is pretty clear to me, Mr Jones, that you have not told me the truth: there could be good reasons for this. Now what about . . .?'. If the interviewer believes the person is not telling the truth, he must not back down or apologize. He must stay in control.

DEALING WITH DENIALS

If the subject denies things he is known to have done – which is effectively a lie – the interviewer should interrupt and point out the evidence. For example: 'That is not correct, Bill, is it? Just look at this . . .'. The interviewer should never gloss over a false denial.

DEALING WITH BODY LANGUAGE

Most inexperienced interviewers overlook the fact that at least 50 per cent of an answer is given through a person's body language or non-verbal communication.

Equally, the interviewer's body language will be interpreted by the subject, and this fact can be used to advantage (see Table 10.4).

Some marketing courses encourage salesmen to copy the body language and postures of people to whom they are trying to make a sale, thus establishing empathy. If you don't believe the power of body language, next time you speak to your boss, put your hand up over your mouth while he is speaking, or pull your ear lobe. See what happens, but be prepared for a change of employment!

DEALING WITH FISHING QUESTIONS

Sometimes, subjects will say something along the lines: 'You tell me what you know, and I will give an answer' or 'I am not prepared to answer general questions: let me see the evidence you have.' In such cases, the subject is simply trying to find out how much the interviewer knows, and is almost certain to have committed much more serious acts than are presently known about.

Table 10.4   Interviewer's body language

Circumstances	Interviewer's body language
When the subject does not tell the truth	• Demonstrators, using fingers • Looking away • Head moving slowly left to right • Leaning forward • Intruding on the suspect's personal space • Hand over mouth
When the subject tells the truth	• Palms-upward gestures with the hands • Looking at the subject and smiling • Head moving slowly up and down • Leaning backwards • Increasing the subject's personal space
When the subject uses a manipulator, such as brushing dust off his clothes	• Look carefully at the movement. • Copy the movement. • Ask if the question is worrying him.

The interviewer's response should be along the following lines: 'I am trying to find out whether you are telling me the whole truth or not. It is a bit like being asked by the Customs whether you have anything to declare. If you don't tell me the whole truth now, I have to draw my own conclusions. Now tell me everything – and I mean everything – you have taken...'. Under no circumstances should the interviewer comply with the interviewee's demands. Instead, he should take the question as an indication that much more serious issues are in the background.

DEALING WITH CONSEQUENCES QUESTIONS

A guilty person will be subject to two opposing forces. The first is the wish to tell the truth; the other is the fear of the consequences. Typically, he might ask about the company's reaction and whether or not it intends to prosecute. Under no circumstances should the interviewer give the subject an untrue answer, but he should respond along the lines that he cannot say, but that his job is to find the truth and to make a report.

However, he should point out that the company would obviously be more sympathetic towards someone who admitted their mistake and helped it recover than someone who tried to lie his way out of a hopeless position. The interviewer should immediately follow up this response with a statement along the lines: 'Come on, Bill, let's sort this out now ... what did you do with the money?'

OFFERING ACCEPTABLE EXCUSES AND PRAISE

The interviewer should consider offering the subject a morally acceptable excuse for what he has done. For example: 'It is obvious to me, Bill, that you are a decent person; did this all start by accident, or what?' Again, the principle is to condemn the act, not the person: we all make mistakes.

Specific Actions in All Cases

LEGAL POSITION AND LETTERS OF AUTHORITY

The interviewer must have a clear understanding of his legal rights to ask questions. This is especially important when the interviewer is working in a country away from his home base. The issues are as follows:

- Is the interviewer permitted to ask questions of the person(s) concerned?
- Is the person required to answer questions under the terms of his employment or some other contract? (If not, think about incorporating such terms for the future.)
- Can the person ask for a union or legal representative to be present? Such representation is not usually helpful in investigative interviews, but the interviewer must take care not to breach disciplinary or other codes.
- Does the interviewer have to tell (or 'caution') the person that he is not obliged to answer questions? This is usually the case where the interviewer is a professional investigator and his objective is to seek criminal prosecution. In these circumstances the interviewer will have to prove to a criminal court that admissions and confessions were obtained voluntarily.
- Can the interviewer tape record the interview without the subject's knowledge?
- Are there disciplinary or other procedures to be followed? In most countries, a distinction is made between fact-finding interviews (at which union representation may be denied), and disciplinary interviews.

The interviewer should consider the advisability of obtaining a letter, signed by the appropriate level of management, authorizing him to conduct the interview (but he should make sure its preparation does not alert the suspects).

Determine the Objectives of Each Interview

The objectives of each interview will be determined, to a large extent, by the general plan for the investigation. In some cases, documentary and other evidence is overwhelming, thus the interview may appear to be a formality. In others, especially where the evidence is weak, interviews can be critical. However, in all cases, effective interviews can make a significant difference, uncover more extensive dishonesty, and lead to greater recoveries. The downside is that in both criminal and civil cases, badly conducted or unfair interviews can lead to serious problems. For this reason, careful planning, legal clearance of the approach and accurate documentation are all vital.

If criminal prosecution is an objective, the police should be informed *before* any internal interviews with subjects take place. The ground rules for internal interviews should be agreed with a senior police officer, but remember:

- The victim's objective is probably to establish the total amount lost, whereas the police will focus on proving a small selection of criminal charges.

- The results of internal company interviews can be made available to the police. However, evidence or internal reports should not be passed to the police without first checking with legal advisers. The reason for this is that the police are obliged to disclose everything they know to the defence, and there may be internal matters that are privileged against disclosure and which your company would wish to protect. The results of police interviews will not normally be made available to the victim organisation.

- Once a suspect has been interviewed by the police and cautioned, he is unlikely to co-operate in an internal investigation.

It is impossible to set down rules that will apply in every case, but usually agreement can be reached that will permit the victim organization to conduct its own interviews, and after-wards make a formal complaint to the police. This is usually the preferred route.

OBTAIN FULL BACKGROUND DETAILS ON THE SUBJECT

It is vital that as much as possible is known about the subject before he is interviewed. Data should be obtained, checked and cross-referenced from:

- **Personnel and contract files** – Special attention should be given to any previous warnings or disciplinary action, and the accuracy of the subject's claimed educational, linguistic and other qualifications.The linguistic factor may be important if the suspect claims not to be able to understand the language spoken by the interviewer. Evidence of any discrepancies or past misdeeds should be summarised and held available for produc-tion in the interview. Note the maiden name of the subject's wife, and surnames of married daughters. Often, shareholdings and assets will be concealed under these names.

- **Expense statements** – these should be analysed in *minute detail*, and any discrepancies noted. Summary schedules and supporting evidence should be prepared for use in the interview. *The fact that the suspect has falsified his expenses will be a telling factor in the interview.*

- **Telephone call logs** – should be analysed showing who the subject has called, when, and in what sequence.

- **A diary of events** – This should cover the period during which the fraud is believed to have taken place. It should be updated as the investigation progresses.

- **Job descriptions and authority tables** – These should be examined and any abuse of authority or deviations from approved procedures fully documented for production during the interview.

- **Computers** – Especially if the employee has been provided with a *laptop* computer. These should be *professionally examined*, and deleted files recovered. Maxima and other firms of leading investigators provide such a service.

- **Voice and e-mail** – A dump of all messages should be obtained, and important details added to the diary of events.

- **Credit ratings** – These should be obtained for the subject and his family. Evidence of financial problems or excesses should be available for discussion during the interview.

- **Press and other databases** – These should be searched for references to the subject, his family or associates, including company registration databases, showing directorships.

DECIDE WHEN AND WHERE THE INTERVIEW WILL BE CONDUCTED

Ideally, interviews should be conducted as part of the First Step, at a time and place where the suspects are most exposed:

- while they are involved in an act of dishonesty
- while they are in possession of stolen goods
- while they are doing anything they are not authorized to do.

The First Step must be taken when the suspects can be caught with their pants down. Whether this is possible or not, interviews should be arranged with minimal advance notice. Where there is more than one suspect, they should be interviewed separately and simultaneously, and under no circumstances should they be given the opportunity to co-ordinate their explanations.

DECIDE HOW THE INTERVIEW WILL BE RECORDED

An accurate record of every interview is vital, and the interviewer should plan how this will be achieved.

In practice, the best method is to use a concealed tape recorder, because it provides an accurate record without disturbing the flow of the interview. However, the legality of covert tape recording in the country concerned should be confirmed. (In the UK, covert tape recording is allowed, and the results may be admitted in evidence in both criminal and civil courts.) If the interview is to be taped covertly, make sure recording lights are not visible and the end-of-tape alarm is deactivated.

If the suspect asks whether the interview is being recorded, he should be told the truth, along the lines: 'Yes. It is in your interest that an accurate record is made, and you can have a copy when we are finished.' Without pausing, the interviewer should move on to a direct question. Remember, it is genuinely in everyone's interest to have an accurate record of what is said. It is also important that the interview should be as natural as possible.

As an alternative to covert recording, the suspect may be asked if he has any objection to the interview being taped. The fact that an accurate record of the interview is in his interests should be stressed. If the suspect has no objection to a recording being made, control of the equipment *must* be outside the interview room, and under no circumstances should the interviewer have to load and change tapes. If taping is invisible, it will be soon be forgotten, and the interview can progress in a natural, free-flowing way.

Careful planning is needed when an interview is to be covertly or overtly taped:

- Use a good-quality recorder with stereo microphones; if necessary, hire suitable equipment.
- Check the audio quality in the room before the interview starts; air conditioning and other barely audible noises can spoil the recording.
- Load the recorder with new batteries, or connect it to a reliable power source.
- Use new tapes; number them uniquely and keep a log of when they were loaded and removed.
- After removal of each tape, break the record-protect lugs to prevent erasure.
- Copy the original tapes as soon as possible, but under no circumstances interfere with them.

- As soon as possible, deposit the original tapes with the company's legal advisers, and retain the receipt.
- Transcribe the copy tapes.
- Check the accuracy of the transcripts.

If the recording is unclear, consider having it professionally enhanced, but take care to ensure that the integrity of the original tape is not compromised, and that the chain of custody – showing by whom and when it was handled – can be established to the satisfaction of the court.

Although the interviewer may have a pad to make the occasional note, under normal circumstances notes should not be made during the interview. Note-taking distracts both the interviewer and the suspect and destroys the timing and spontaneity of the interview. Notes may be written after the interview, possibly in conjunction with the suspect. For example, at the end of the interview, the interviewer may say something along the lines: 'Bill, we need to get an accurate record of what you have said. You told me xx and yy.' The subject should be asked to agree and sign the notes. *However, in a long interview which is being covertly recorded, not taking any notes may alert the subject to the fact that a recording is being made, and lead to questions and conflict.*

Interviews with Witnesses

OBJECTIVES

Interviews with witnesses can be conducted at any stage in an investigation, but great care must be taken that:

- such interviews do not alert the suspects
- the witness is not himself involved
- the witness is reliable, and has no hidden motives.

The ultimate objective of interviews with witnesses is to obtain information and evidence which can be used in court, an industrial tribunal or for making a claim under insurance. However, the value of intelligence or opinions provided by a witness should never be underestimated.

A witness can be summoned to give evidence in legal proceedings even though he does not want to attend and has refused to make a written statement. However, most lawyers are unhappy about calling a witness without knowing precisely what he is going to say. Thus a written statement has the following value:

- It enables counsel to understand exactly what a witness will say.
- When the evidence concerned is not challenged by the opposition, the statement may be read without going to the expense of asking the witness to attend court.
- If the witness fails to stick to his statement, he may, with the leave of the trial judge, be questioned by counsel as a hostile witness.

Thus the final object of interviews with witnesses is to obtain formal evidence in a statement or written form:

- to prove a loss
- to establish responsibility
- to prove the method of fraud
- to establish the suspect's guilty intent
- to obtain expert testimony
- to uncover other losses, trace assets, and to identify any other people involved.

CONDUCTING INTERVIEWS WITH WITNESSES

Interviews should be conducted in *private* in a low-key and professional way. The witness should be:

- asked to relate *everything he knows* about the crime or event in question in his own words; he should not be interrupted; open questions should be used as much as possible
- questioned about specific points in his evidence
- asked to produce documents or other evidence in his possession
- shown all relevant documents or other exhibits, to identify them and to refresh his memory
- asked to go over his evidence again
- asked to resolve discrepancies between his first and subsequent statements.

If the witness's evidence is relevant, it should be written down in a Proof of Evidence. If not, the interviewer should prepare a short file note. It is essential that a note is kept of every interview conducted during an investigation.

STATEMENTS AND PROOFS OF EVIDENCE

A *Proof of Evidence* is a written account of what a witness says. It may contain hearsay and other details not directly related to the facts in issue. Lawyers can use a Proof as the basis for preparing a formal statement or affidavit.

Although in both criminal and civil proceedings in the United Kingdom statements will normally be made available to the opposing side, this is not true of Proofs of Evidence, providing they are prefaced as follows:

> This Proof of Evidence has been prepared for the Legal Advisers of X Ltd., for information and in contemplation of legal proceedings relating to the matters referred to in it.

This caveat should establish the privileged nature of the document. It is therefore much safer for inexperienced investigators to obtain Proofs of Evidence, rather than formal signed statements.

When criminal proceedings are contemplated in the UK, witnesses may be asked to sign a statement, bearing an endorsement under the Criminal Justice Act (CJA):

> This statement consisting of ... pages each signed by me is true to the best of my knowledge and belief and I make it knowing that if it is tendered in evidence, I shall be liable to prosecution if I have wilfully stated in it anything which I know to be false or do not believe to be true.

Statements of this type are invaluable, and they can be introduced directly into evidence without the need for the witness to attend. However, they should only be taken by experienced investigators.

OBSTRUCTIVE AND UNWILLING WITNESSES

If a witness is deliberately obstructive or deceitful, the interviewer should:

- seek to break the bond between him and the suspect, or try to establish why he is reluctant to tell the truth, and then deal with that reason

- if all else fails, the interviewer should take a *CJA statement* in writing and, after signature, point out the seriousness of perjury; the interviewer should point out the untruths in the statement, and explain that unless they are corrected, the witness could be at risk of prosecution for perjury.

If a witness refuses to sign a Proof of Evidence or statement, the draft should be read over to him – word for word – and he should then be asked to read it himself. He should be asked if it is correct and, if not, corrections or additions should be made. These should be initialled by the witness even though he may refuse to sign the statement itself.

   If the witness still refuses to sign or even initial the corrections, the interviewer should endorse the document – in front of the witness – in the following way:

   The above Statement/Proof of Evidence was read by ... to ... and he agreed that it is true and correct. He declined to sign the Statement because ... enter reason (for example, because he did not wish to become involved).

   Signed .... (Interviewer) Date and Time.
   Witnessed.............................. (Suspect)

The interviewer should point out that the witness may be called to give evidence. If the witness makes it clear that he will not attend voluntarily, a Witness Order may be obtained from the court directing his attendance on a specified date and, where appropriate, listing the documents(s) he is to produce.

   Failure to attend after being served with a Witness Order may lead to the witness being arrested and taken to court. If he fails to testify, he may be prosecuted for contempt of court, and false evidence could result in an allegation of perjury. This process should be made clear to the obdurate witness: it sometimes focuses his attention.

TAKING STATEMENTS FROM EXPERT WITNESSES

Normally, witnesses can only testify to facts from their firsthand knowledge, and cannot give hearsay evidence, nor can they express an opinion. The one exception to this general rule arises in the case of *expert witnesses* who have a recognized expertise in a particular subject and who are allowed to express *an opinion* and advise the court generally. For example, a medical doctor may give an opinion as to the cause of death, or an accountant can express an opinion about the reasons for a company's failure or the efficiency of its controls.

Before being called to give evidence, the expert witness must satisfy the trial judge that he is qualified by learning and experience to give an opinion within his field. Any statement taken from him should set out his qualifications in full, and his past experience as an expert witness. It is absolutely vital that the background of an expert witness is checked out thoroughly and that any padding of his qualifications or experience is removed. It can be catastrophic if an expert witness is discredited in court.

Statements by expert witnesses will usually be taken under the guidance of lawyers, although the task of interviewing and obtaining a draft of his evidence might be delegated to an investigator, auditor or manager.

Expert testimony is intended to inform and be helpful, and not simply to impress the court with the skill of the witness, nor to bamboozle the jury. The quality of expert testimony is its simplicity.

This objective can be achieved as follows:

• The expert should understand exactly what is required of him and what the problem is. Each question should be framed *in writing*, and should deal with a single matter upon which an opinion is required.

• The conclusions that the expert is expected to reach should not be suggested to him. He must be free to make up his own mind.

• The expert should be given a realistic amount of time to study the facts and to form an opinion.

• The expert should provide an initial report, addressed to the company's lawyers, which should be read carefully, and all ambiguities resolved.

• Technicalities, acronyms and abbreviations should be avoided. The Proof of Evidence should be written down in the most simple terms.

• If the subject is complex, charts, diagrams or working models should be used to assist in the understanding of his testimony.

• The draft Proof of Evidence should be submitted, by the company's lawyers, to two or three laymen who are not familiar with the case. They should be questioned on their understanding. The Proof of Evidence should be revised if necessary.

• In complex cases, a glossary of terms should be prepared.

The procedure outlined above should result in clear-cut and simple evidence, and not, as often happens, in technical gobbledegook that confuses the judge, jury and even other expert witnesses.

Planning Interviews with Suspects

GENERAL STRUCTURE

In most investigations, there is only one opportunity to interview suspects, thus they must be carefully planned and conclusive.

Such interviews can normally be divided into four phases, as shown in Figure 10.2.

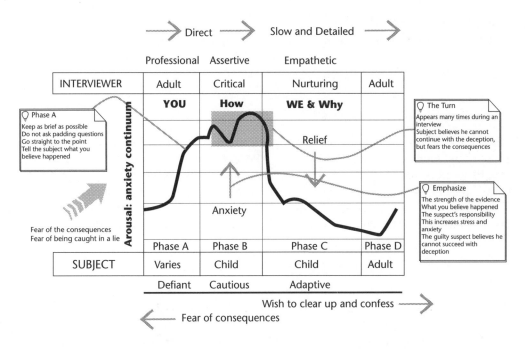

Figure 10.2   Interview road map: the four phases, showing the requirement to change roles

Phase A: The Human Lie Detector

Selected questions are asked, which, from their responses, distinguish guilt from innocence and truth from lies. In this phase, the interviewer acts like a human polygraph machine, with all of his sensors switched on. He may also use a number of blocking questions to prevent the suspect claiming a plausible excuse for his dishonesty later in the interview.

Phase B: Increasing the Stakes

In this phase, the interviewer deliberately attempts to convince the subject that it is inevitable that the truth will be established. He will follow an accusatory line of questioning, much like a critical parent disciplining a child. Professional, determined questioning around the central issues, statements that the subject is believed to be responsible, and powerful summary statements all increase the prospect of the inevitability of detection. The interviewer should focus on how the transgression occurred, and the subject's responsibility for it.

A critical point, called the 'X' point, will be reached many times throughout the interview, at which the subject will carefully balance his inclination to tell the truth against his fear of the consequences. These pressures are in conflict, and will often cause the subject to become more and more passive.

Phase C: Admission-Seeking

At the 'X' point, the interviewer turns from being a critical into a nurturing parent, and focuses on how the matter can be resolved and why it happened. He creates an atmosphere in which the truth can be admitted. This is the most critical phase, and one which many interviewers find difficult to handle.

Phase D: Getting the Detail

In this phase, the subject may have already made some small admissions, and the relationship between him and the interviewer is likely to be that of a nurturing parent and an adaptive child. This phase should be taken slowly.

CATALOGUE MINOR BREACHES

Minor breaches of procedures, incorrect application forms, previous false explanations, abuse of discretion or expense fiddles should be identified, catalogued and summarized so that they can be produced during the interview. These, although not directly a part of the worst case, may be used to demonstrate to the suspect that, whether he admits to the more serious matters or not, he is already exposed to disciplinary or other action. This may lead him to conclude that he has little to lose in clearing up the more serious matters.

CONSIDER HOW THE EVIDENCE WILL BE PRESENTED

How evidence is to be handled in the interview calls for careful planning. In some cases, important evidence may be held in reserve and shown to the suspect after he has denied its existence or given a false explanation about it. In other cases, the interviewer may decide to maximize the impact of the evidence by displaying it in the interview room.

For example, in a forgery case, cheques may be enlarged and mounted on the walls in the suspect's direct line of sight. These will be a constant reminder of the strength of the evidence.

In any event, before the interview begins, the evidence must be assembled in a logical order. *Schedules summarizing the key points* and a timetable of events relating to the case concerned should be prepared. Important documents may be enclosed in clear plastic envelopes with 'exhibit labels'. However, be very careful with photocopies which can be corrupted by plastic. Also, don't expose documents which might be required for an ESDA examination to plastic.

The possibility of having some or all of the evidence forensically examined should be considered:

- ESDA testing for latent impressions of other writings. (The leading company in the UK is Berkeley Security Bureau Ltd, 10 Grosvenor Avenue, London SW1 0DH.)
- handwriting analysis, to prove who wrote a document
- fingerprinting, to prove who handled a document
- enhancement of audio tapes from answering, voice mail, dealing and dictation machines
- recovery of deleted computer files and e-mail.

The interviewer should identify the strongest evidence and make sure he understands its significance. He should consider summarizing complex facts onto easy-to-understand schedules. In the interview, the production of, and reference to, evidence must be slick and professional. Fumbling with papers reduces the chances of finding the truth, as it makes the interviewer appear incompetent and childish, and thus destroys his ability to assume the role of a critical parent.

CONSIDER THE SUSPECT'S POSITION

The suspect's likely reaction to the interview should be evaluated. Remember that in fraud cases remorse is seldom a reason why a suspect confesses. This is especially true of very senior employees, who appear to be able to minimize, rationalize and justify their dishonesty. They often deceive themselves, and usually have a plausible excuse. However, lying is stressful, and to an extent self-defeating – the more a person is compelled to lie, the greater his anxiety. This leads to a leakage of clues, and a spiral of increasing anxiety.

Usually, a full confession will be made only when the suspect believes he has nothing to lose, will obtain an advantage by telling the truth, or when he is convinced that the evidence against him is overwhelming.

Contrary to popular detective films, it is not essential that a suspect admits his guilt. In fact, failure to explain, when given the opportunity, and patently untrue answers will be to the suspect's disadvantage. Thus, if a suspect is not prepared to face the truth, make sure he commits himself to detailed and outrageous lies which can be disproved by other evidence.

Consider the possible excuses and explanations the suspect is likely to offer. Some may be true, but many will be false. Identify counter-arguments to all potential excuses. These should be reviewed and polished in the rehearsal phase (see page 172).

PLAN THE INTERVIEW ROOM

Always make the suspect play away from home. Only in exceptional circumstances should an interview be held in the suspect's home or office. There are two reasons for this. The first is that the interview can be deliberately disrupted. Secondly, in his own home, the suspect is in control. Also, the interviewer should think carefully before holding the interview in his own office, especially if it is small, untidy or displays his golfing memorabilia and photographs of his wife and kids.

Ideally, the interview room should be small, clinical, with no telephones or other distractions. At the start of the interview, the interviewer should sit behind a desk and opposite the suspect. If a witness is present, he should sit outside the suspect's direct line of sight and should keep quiet throughout, unless the interviewer asks him to participate.

In the later phases, the interviewer may move from behind the desk and sit alongside the suspect (thus reinforcing the nurturing parent role), but movements of this sort must appear spontaneous and natural.

Depending on the overall strategy of the investigation, important exhibits may be displayed in the interview room. Before the interview begins, a colleague who is not involved in the case should evaluate the impact the room and any displayed exhibits would have on him if *he* were the suspect. If necessary, adjustments should be made.

CONSIDER USING INTERPRETERS

In some cases, interviews have to be conducted through interpreters, and this increases the difficulty. First, the intervention of an interpreter disturbs the transactional relationship between the interviewer and the suspect: it slows down the pace of the interview, and can lead to misunderstanding. If an interpreter has to be used (and bear in mind that some crooks will underplay their linguistic skills to give themselves more time to plan their answers):

- Make sure the interpreter speaks and reads both languages fluently. Choose an interpreter with experience of working with the local police or litigation lawyers.

- Check the interpreter's background fully, and especially his experience of giving evidence.

- Make sure he has no connection with the suspect, or anyone else involved in the case.

- Translate the key documents so that both versions can be shown to the suspect during the interview.

- Obtain a letter of engagement and confidentiality agreement, signed by the interpreter, and check his references. Explain the case fully, and make sure he understands the evidence and the approach the interviewer plans to take. The interview should be rehearsed. In the first dry run, the interpreter should play the role of the suspect, and in the second the interviewer. The real interview should be tape recorded. This is a prudent step, and the recordings can be used to resolve any misunderstanding.

CASE FILE

The interview was going badly, and the interpreter did not seem interested. The interviewer suggested that they should take a break, and he walked out of the room leaving the interpreter and the suspect together. Unbeknown to either of them, the interview had been, and was still being, taped. The interviewer returned to the room and terminated the interview. A few days later when the tape was transcribed, part of the conversation between the interpreter and the suspect during the break read:

Suspect: I thought I was in trouble there for a moment.

Interpreter: Trust me, the man's a fool. Keep calm.
Suspect: How much longer will it be?
Interpreter: Not long. He is giving up. He is a cretin: don't worry, my friend.

It transpired that the suspect and the interpreter were first cousins who often went clubbing together. The real insult was that the off-record conversation was in English, a language the suspect said he could not understand.

Plans for Stage A

GENERAL

Before the interview begins, the interviewer *must* plan and rehearse the approach and techniques he will use. With effective planning, interviews become simple.

Although it is usual for even experienced investigators to feel a little nervous, the interviewer should remember, deep down, the suspect is under much greater stress. The interviewer's nervousness can be reduced by good planning, knowing the facts inside out, and through rehearsal.

The interviewer should not read too much into the suspect's initial nervousness. Innocent people may be frightened of being disbelieved, and some crooks are very confident. The interviewer can, however, read a great deal into the suspect's anxiety in other phases of the interview.

APPROACH IF THE SUBJECT'S GUILT IS NOT OBVIOUS

The interviewer's approach in Phase A should be carefully planned, and he should highlight on Table 10.5 the approaches he intends to take.

Table 10.5   Approach in Phase A

Select the techniques and questions to be used in the interview	
Question or statement	*Significance of response*
Don't ask unnecessary questions, discuss the weather, or golf, but go straight to the point along the lines: 'We are investigating a serious case of xxx and believe you can help.' Emphasize that your job is to find the truth, that the company is taking the matter very seriously and that you have **limitless time** and resources at your disposal.	Don't be deterred by a response such as: 'Are you accusing me?', but say something to the effect 'At this stage I am trying to find the facts and I think you have some questions to answer. Now . . .' (then move on to a direct question).
Do not make wild allegations, promises or threats.	If you do, any evidence obtained may be compromised.
Use **open questions** that invite **detailed answers**. Ask the suspect to tell you everything he knows about the matters in question. These are sometimes called 'blocking questions', and they are very important.	Guilty and deceitful suspects will usually be reluctant to provide detail. Open questions give innocent people the chance to volunteer facts. If a suspect does not volunteer information in reply to open questions, he may be denied a plausible, innocent excuse later.
Test the suspect's memory of uncontroversial events in the time frame concerned.	The liar will usually have a good memory of uncontroversial events and facts which support his innocence, but a poor recollection (spontaneous forgetfulness) of events and facts establishing his guilt.
Ask the suspect if he knows why you have asked to speak to him.	The guilty suspect is likely to say that he does not know, or to give a vague and untruthful answer.
Show him the key evidence, and ask for his explanation. Repeat your theory of the fraud. Show him the key pieces of evidence, and ask detailed questions about them.	Usually a guilty or deceitful suspect will have a passive, low-key response to inferences or accusations of responsibility. He is very unlikely to retain incriminating evidence within his personal space. Typically, guilty people will gradually push evidence away from them.
Ask questions where the **answers are already known**, and test the suspect's truthfulness.	Don't allow the suspect to escape with lies.
Ask the suspect whom he believes is responsible.	The guilty person will not normally name anyone.
Ask the suspect whether there is anyone he can definitely clear of responsibility.	The innocent person will usually immediately clear himself; a guilty person is less likely to do so.
Ask the suspect whether he has ever considered the act in question.	The guilty person is more likely to admit he has 'considered' the act.
	Continued

Table 10.5   Approach in Phase A – *concluded*

Select the techniques and questions to be used in the interview	
Question or statement	*Significance of response*
Ask the suspect how he would have committed the act in question.	An innocent person is unlikely to given an answer. A guilty person is more likely to respond. He may give deliberately misleading information, or may accidentally reveal something known only to the perpetrator.
Explain exactly what you think has happened (the FRAUD THEORY), and how he can assist. Tell him what you believe he has done.	Monitor the suspect's reaction carefully. A guilty suspect's response is more likely to be low-key.
Ask the suspect how he would feel if you proved his responsibility beyond doubt or showed that he was not telling the truth.	A guilty person's reaction is more likely to be passive or along the lines of: 'If you can do that, fine. I will go to prison.'
Ask the suspect if he would like to give a different explanation.	A guilty or deceitful person is more likely to consider this option.
Tell the suspect that going temporarily off the rails is one thing; telling lies and throwing suspicion on his colleagues is another. Challenge his honour to tell the truth.	A guilty suspect will normally consider his answer to this statement carefully. An innocent person is likely to become angry.
Ask the suspect whether he would like to make restitution or resign.	Great care has to be taken with this, but the innocent person is more likely to respond in the negative.

During this phase, the interviewer will form an opinion about whether the suspect is telling the truth:

- Establish the *baselines* between honest and dishonest responses.

- The interviewer must concentrate on the mechanics, or the 'how' of the case, on minor wrongdoings, emphasizing the evidence he has or which he believes he can get, taking a professional, relentless and adult role.

- If the interviewer is sure the subject is being *truthful* and is not responsible for the wrong-doing in question or any other misdeed, he should seek his co-operation as a potential witness.

- If the interviewer believes the subject is responsible, *or is not sure*, he should move to Phase B.

APPROACH IF THE SUSPECT'S GUILT IS OBVIOUS

If evidence of the suspect's guilt is overwhelming, the interviewer should *plan* to open the interview with a direct confrontation along the lines: 'We are investigating a serious case of *x* and I need to see you to give you the opportunity to explain.' The interviewer should then progress directly to Phase B.

Plans for Stage B

If the suspect appears guilty, or if the interviewer is not sure one way or the other, he should *plan* to move into Phase B, adopt the role of a *critical parent* and draw on the methods shown in Table 10.6.

Table 10.6   Approach in Phase B

Select the techniques and questions to be used in the interview	
Question or statement	*Significance of response*
Emphasize the most convincing evidence you have, stating directly or by inference that you believe the suspect is responsible. WORK ON YOUR THEORY OF THE WORST CASE, AND EMPHASIZE THE EVIDENCE.	Such statements should be repeated throughout this phase: an innocent person's reactions will usually become stronger.
Use pointing, accusatory hand movements. Move into the suspect's personal space.	Increases the suspect's non-verbal communications and emphasizes your verbal points.
Use emotive words like 'thief', 'steal' and 'fraud'.	The guilty suspect is unlikely to repeat such hard words, and in his own mind will minimize the crime.
Use silence to your advantage.	You may say, 'If you are not prepared to tell me the truth, I suggest you say nothing.' You must then remain silent and wait.
Explain how you intend to obtain other evidence: especially from people in collusion with the suspect. Describe the INVESTIGATION PLAN and the inevitability of the outcome.	The guilty person may say something along the line: 'If you can do that, fine.'
Focus on the mechanics of the fraud and 'YOU'.	**The guilty person is likely to listen passively.**
Move quickly from one incriminating piece of evidence to another. This makes it more difficult for the suspect to plan his answers.	A deceitful suspect is more likely to object to this approach. He will find the change of topics uncomfortable.
Press for more detail.	The guilty person is likely to resist giving detail.
Make the suspect touch and examine incriminating evidence, but make sure he does not destroy it.	The guilty person will not wish to do this, and is likely to push papers, etc. away from his personal space.
Use closed questions which call for a 'Yes' or 'No' answer.	Closed questions speed up the interview and give the deceitful suspect little time to think. They also pin him down to specific positions.
Enhance the importance of selected questions by prefacing them with phrases such as: 'I want you to be very careful how you answer this . . . Take your time and think carefully over the next question . . .'.	The deceitful suspect is more likely to remain silent, think carefully and deliver his answer. An innocent person is more likely to object to the inference that he might tell less than the truth.
Repeatedly explain **how** you believe the dishonesty occurred and the mechanics, based on the FRAUD THEORY.	The guilty person will usually listen passively.

Continued

Table 10.6   Approach in Phase B – *concluded*

Select the techniques and questions to be used in the interview	
Question or statement	*Significance of response*
Repeat important questions, and remain alert to inconsistent answers.	The guilty person is more likely to object. Also, his replies may be inconsistent and lacking in detail.
Point out discrepancies in his explanation.	It is less likely that there will be discrepancies in a truthful explanation.
Use summary statements such as: 'So far, you have told me . . .'.	These act as benchmarks and fallback points if the interview goes off track.
Point out the minor expense and other infringements that could lead to his dismissal or prosecution. Explain that it may be in his interest to clear up everything.	The guilty person is more likely to dismiss these as irrelevant. An innocent person may become genuinely angry or upset.
Point out that it does not matter whether the suspect has the courage to admit his mistakes or not, the result will be the same. Admissions will help the company clear up the case more quickly and quietly than otherwise would be the case. If the suspect refuses to accept his responsibility, the company may have no option other than to prosecute.	The guilty person is more likely to ask a question. An innocent person may become angry.
Pin the suspect down: 'So what you are telling me is . . . and you say you are sure about this. You have not misunderstood the questions. So if I show you that . . . what you have told me would be a bare-faced lie; wouldn't it? You would have absolutely no excuse, would you?'	A liar will find such a statement extremely stressful. He may challenge the proof, or attempt to weaken the commitment of his explanation.
Point out the damage the dishonesty has done to innocent colleagues. Tell the suspect he has an obligation to remove the cloud of suspicion hanging over them.	A guilty suspect will normally consider his answer to this statement carefully. An innocent person is likely to become angry.
If the suspect continues to tell lies, obtain a statement in writing and point out the seriousness.	The deceitful suspect is more likely to resist making a statement.

During this phase, a guilty suspect will consider confessing or admitting some of the truth:

- The interviewer must emphasize the strength of the evidence and the inevitability of the outcome, with or without a confession. The subject is likely to be hesitant and thoughtful. On one hand he will want to tell the truth, and on the other will be fearful of the immediate consequences. His dilemma will be obvious, mainly from non-verbal clues. At such points, which will be repeated throughout Phase C, the interviewer must adopt the role of a nurturing parent and emphasize how '*we* can resolve the matter'.

- If, on the other hand, the interviewer is sure that the subject has been truthful and is not responsible for the wrongdoing in question or some other misdeed, he should seek his co-operation as a potential witness.

Plans for Stage C

This phase is critical. Confessions are obtained when the interviewer adopts the role of a nurturing parent and the suspect is willing to accept the role of an adaptive child:

- If the suspect's guilt is reasonably obvious, in Phase C the interviewer should *plan* to focus on five main themes:
  - the absolute *inevitability* that the facts will be established
  - that the interviewer has *limitless time* and resources to find the truth
  - the *weaknesses* in and hopelessness of his explanations
  - *why* the problem started
  - how *the interviewer and the subject* can resolve the problem *together*.
- The interviewer can plan to reinforce his role as a nurturing parent by:
  - pushing incriminating documents to one side
  - calling the suspect by his first name
  - using friendly, palm-upwards hand movements and other positive body language
  - moving to sit alongside the subject, inside his personal space, so that on occasions their bodies touch; this may seem a strange sort of move, and it is important that the touching is very discreet; experiments show that waitresses and waiters who touch their customers – but very discreetly – increase their tips by 80 per cent; touching is consistent with a nurturing parent–adaptive child relationship
  - offering an acceptable excuse or alternatives such as: 'Did all this start by accident, Joe, or what?'
  - pointing out that he is basically a decent person who has simply made a mistake.

The interviewer should be prepared to compliment the suspect when he makes small admissions (as a parent would a child) and continue stressing the inevitability of the investigation. The interviewer should emphasize that it is obvious the suspect is finding it very difficult to hold back the truth and that the interviewer knows how he feels and what he is thinking. (Most liars hate this statement, and will react along the lines that you cannot possibly know.)

Plans for Stage D

If all has gone to plan, the interviewer will either be convinced that the suspect is innocent, or will have obtained admissions to some or all of his misdeeds.

- If the interviewer is satisfied that the suspect is innocent, he should not close the interview too quickly, but explain why he had taken the approach he did and, if necessary, apologize. If the subject is sensible, he will understand. The interviewer should discuss the case generally, and ask the subject for his advice.

- If the suspect has confessed or made admissions, the interviewer should *plan* to obtain details to help recover funds and track dishonesty by others. By gaining access to details known only to the suspect, the interviewer will make it less likely that the subject can withdraw his confession. The interviewer must take time and:

- ask open questions
- establish when the dishonesty started, why, and who else was involved
- find out what the suspect thought when the problem first started
- establish the amount lost and how it might be recovered
- try to recover tangible evidence
- find out about any other dishonesty involving the suspect or others
- ask the suspect if he would like to write a letter of apology to his manager.

If appropriate, the interviewer should take a written statement or prepare a note with the suspect setting out the main admissions and his estimate of the amount the company has lost. The subject should be asked to sign the statement or file note.

If the person has made only minor admissions and has generally lied, the interviewer should plan to take a statement in writing, incorporating as many details, obvious lies and evasions as possible. This, in itself, may be sufficient to establish his guilt. *A confession is not essential.*

Rehearsing the Interview

If the interviewer has completed the preparatory stages described above, he will have a clear plan for the way in which the interview will be conducted and the questions he will ask.

Important interviews must be rehearsed in two stages:

- The interviewer should interview a colleague who plays the role of the suspect.
- The interviewer should play the role of the suspect in an interview by a colleague. This is a very important step.

Often, the rehearsal in which the interviewer *plays the role of the suspect* is the most important. He will understand where the evidence is the strongest; he will be able to anticipate, and then defeat, false excuses. Rehearsal will make the interviewer more confident. Where an interpreter is to be used, he must be involved in the rehearsals.

A Final Check with Legal Advisers

In all serious investigations, the advice of top-quality litigation lawyers is recommended. The interviewer should make sure the approach he plans to take will not cause problems or result in evidence being inadmissible.

Actually Conducting the Interview

Interviews are 90 per cent preparation and ten per cent execution. The careful planning and rehearsal discussed earlier will have built up the interviewer's confidence, and he should have a clear approach for every interview within the general Investigation Plan.

The interviewer should not drink alcohol nor eat a heavy meal immediately before the interview. He should get a good night's sleep. He should dress professionally, arrive early at the interview room and *check everything*. He should be in place in the room before the suspect enters. He should concentrate on the suspect's anxiety, not his own.

Actions After the Interview

It is probable that during the interview, the interviewer will have established a close relationship with the suspect. If the interviewer has told him he is going to do something, he should stick to his word and treat him with respect.

As soon as possible, the interviewer should write up notes or transcribe tape recordings and check them carefully, identifying other aspects that require investigation.

'They're fraud investigators – they never relax.'

11 *Stage F: Follow-up*

Principles

- Concentrate on the important elements listed in the Investigations Plan.
- Aim to complete the investigation as quickly as possible.
- Remember that all of your working papers and reports must be catalogued so that disclosure can be made to the defence at the appropriate time.

Continue with Parallel Actions

Use appropriate techniques to complete the investigation quickly. There are three vital aspects:

- good and complete documentary and computerized evidence
- good and effective interviews with witnesses and suspects
- selected legal actions.

Keep up the pressure to complete the investigation as quickly as possible, and do not give the fraudsters time to cover their tracks. Keep the Investigations Plan up to date, and hold regular progress meetings with the project team.

Freeze Assets

As soon as possible, obtain orders to freeze assets and to force suspects and others to disclose the source of their wealth. At this point, you will come to understand how good or bad your lawyers are!

Keep in Contact with the Police

Keep in close contact with the police. As the investigation progresses, the most natural point of contact between the police and the company may appear to be through the investigators, but this is not necessarily the best channel. Obviously, on a day-to-day basis there should be close contact between investigators and the police, but a formal channel between the police and the company's lawyer should be established.

Copies of reports and other information should, where possible, be passed through the legal channel to preserve privilege. The Documents Co-ordinator should keep a record and copies of all documents and other evidence handed over to the police.

Conduct Final Interviews

Conduct final interviews with all the suspects. These are normally held towards the end of the investigation and are usually very important. Detailed guidelines on planning and conducting interviews are set out in Appendix 4.

Consider Disciplinary Action

Consider dismissing employees against whom there is evidence of dishonesty. Again, there should already be a defined procedure. It is not necessary to wait for the outcome of police investigations before taking this action. Immediate dismissal can be justified on the grounds identified in Table 11.1.

Table 11.1   Grounds for immediate dismissal

Justified grounds for dismissal	Examples
Admission to management of guilt	The admission does not need to comply with the standards required in a criminal court, although pressure or promises should not be used to obtain a confession
Evidence available to management	The evidence should, on the balance of probabilities, establish the employee's guilt
Conviction by a court or tribunal in relation to his job	Criminal conviction directly relating to work for the employer
Conviction by a court making it impossible for the person to carry out his job	This would apply, for example, to a truck driver who loses his licence for drunken driving
Conviction by a court, discrediting the employee's reputation	This would apply, for example, to a professional person convicted of an offence – not in relation to his job – to such an extent that his credibility is destroyed

In all cases, the dismissal must take place as soon as possible after one of the above grounds becomes known to management, and should be conducted in a reasonable manner.

In some cases, it may be preferable to delay the dismissal of an employee suspected of fraud until after the investigation is more or less complete. He may be suspended without pay (definitely not *on* pay), pending the outcome of enquiries, on the understanding that he agrees to co-operate.

However, where criminal prosecution is contemplated, care has to be taken to make sure that the employee is not induced by fear of dismissal or in response to a promise to act in a way which it could later be argued to have been against his interests. Threats, promises and pressure will most likely render any evidence obtained inadmissible in criminal courts, although it may still be accepted in civil proceedings.

Terminate Contracts and Negotiate

The team should remain alert to opportunities to negotiate with the suspects or others involved. Contracts with suppliers, customers and others should be terminated if they fail to co-operate in the investigation or if they are in any way culpable. The object is to keep the pressure (in the nicest sort of way) on the crooks and their associates.

'I love the synopsis, but in the circumstances I don't think we can offer you an advance.'

12 *Stage G: Investigation Reports*

Principle

- Each stage of the investigation should be documented, and interim and final reports prepared, addressed to the company's legal advisers.

Prepare a Final Report

As soon as possible, prepare a final report addressed to the company's lawyers for the primary purpose of obtaining legal advice and for pursuing recoveries.

The report should be professionally written and indexed. It should be supported by copies of all exhibits, statements and detailed schedules. The pages of the report should be numbered, and they should be bound in one or more folders. Each page should be marked:

> CONFIDENTIAL. This report has been prepared for the legal advisers of Company X for information and advice and in contemplation of legal proceedings relating to matters referred to in it.

Exhibits, statements and schedules should also be numbered and bound in separate folders. This makes it much easier for readers to cross-refer between the report and the supporting documentation. If you like using abbreviations in place of proper nouns, avoid initials. For example, do not refer to J.A. Jones as 'JAJ' or the Interballistic Mining Company UK PTE Limited as 'IMBUPL', as it is all too confusing. Instead use 'Jones' and 'Interballistic'. Make the report easy for readers. Imagine you are writing a letter to your Mum.

The report should be carefully structured and *should not include anything you would not want released to the opposing side.*

PART 1: MANAGEMENT SUMMARY

This should provide an overview of the case for a layman. The key elements of the investigation should be presented. The report must be factual, and any conclusions should be supported by evidence. Never let the report run ahead of the evidence, and when you express an opinion, make sure it is flagged as such.

'The case was going fine until we had to write a report.'

PART 2: BACKGROUND OF THE PEOPLE AND COMPANIES INVOLVED

This should present a detailed biography of the characters and companies involved in the case.

PART 3: CHRONOLOGY

This should set out the precise mechanics of the fraud and the investigation, in strictly chronological order. It may be included in the body of the report, or as an appendix.

PART 4: PROOF OF DISHONESTY OR NEGLIGENCE

Facts which prove dishonesty or negligence should be summarized and emphasized in this section. The various theories or opinions of how and why the fraud or loss occurred may be discussed, but opinions should be clearly distinguished from evidence.

PART 5: PROOF OF LOSS

This should explain how the loss schedules have been prepared, and should show cross-references to other supporting documentation, such as statements, affidavits and exhibits. It is vital that claims are not exaggerated. To do so will invalidate any insurance claim and expose you to allegations of perjury if the Proof of Loss has to be sworn under oath.

PART 6: SUMMARY OF OFFENCES

A list of all criminal or civil actions brought against the perpetrators and their accomplices should be provided. The status of these actions should be explained.

APPENDICES

Bind these in separate bundles (clearly separated with tabs), and not as part of the report. This makes them much easier to reference.

Review the Evidence

In major cases, a lawyer who has not been involved in the investigation should review the report and the supporting evidence in detail, and consider, if he were asked to defend the suspects or the fidelity insurance company, what line he would take and which evidence he would attack. Appropriate counter-arguments should be prepared and incorporated in the report.

'It's hard to believe that is someone's intellectual property.'

13 *Stage H: Recoveries*

Principle

- Get your money back, with costs and interest.

Background

A victim of fraud of is free to negotiate with the people and companies responsible for his loss and to obtain restitution from them. However, in the UK a victim of fraud has to note the provisions of the Criminal Justice Acts, which require that only the amount proven to have been lost can be recovered as a condition of dropping criminal charges. The intent is to ensure that the victim cannot use the threat of prosecution as a means of profiting from a loss.

This only applies to *criminal* proceedings, and under the civil law, or in a negotiated settlement, a victim is entitled to apply for compensation for lost interest, business interruption and the cost of any investigation or legal action, providing there is reasonable justification for doing so.

Negotiation with the perpetrators of fraud is recommended in the following circumstances:

- they have admitted their dishonesty

- they will provide unrestricted access to all records under their control, including bank accounts, so that the full extent of the loss can be established

- they have funds available to repay

- settlement does not depend upon the withdrawal of criminal or civil complaints or other actions which would prejudice the Fidelity Insurer's rights to recover any amounts it has paid out to the victim.

Every effort should be made in negotiations to recover consequential losses and other costs not covered by insurance.

Sometimes frauds occur because of the negligence of professional advisers such as bankers, accountants, government departments, telephone and public communications providers, insurers, lawyers, security companies or automated clearing houses retained or relied upon by the victim. Similarly, past employers of the perpetrator, if they did not provide an honest reference, may be prime targets for recovery.

Thus the possibility of making recoveries from third parties should be considered. Emphasis is placed on the word 'considered'. The usual knee-jerk reaction to sue the auditors is usually wrong, and often unethical. In some cases, settlement can be negotiated, in others litigation may be necessary.

Much will depend on the circumstances of the case and the evidence available, the ethical justification for bringing legal action, and its effect on future relationships with the third parties concerned. However, in most cases of large-scale fraud, Company X will attempt to make recoveries under its Fidelity Insurance. For most auditors, the following notes will not be relevant, as insurance claims will be handled by Risk Management. However, they are included to show the difficulties involved in making insurance recoveries.

Insurance Recoveries

PRINCIPLES

Making recoveries under fidelity and other insurance policies is seldom easy. The insurer has every right to minimize its payout, and the victim should be prepared for a very tough fight.

GIVE PRELIMINARY NOTICE TO THE INSURER

Give Preliminary Notification, if this has not already been done.

The litigation lawyer on the project team should be instructed to notify the current and previous fidelity insurance company(s) and broker(s) in writing that a loss has been discovered and that investigations are under way. Whenever possible, dealings should be directly with the fidelity insurance company, rather than through a broker. The broker should not be given responsibility for the settlement of the claim, but may be copied on all correspondence and invited to attend appropriate meetings.

The fidelity insurer might sue, or threaten to sue, your directors, external accountants or others for negligence. To minimize the consequences of such actions, the directors' and officers' liability insurer should be informed in writing of a potential claim.

All senior managers and appropriate employees should be informed that a claim against insurance has been made. They should be instructed:

- not to discuss the case
- not to make off-the-record comments to the press, brokers nor to the fidelity insurer's representatives
- not to release documents or information relating to the case, without first obtaining the consent of the claims co-ordinator and the litigation lawyer.

They should also be asked to submit any evidence or information that might support or influence the claim to the co-ordinator.

BRIEF EXTERNAL AUDITORS

Advise accountants and other third parties that a claim has been made.

The claims co-ordinator should also inform the external accountants and any other advisers, such as bankers and lawyers, that a claim has been filed, so that they can consider the likelihood of an action being brought against them by the fidelity insurance company.

The insurer should be pressed to acknowledge receipt of the preliminary notice, but in most cases the response may be non-committal, or it may deny liability altogether. In some recent cases, the first response by the insurer has been to make *ex parte* application to the courts for a declaratory judgment denying liability. The company should not be alarmed if this happens, but should continue with the investigation and all other actions as quickly as possible.

ASK FOR THE INSURER'S SUPPORT

Ask for the fidelity insurance company's support in civil actions.

The victim must not prejudice the rights of the fidelity insurer under the subrogation clauses. To minimize later argument on these grounds, the insurer should be invited to agree on a general recovery and prosecution strategy.

The litigation lawyer should establish whether the insurer would support a civil action against some or all of the perpetrators, or against advisers whose actions could be regarded as negligent. If the insurer is unsupportive or – more likely – non-committal, the litigator should confirm the company's recovery strategy in writing, and the project team should press ahead. In the final analysis, the insurer's unwillingness to co-operate would harm its own cause.

MONITOR REPORTING DEADLINES

The claims co-ordinator should monitor the date by which a Proof of Loss must be filed, which is based on the date of discovery, and not on the date that preliminary notice was given. The project team should complete all investigations as quickly as possible. Lack of detailed proof may encourage the fidelity insurer to prevaricate, or to undervalue the importance of the claim and your determination to pursue it.

REQUESTS FOR FURTHER INFORMATION

It is usual for a fidelity insurer to push for further information and, if the claim is large, to suggest that its loss adjusters, lawyers or investigators should become involved without delay. Requests of this nature should be considered carefully. If the insurer instructs a lawyer of dubious reputation to adjust the claim, the project team should anticipate trouble.

However, you should co-operate with whoever is appointed by the insurer, as refusal to do so may reflect badly if a disputed claim goes to trial. On the other hand, the obligation to prove the claim falls on the project team, and interference in the investigation by the insurer or its agents – particularly if it is self-serving or discouraging – can be a handicap.

The track records and reputations of loss adjusters or investigators representing the insurer should be carefully checked before they are allowed access to company premises, records or witnesses. Although most firms are honest and reliable, there are some overzealous, aggressive and unethical operators. In one case, the investigator nominated by the insurer was totally unacceptable, having been prosecuted for perjury. Representatives of the insurer should never be allowed uncontrolled access to your premises, employees or records. File notes should be prepared after each meeting.

Ideally, the insurer should be asked to confirm in writing that investigators or loss adjusters are acting as its agents, and that it will assume responsibility for their actions.

Further, the litigator should try to get an agreement that any reports produced for the insurer will be made available to him.

It is more usual, however, for the insurer to take a passive or even negative role in an investigation, and to refuse to allow their investigators or loss adjusters to discuss the case. Short of full and open co-operation, this is the second best position, because the more unreasonable the insurer becomes, the more its interests will be harmed in the long run.

It often takes months, and sometimes years, to document a loss fully. During this time, the insurer may press for more and more information, to which it may or may not be entitled. To a large extent, this pressure may result from political posturing rather than reflecting a genuine desire to reach agreement. It is in the interest of an insurer to delay settlement.

The project team should try to avoid requests to provide further information until the Proof of Loss has been finalized. If it appears that the Proof cannot be completed within the specified period, the claims co-ordinator should ask the insurer for an extension. Normally, this will be granted without argument, but if refused, the co-ordinator should consult the litigator without delay. If the insurer acts reasonably, the project team may provide further information, but this should always be furnished through the litigator:

- Originals of all documents and statements should be retained by the project team. The insurer should be provided with copies, and should be allowed to inspect original documents on request and under close supervision.

- All files should be read very carefully by the litigator and investigators before being copied to the insurer.

- Under no circumstances should unchecked or unread documents be released to the insurer or its representatives, no matter how friendly they might seem.

- Copies of all documents released by the project team should be covertly marked, so that if they are disseminated without authority, that fact can be established in a court if necessary.

- The insurer should be required to give an undertaking that it will treat as confidential all documents submitted in respect of the claim, and will accept liability if they are released to third parties.

GIVING THE GAME AWAY

In one recent case, a confidential investigation report, passed to the representative of a fidelity insurance company, was copied to the perpetrator, who then threatened to sue for defamation. He subsequently used confidential information from the report for his defence on criminal charges:

- covering letters should accompany all information passed to the insurer.

Copies of the letters and all attachments should be filed chronologically by the documents co-ordinator. This file can be used to establish at a later date exactly what information was passed over, and when.

- File notes covering discussions with the insurer and broker should also be copied to the chronological file.

- All schedules purporting to calculate losses should be marked 'Provisional'.

Sometimes, regulatory and law enforcement bodies will become involved in a claim, and may ask for information. In general, the project team should co-operate in full, but should never release documents to official agencies unless ordered by subpoena to do so. Taking this precaution makes it less likely that the victim could be held responsible for disclosing information without authority or for libel and slander.

DEAL WITH THE INSURER'S REACTION

If a claim has any defects, the insurer is justified in exploiting them, either to deny liability or to compromise for a lower amount than would otherwise be the case. This is a hard fact of life, which need not take us by surprise.

An insurance company always has to be on the lookout for spurious claims. It is an unfortunate fact that some people consider insurance companies as legitimate targets for fraud. There is a valid distinction, but a fine balance, between the obligations of a fidelity insurer to pay out genuine losses and to reject spurious claims.

ANTICIPATE CANCELLATION

In some cases, the insurer could respond to the claim by giving immediate notice that the policy has been cancelled. Unless there are any legal requirements to hold coverage, it is usually better to accept the cancellation, rather than to accept exorbitant rates for reduced protection. However, this decision will need to be taken at Board level.

You should never assume that a claim will be paid quickly or without argument. Rather, anticipate a deteriorating relationship in which your patience and resolve may be tested to the full. If the claim is valid, you should not be bullied into accepting less than the amount due. Prepare for a fight.

You should consider any initial points or arguments advanced by the insurer. All responses should be made in writing through the litigator. If the good faith of the insurer is in doubt, you should be prepared to take an extremely tough line immediately.

In particular, if the insurer does not make a sensible response within 60 days, or other contractual period, from the filing of the detailed Proof of Loss, legal proceedings should be considered.

FINALIZE THE PROOF OF LOSS

The litigator should decide how the Proof of Loss is to be submitted, and what items are to be included. He should structure it based on a sensible and honest interpretation of the evidence, in a way that enables the opportunity to recover the maximum amount possible. For example, it is permissible to argue a claim as separate incidents to benefit from individual occurrence limits, or to consolidate losses to avoid multiple deductibles.

In most large cases, the victim will be required to swear the accuracy of the Proof of Loss under oath. Any deliberate misstatement could result in prosecution for perjury and the dismissal of the claim. Extreme care is necessary. Never inflate a claim.

DEAL WITH PREVARICATION

The fidelity insurer has a set period of time after receiving the Proof of Loss to respond.

During this time, the claimant cannot start legal action for non-payment. The time period for litigation is typically 60 days from filing the Proof of Loss, and within two years of the date of discovery. Thus if the claimant lets the insurer delay beyond the two-year period, it is prevented from taking any legal action for non-payment.

You may have to decide on the bona fides of the insurer's attitude. If there are any doubts about the honesty of the insurer's intentions, legal action should not be delayed. Although it may not be necessary to finalize these actions, they may help to bring the insurer to the negotiating table and to speed up settlement.

In extreme circumstances, the victim can consider giving maximum publicity to the case, to heighten the profile of the claim.

RECOVERY ACCOUNTING

Genuine but as yet unsettled claims have a value. How that value can and should be entered in the accounts will vary from case to case. If the loss is large, you might consider having your claim valued by experienced insurance lawyers. An 'expert opinion' letter may be used as the basis for including at least part of the possible settlement in the accounts.

If not already done in Stage C4, as soon as the claim has been filed, the victim should then set up the following accounts in the general ledger.

Primary loss account

The primary loss account should show the total indebtedness of the fidelity insurer to Company X, and include calculations of the direct loss sustained as a result of the fraud or incident concerned, subject to the limit of the policy. When individual rather than aggregated claims are to be made, separate accounts should be established for each line.

The accounts should be compiled in the currency in which the loss was sustained, and converted to the currency in which the insurer normally operates, effective on the dates on which the losses were suffered. This is normally taken to be the date on which funds were disbursed or assets removed.

Interest due from the date a judgement by the court was given against the fidelity insurer, or on which settlement was agreed, should be debited to this account

Excess loss account

The excess loss account should show the amount by which direct losses exceed the applicable policy limit.

Secondary loss account

The secondary loss account should include consequential and other losses, such as business interruption, lost interest and so on, which cannot be claimed against insurance, but might be recovered by negotiation or civil litigation.

Investigation costs

External investigators' charges devoted to identifying and making recoveries can be offset as the first priority against funds received from the perpetrators or third parties. These receipts do not reduce the policy limits, nor the insurer's liability for reimbursing direct losses. However, the victim's own payroll and administration costs cannot be deducted from recoveries.

Legal fees

All legal fees incurred in recovering losses, other than suits against the fidelity insurer, should be debited to this account, as should legal expenses approved by the insurer for defending liabilities under the policy.

Application of recoveries

Fidelity insurers are only liable for direct losses and interest from the date judgment is given against them by a court, or from the date on which they agreed to settle a claim.

The victim is free to negotiate or take civil action against the perpetrators or third parties to recover direct losses and consequential costs. Any recoveries of direct losses should be credited in the following order:

1 investigation costs account until cleared
2 excess loss account until cleared
3 primary loss account for the benefit of the fidelity insurer.

However, any recovery of consequential, uninsured costs or losses can be applied in whichever way the victim chooses. Ideally, the secondary loss account should be credited as first priority. The fidelity insurer may argue that recoveries of this nature prejudice its subrogation rights, although it is doubtful that it would succeed with this argument.

NEGOTIATION WITH THE INSURER

At one time, it was unusual for an insurer to let disputed claims go forward for full trial, mainly because the bad publicity caused by such actions was a major disincentive for other insurance buyers. These days, many fidelity insurers fight to the death, regardless of the bad publicity.

However, at various stages, the victim may be presented with the opportunity to negotiate with the insurer. These opportunities should be considered carefully, but if the victim is convinced about the strength of its claim, it should concede nothing unless an equivalent benefit is obtained. In some jurisdictions, notably the UK, courts have taken a very robust view of an insurer's responsibilities, and are unlikely to be impressed by crafty dodges to deny liability. This means that the victim may be in a powerful position if a claim goes forward for full trial.

'Cash? That will do nicely.'

14 *Stage I: Asset Tracing*

Background

Reliable estimates show that up to US$2.8 trillion is laundered annually, sponsored by terrorists, organized crime and drug gangs down to run-of-the-mill tax dodgers and company fraudsters. Historically, both crooks and many regulators have considered Liechtenstein, Switzerland and the Cayman Islands as preferred countries for hiding assets and laundering funds. However, there are now serious new contenders and new methods of asset stealth. But, as always, tracing hidden assets is not a job for amateurs or for the faint-hearted. This chapter explains how victims can trace and recover assets. First, it is important to agree the principles of asset stealth.

The Essentials

There are four main aspects to asset stealth:

- **Someone having interests** worth hiding – these days, many people do, if only to genuinely shelter their assets from opportunistic litigation; for example, in the USA there are 14 malpractice claims per 100 doctors: every year, 1 in 10 citizens are sued: accounting firms now face more than 3000 suits, seeking more than US$13 billion in damages; thus not all people who wish to hide assets are crooks

- **Establishing a cut-out** (blurring ownership) between the true owner and the assets, so that they cannot be seized

- **Handling the funds safely** in a way that leaves the owner in control of them

- **Controlling investments** and monitoring their progress.

In asset stealth cases, there is a critical relationship between the opacity needed to shelter the identity of the owner, and control of the assets concerned. If the connection is too obscure, the owner may lose his money. This is a serious risk for all stealthists, as they are vulnerable to dishonesty by others.

Trends in Asset Stealth

THE PRINCIPLES

It is critical that the stealthist keeps control of his assets while obscuring ownership. There are a number of options available to him, as Figure 14.1 indicates.

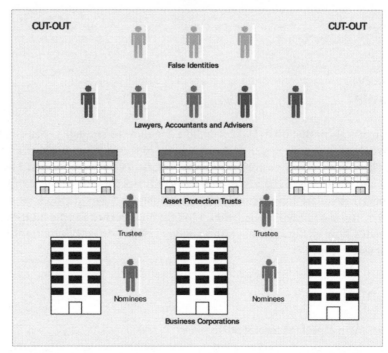

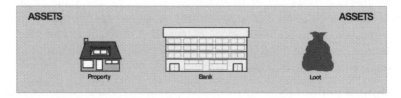

Figure 14.1   Cut-outs and destinations

The roles of the various people and entities are discussed later.

The countries and flows chosen by the stealthist can be viewed in three groups, although in many cases there will be an overlap (see Table 14.1).

Table 14.1   Fronts used by stealthists

The country	*Comment*
Originating: usually in which the stealthist has his base of operations	The country in which illicit funds are generated through fraud, tax evasion, narcotics, etc.
The cut-outs: usually offshore	The countries in which fronts, such as International Business Corporations (IBCs) and Asset Protection Trusts (APTs), etc. are created
Destination: usually a safe haven	The countries to which funds flow and are invested. Usually these are stable, well-regulated democracies

An excellent website run by John Walker, <http://members.ozemail.com.au/~born1820>, contains extensive statistics on money laundering which may be summarized as shown in Table 14.2.

Table 14.2   Sources and disposition of funds

	ORIGINATING COUNTRIES *Where illicit money is created*				DESTINATION COUNTRIES *Where illicit funds are invested*		
Rank	Country	Amount US$ millions p.a.	%	Rank	Country	Amount US$ millions p.a.	%
1	United States	1 320 228	46.3	1	United States	1 538 145	54.0
2	Italy	150 054	5.3	2	Cayman Islands	138 329	4.9
3	Russia	147 187	5.2	3	Russia	120 493	4.2
4	China	131 360	4.6	4	Italy	105 688	3.7
5	Germany	128 266	4.5	5	China	94 726	3.3
6	France	124 748	4.4	6	Romania	89 595	3.1
7	Romania	115 585	4.1	7	Canada	85 444	3.0
8	Canada	82 347	2.9	8	Vatican City	80 596	2.8
9	United Kingdom	68 740	2.4	9	Luxembourg	78 468	2.8
10	Hong Kong	62 856	2.2	10	France	68 471	2.4
Other	Other	519 072	18.2		Other	450 515	15.8
Total		2 850 470				2 850 470	

Source: John Walker, November 1998.

These results accord with Maxima's experience, and suggest that in most cases, stealth assets are invested in the originating and safe countries rather than being transferred overseas. However, the cut-out is usually through obscure jurisdictions.

For obvious reasons, statistics on money laundering must be unreliable, especially since they usually exclude massive movements of cash through Hawala or similar unofficial compensation schemes extensively operated by Asian and Arabic groups (see <http://www.kalchakra.org> for a description of Hawala transactions).

The bottom line is that stealth funds are hidden through obscure cut-outs but are usually invested in stable countries (see Table 14.3). Column 5 shows the percentage of funds transferred overseas or cross-jurisdictional. Column 6 shows the total transfers offshore by countries listed in Column 1. Use of italics signifies amounts transferred outside of the country.

Table 14.3 indicates that most stealthists retain significant assets in the countries in which they live. The largest percentage of overseas transfers are from Italy to the Vatican (37 per cent) and from Hong Kong to Taiwan (30 per cent). There is a 70 per cent chance that a stealthist originating funds in the UK will transfer them overseas, whereas most Russian 'black money' will remain invested locally.

However, in asset stealth there is an exception to every rule, and new schemes emerge by the day. *Each case must be treated on its own merits.*

USING FALSE IDENTITIES

One of the easiest steps for an asset stealthist is to create a false identity either through a 'Day of the Jackal'-type false passport in the name of either a dead person, some poor wretch who

Table 14.3   Main internal and cross-border flows

Originating country	Amount created US$ millions	Transferred to US$ millions	Amount US$ millions	Per cent transferred	Total transferred offshore %
1	2	3	4	5	6
United States	1 320 228	United States	528 091	40	
United States		Cayman Islands	129 755	10	
United States		Canada	63 087	5	
United States		Bahamas	61 378	5	60
United States		Bermuda	46 745	4	
United States		Luxembourg	18 804	1	
Russia	147 187	Russia	118 927	81	19
Italy		Italy	94 834	63	
Italy	150 054	Vatican City	55 056		37
China	131 360	China	94 579	72	28
Romania	115 585	Romania	87 845	76	24
France	124 748	France	57 883	46	54
Germany		Germany	47 202	37	
Germany	128 266	Luxembourg	18 804	15	63
Spain	56 287	Spain	28 818	51	49
Thailand	32 834	Thailand	24 953	76	24
Hong Kong		Hong Kong	23 634	38	
Hong Kong	62 856	Taiwan	18 796	30	62
Canada	82 374	Canada	21 747	26	74
United Kingdom	68 740	United Kingdom	20 897	30	70

is unlikely to travel, or someone who has alternative documentation issued by the military or another government agency. Alternatively, the stealthist may obtain what is known as a 'camouflage passport' (<http://www.passportworld.co.uk>; see Figure 14.2), which states:

> The camouflage passport looks exactly like a real passport but the issuer is a non-existent country. It has a richly authentic vinyl cover which is embossed with gold lettering and contains your photograph, entry and exit stamps and an official seal. You can also obtain official looking identity cards and supporting documentation. You can even return your passport to us to obtain more recent exit and entry stamps.

This may be sufficient to convince a banker to open an account. The trouble is that if the false identity is exposed, the asset stealthist may have trouble establishing title to his assets. This is a serious problem.

OFFSHORE FINANCIAL CENTRES AND IBCs

Many asset stealthists choose one or more of 200 Offshore Financial Centres (OFCs) to establish an International Business Corporation (IBC: a company that is exempt from legal

Figure 14.2 Illustration of a camouflage passport
Source: reproduced from <http://www.passportworld.co.uk>

reporting requirements), a Limited Partnership or an Asset Protection Trust (APT). Such fronts are often created through a chain of lawyers, accountants, fiduciary or company formation agents.

The astute asset stealthist – acting through a web of agents and lawyers – may create a number of IBCs and domestic companies in different jurisdictions, sometimes using the same or similar names to confuse the trail. In some countries, IBCs can be registered with bearer shares, but more often only the names of nominee directors appear in public records, most of whom have absolutely no knowledge of the beneficial owners of the companies they represent. *Public* records are not very useful in tracing *hidden* assets.

The countries in which the IBCs or trusts are formed can be critical. For example, in the Cayman Islands it is a criminal offence for anyone to try and break the veil of corporate secrecy or to attempt to obtain banking information, and this applies regardless of whether or not the investigators or lawyers enter the jurisdiction. Switzerland also has penal anti-commercial espionage laws.

The astute asset stealthist will choose a country whose laws best protect him and punish those who try to investigate his activities.

SECURITY OF LOCAL AGENTS

Asset stealthists are also concerned about the security of the lawyers' and agents' offices they use to set up and maintain fronts. The more professional agents impose watertight security and have only a few employees, all of whom are trustworthy.

Some of the larger (and, ironically, better-known) formation agents are slack on security and have so many employees they can be infiltrated. And, as clearly demonstrated in the UK by the case of Benji 'the Binman' Pell, lawyers and bankers are notoriously careless with the papers they throw into the trash bin.

The wise asset stealthist may decide to work through sole practitioners, who can maintain high levels of security and cannot be infiltrated easily.

About Asset Protection Trusts and IBCs

TRUST DEEDS

APTs come in all shapes and sizes, but are usually based on a Trust Deed, which may or may not have to be filed with tax and other authorities. In asset stealth cases, it is pretty certain that the deeds will be bland. Again, public records are of little value.

KEY ROLES IN TRUSTS

Generally, each Trust has a 'Settlor', who is the person who puts assets – often his own – into it, into an IBC, or a limited partnership. Sometimes, a person or company paying bribes will set up a Trust for the bribee and act as Settlor.

There is always a danger for the stealthist that both initial and subsequent transfers of assets will be unravelled.

There is usually a 'Protector' who ensures that the Trust works as intended. Then there are the Trustees, who are generally appointed by the 'Settlor' to manage the Trust. The typical Trustee will be involved in hundreds of different Trusts, and will probably have no knowledge of the Settlor or Beneficiaries.

BENEFICIARIES AND LETTERS OF WISHES

Finally, there is always one or more 'Beneficiary' who may be named in the Trust Deed. More often, a stealth Trust gives the illusion of being discretionary, in which case the Trustees supposedly decide who will benefit, under what circumstances, and when. In practice, asset stealth Trusts are never truly discretionary. Instead, the Settlor writes a 'Letter of Wishes' which names the Beneficiaries. The letter may be given to the Trustees, the Protector or to some other third party, and becomes effective at the appropriate time. Thus to break the veil of secrecy of discretionary Trusts, it is essential to discover the Letter of Wishes, and for obvious reasons, this is extremely difficult.

TRUSTS AND IBCs

A Trust may be linked to an IBC, a number of IBCs, limited partnerships, to domestic corporations, or to other Trusts and fronts, but the asset stealthist always has to balance anonymity against control, and take care that his assets are not stolen by others.

EVEN MORE OBSCURE TRUSTS

Some offshore banks and fiduciary companies offer special services where Trusts are created along the lines of a conventional mutual fund, with shares being issued to individual Trustees on behalf of various beneficiaries. For example, 'Bank X: Trust 452' may be created and funds invested in property, in publicly listed or private shares, or in other assets. A particular Settlor or beneficiary may hold 14.23 per cent of the Trust. Getting behind such Trusts is even more difficult than usual.

Bank Accounts

Both the Trust and the IBC will have one or more bank accounts which may be personal, corporate, named, numbered or in fictitious names. Some banks offer anonymous 'Bearer Accounts' where proof of ownership relies only on the presentation of a pass book and code. The astute asset stealthist will avoid any direct contact with the bank accounts into which funds are first deposited, but may have signatory powers over accounts which they later feed. He may also have credit or debit cards issued on some or all of the accounts in his own, company or false names.

Sometimes, the accounts will be in countries that do not co-operate with international law enforcement agencies and where money laundering reporting requirements are optional or don't exist at all.

However, the astute asset stealthist will ensure that, whatever obscure cut-outs are used, his funds or other assets are in totally safe jurisdictions.

The asset stealthist's requirement for banking facilities will depend on the type of transaction or fraud concerned. These days a Swiss bank account can be obtained online through <http://www.swissnetbank.com>. In narcotics and some other cases, the main problem for the stealthist is the initial placement of cash into the banking system. Typically, cash launderers accept that the costs of placement vary from 5 to 40 per cent of the amounts involved. In other cases, bank officers will be misled or corrupted into accepting large cash deposits without question.

In larger cases, the stealthist may work with a private banker to manage his investments, and this is sometimes the weak link, with telephone and other records exposing a direct connection. For this reason, telephone call logging records can be invaluable.

Stealth Objectives and Assets

The stealthist may have a number of reasons for hiding his assets, but his longer-term objectives will normally include anonymity and security for:

- **Capital** growth
- **Earnings**
- Beneficial **use**.

Every investment he chooses will leave clues to his ownership. These are summarized in Table 14.4.

Table 14.4   Assets and examples of clues to ownership

Type of asset	Primary objective Security and . . .	Comments and examples of clues
Currency (notes) **Travellers' cheques**	Earnings Use	No capital growth Exchange rate fluctuations Difficulty of placement into the financial mainstream Living beyond visible means Excessive credit card expenditure Luxury travel (especially extended trips to country of origin) Obsessive hobbies (motor racing, horses, sailing, etc.) Excessive charitable or religious donations or sponsorship Political donations and power broking Gambling Drugs abuse Family support (parents' houses, etc.) Domestic borrowings secured by overseas collateral Disgruntled associates and former sexual partners
Certificates of deposit **Bank accounts** Investment accounts and private banking Cash investment loans to third parties		Trading accounts Discarded papers and envelopes Telephone records Meetings, especially when accounts are overseas Meetings Telephone records
Shares Privately owned businesses Publicly traded shares, options and bonds Commodity and other warrants	Capital growth Earnings	Trading accounts Discarded papers and envelopes Telephone records Meetings, especially when accounts are overseas Access to esoteric information sources
Residential property Commercial property		Registry records Improvements paid in cash Unexplained visits and meetings Excessive for visible means Utility bills and payments Insurance policies
Development land Vacation property	Use	Land registry records Registry records
Cars, aircraft, boats, etc.		Improvements paid in cash Unexplained visits and meetings Excessive for visible means Utility bills and payments Insurance policies
Jewellery (including gems and gold) **Antiques** **Paintings**	Use Capital growth	Photographs Insurance policies Obsessive knowledge
Other, possibly obsessional, collections (e.g. stamps, etc.)		Club memberships Journal subscriptions

The lifestyle of the stealthist is nearly always too extravagant for his visible earnings. This is an obvious indication that assets have been hidden.

The more time the stealthist has to plan his end game, the deeper he can bury his assets.

THE BEST CUT-OUTS

The most attractive countries for *establishing cut-outs* appear to be those shown in Table 14.5.

Table 14.5 Countries as cut-outs

Country	Perception	Penetrability	Rating as a cut-out	Rating as a destination
1	2	3	4	5
Mauritius	80	6	2500	56
Vatican City	70	7	2409	24
Macao	90	5	2300	9
Nauru	80	6	1945	8
Luxembourg	100	9	1586	100
Saudi Arabia	60	8	1540	8
United States	60	5	1534	100
Andorra	70	6	1510	18
Niue	90	4	1490	8
Samoa	90	4	1490	6
Marshall Islands	80	6	1465	4

The rating of perception (Column 2) is subjective and based on interviews with – and vast experience of – successful asset stealthists. Column 3 indicates, again based on experience, the difficulties of breaking the veils of corporate secrecy in the countries concerned. Column 4 is based on an algorithm taking all of the 'evaluation factors' into account.

THE BEST FINAL DESTINATIONS

The most attractive countries for *holding assets* outside the country in which they originate are shown in Table 14.6.

Surprisingly, Switzerland does not feature in Table 14.6, but this is mainly because of the many cases in which bank secrecy has been broken by French tax authorities and creditors.

Tracing Options

BACKGROUND

Even for government agencies, tracing assets is not easy. For the commercial victim, there are four options: 'inside to out' and 'outside to in' field investigations, legal action, or ideally, a combination of each. The benefits and problems of each of these methods are discussed below.

Table 14.6   Destinations for asset stealth

Country	How assets are most likely to be held	Perception	Penetrability	Rating as a cut-out	Rating as a destination
1	2	3	4	5	6
Liechtenstein	Financial Institutions	100	9	1366	100
Luxembourg		100	9	1586	100
United Kingdom		50	5	1439	100
United States	General	60	5	1534	100
Isle of Man		80	4	370	90
Jersey		80	4	370	90
Guernsey	Financial Institutions	80	4	370	81
Sark		70	4	660	81
Canada	General	50	5	750	80
Gibraltar	Financial Institutions	80	8	790	72
Ireland	Financial Institutions	50	5	606	72
Belgium	General	40	5	600	64
Bermuda	Financial Institutions	50	3	463	64
France	General	50	5	650	64

Note: In Column 2, 'General' includes Financial Institutions, physical and other assets.

'INSIDE TO OUT' FIELD INVESTIGATIONS

Business and other records available to the victim are used as the beginning of a thread, leading to hidden assets. They are focused from a defined starting point and call for forensic accounting and investigative skills. Experience shows that victims pay far too little attention to this form of asset tracing, simply because it is not 'sexy'!

'OUTSIDE TO IN' FIELD INVESTIGATIONS

Under this approach, a wide net is thrown around banks, lawyers and others with whom the villain is known to have contact, in the hope they will reveal information. The first thing to appreciate is that very little is ever achieved by searches of public databases, simply because the primary objective of asset stealth is to conceal. Another common method used to track assets is to approach some or all of the *bankers* or *advisers* involved on a pretext basis.

THE DANGERS OF PRETEXT CALLS

For example, the investigator – who has discovered that James Smith, a stealthist, has telephoned an overseas bank – may pose as a Settlor or someone wishing to transfer funds into an account.

Investigator: This is ABC bank, Copenhagen here. We have $100 000 to transfer to the account of James Smith. We do not have the account co-ordinates.

Bank: Wait one minute. Yes, please transfer by SWIFT sort code xxxxxx account number yyyyyyyy.

Based on this, the investigator reports that James Smith has an account number yyyyyyyy at ABC Bank, which has the sort code xxxxxx. However, the hard, but true, fact is that such references may relate only to an internal suspense account for unallocated incoming funds. Most bank officers and advisers:

- are well aware of the danger of pretext calls
- are keen to get money into their bank for overnight deposit
- will worry about the internal allocation to a private or corporate account at the appropriate time.

The fact that a bank is prepared to accept an incoming transfer usually means nothing: the pretext call may be illegal, and may do little but embarrass the creditor or even compromise its legal case.

However, pretexts directly against the asset stealthist, his family members or business associates are usually much more productive, but they call for careful planning under professional legal advice, and they are expensive and time-consuming.

LEGAL ACTIONS

In many cases, legal actions (in England and in countries whose laws devolve from English law), search and freezing orders are used to uncover assets. It is essential that these take the villain by surprise and are hard and fast. The routine service of a conventional Statement of Claim or writ simply gives the asset stealthist time to hide his assets even deeper.

Effective asset recovery calls for close co-operation between expert litigators and investigators, who, based on a legal and effective strategy, use selected civil actions and field investigations.

The Big Question

The big question is always: 'Is it worthwhile spending time and effort trying to track and recover the villain's assets?' The truth is that in 80 per cent of cases, victims fail to make meaningful recoveries because:

- They fail to understand the nature of asset stealth, but expect immediate results and at no cost.

- They put a manager under whose control the loss occurred in charge of making the recovery: this puts Billy Bunter in charge of the cream cakes, and never works.

- They do not invest sufficient time or money in the recovery effort, supposedly on the basis that they 'do not want to throw good money after bad'.

- They end up in a fight with other creditors over limited assets.

- They retain ineffective lawyers and investigators.

Creditors should always question the likelihood that assets can be recovered, and the cost benefits involved.

As a general rule, in large cases, a budget for legal, investigative and other fees of between 5 and 10 per cent of the amount involved is appropriate, but most of these can also be recovered.

The art in asset recovery is to focus on cost-effectiveness, and not simply costs.

Assessing the Possibilities

The checklist in Table 14.7 is based on the experience of Maxima Group Plc and its associates, and shows the likelihood of making recoveries through a combination of field investigations and legal action.

Table 14.7   Asset recovery checklist

Factor	Comment	Weight (one only)
AMOUNT INVOLVED		
The amount involved is:		
• Less than $500 000	The greater the amount involved, the	0
• More than $1 million less than $5 million	more likely it is that significant assets will	1
• More than $5 million less than $10 million	have been hidden. But experience shows	4
• More than $10 million less than $50 million	that very large losses are difficult to	6
• Over $50 million	recover and usually involve competing creditors	2
TOTAL (Transfer to page 206)		

Table 14.7   Asset recovery checklist – *continued*

SCORE *(Score all of the appropriate boxes)*

Factor	Comment	Score all boxes
THE PERPETRATOR There is more than one perpetrator, and their present whereabouts are known.	Collusion makes it more likely that confidential informants will be found.	50
He is located in a well-regulated jurisdiction.	Where civil action should succeed.	80
There is evidence against him of civil or criminal fraud.	Actions may be dropped in return for a negotiated settlement.	100
Discovery of his actions took the perpetrator by surprise.	Making it unlikely that he had time to plan an end game and to effectively hide assets.	100
The perpetrator used a number of different banks, not all of which have incurred losses. Information obtained on discovery can be used for inside-out tracing.	The larger the number of banks involved, the greater the chance of developing leads to hidden assets.	50
The perpetrator has not been involved in previous incidents of a similar nature.	And is not thought to have asset concealment knowledge.	40
The perpetrator and his close associates currently have expensive lifestyles not justified by their visible incomes.	Usually suggesting that he believes he has put recoverable assets beyond recovery. The veil can usually be penetrated.	100
He and his close associates own or control a bank or financial institution.	This is a common feature of many international frauds. It is estimated that more than fifty Russian banks are owned by criminal groups.	–100
The perpetrator has owned/does own a business or residential property.	Property is usually an easily recoverable asset.	40
TOTAL (Transfer to page 206)		

Table 14.7   Asset recovery checklist – *continued*

SCORE *(Score all of the appropriate boxes)*

Factor	Comment	Score all boxes
NATURE OF THE CASE The dishonest acts took place in a well-regulated jurisdiction.	Civil and criminal laws are effective.	60
The loss was the result of: • Employee fraud • Credit fraud • Mortgage or insurance fraud • Lending, trade finance or documentary credit fraud • Trading or investment problems • Other	Scores are subjective, based on experience.	100 30 50 10 10
There is evidence of criminal acts, tax evasion or frauds against a government agency. The fact that a crime has been committed allows more flexibility under data protection and human rights legislation for the investigation.	Against which the police can take action. However, the amount of assistance the police can give the creditor is limited. Also claims for compensation by police and tax authorities take precedence over other creditors.	−100
The loss has been/will be reported to the police.		−50
One or more government agencies are creditors.	With secured or preferential creditors, the victim's chances of recovery are reduced.	−100
The proceeds of the dishonest acts were not initially disbursed in cash.	Assets are easier to trace on an inside to out basis, i.e. from source to destination.	50
The victim has access to records showing the initial disbursement of funds.		50
The dishonest acts involved employees of the victim company and collusion.	This may provide grounds for recovery under fidelity insurance.	100
There is evidence of involvement by organized crime or terrorist groups.	Such groups are expert in laundering funds.	−100
There are commercial reasons for not pursuing the debt.	This decision must be taken at the highest level.	−100
The loss was discovered • Less than a week ago • More than a week and less than 6 months ago • More than 6 months and less than 12 months ago • More than 2 years ago	Speed is critical but the likelihood of recovery diminishes six months after discovery. However, the chances increase again after the initial flurry of activity by creditors, most of whom lose interest.	50 20 0 50
TOTAL (Transfer to page 206)		

Table 14.7   Asset recovery checklist – *concluded*

SCORE *(Score all of the appropriate boxes)*

Factor	Comment	Score all boxes
OTHER CREDITORS The victim is the only creditor.	Thus assets will not be contested by others.	100
A receiver or administrator has been appointed by other creditors.	Experience shows that recovery chances are severely reduced.	−100
A committee of creditors has been/will be formed.	Nothing is ever achieved by a committee.	−100
TOTAL (Transfer to page 206)		

SCORE *(Score all of the appropriate boxes)*

Factor	Comment	Score all boxes
LEGAL ACTION Civil action has been or will be taken by other creditors.	This makes it less likely that the victim will have any enforceable claim on assets.	−100
A civil judgment has already been obtained by the victim for most or all of the amount involved through a conventional writ.	If not carried out without warning, funds will have been disbursed.	−50
Pre-emptive civil action including Search and Seizure orders are possible (e.g. Search, Discovery and Freezing Orders).	Such actions must be handled by experienced litigation lawyers and with an element of surprise.	100
TOTAL (Transfer to page 206)		

SCORE *(Score all of the appropriate boxes)*

Factor	Comment	Score all boxes
CONTROL OF THE RECOVERY PROCESS Recovery is being handled by a senior manager not previously responsible for the operations in which the loss took place.	Independence is vital.	100
The loser is prepared to create a reasonable legal and investigative budget for recovery action.	Focus must be on cost-effectiveness, and not just on cost of recovery.	100
TOTAL (Transfer to page 206)		

SCORE *(Score all of the appropriate boxes)*

Factor	Comment	Score all boxes
OTHER RECOVERY POSSIBILITIES Banks or professional advisers were involved, through dishonesty, wrongful acts or negligence.	Civil actions against third parties are generally unsuccessful.	30
TOTAL (Transfer to page 206)		

Assessment

The above factors should be transferred to Table 14.8.

Obviously, the checklist is no more than a guide, but the fact is that most victims recover nothing simply because they don't plan and don't recognize the difficulties.

Table 14.8   Asset recovery checklist: summary of findings

Weight	2.1	2.2	2.3	2.4	2.5	2.6	ASSESSMENT =
Size	Perpetrator	Case	Creditors	Legal	Process	Other	*a multiplied by*
a	b	c	d	e	f	g	*(b+c+d+e+f+g)*

10 000 plus	Very good chance of identifying and recovering assets
2000	Borderline
<2000	Requires careful cost justification

Recommended Actions

THE VITAL STEPS

Let's assume you have been victimized and believe the people responsible have assets tucked away which you would like to recover: what should you do?

- First, seriously consider whether it is worth trying to make recoveries at all; in many cases it is not. Sometimes, it is better to learn the lessons and get on with life. However,

Table 14.9   Recovery options

Recoveries from	Comment
The perpetrators and their associates	May be possible by: • Negotiation • Litigation Prior knowledge, from field investigations, of where their assets are located is a great advantage
Fidelity insurance	When employee dishonesty is provable
Advisers and third parties who were complicit in the loss through negligence, etc.	Despite the fact that external auditors and bankers are usually a target for such recoveries, the actual success rates are very low Field investigations may be justified to obtain evidence of third party negligence
Other • Offsets • Directors' and officers' liability insurance • Other	Other options will vary on a case-to-case basis

document the reasons for your decisions, because at some point in the future, shareholders or regulators may accuse you of not pursuing recoverable assets.

- Identify, based on the advice of lawyers, investigators and recovery experts, all your *options* as part of a strategic plan (Table 14.9).

- If you have not already done so, appoint a sensible, determined, *senior manager*, who was not in any way involved in the loss to be in charge of the recovery. Set sensible objectives, timescales and budgets (possibly up to 10 per cent of the amount at stake), and take the toughest line possible. The rule is that when you have the villains by their 'goolies', their hearts, minds and money will follow, but always operate within the law.

- If you have not already done so, appoint tough *external litigation lawyers* who have a track record in fraud and asset recovery: if necessary conduct a beauty parade and remember you are appointing the best lawyer and not necessarily the biggest or most prestigious firm. Agree a realistic budget and timescale in a letter of appointment and obtain a confidentiality agreement. Their objectives are to act on intelligence and other data and to obtain search, seizure and disclosure orders to identify and recover assets.

- If you have not already done so, appoint a firm of qualified specialist investigators, but never your own external accountants. Again, if necessary, conduct a beauty parade, and pick the best.

- Develop an overall plan, setting out the steps to be taken, the manpower required, and possible costs. Keep this plan under review, and make balanced decisions. Focus on cost-effectiveness rather than pure cost. Make sure all investigative steps are legal and that admissible evidence will result.

- Use a combination of investigative and legal actions.

If you follow this advice, your chances of success are greatly increased. However, don't expect results too quickly, or an easy ride. *And never expect to find hidden assets in the public records.* You will simply be wasting your time.

Planning Now

Finally, if you work for a bank or financial institution, the time to establish the trail to assets is *now*, before problems arise. Make sure that in meetings with customers you obtain specific detail, and record it so that, if at some later time you have to trace their assets, you can do so on an 'inside to out' basis. This will make things much easier.

'All I did was give the judge a Masonic greeting.'

15 *Stage J: Giving Evidence*

Background

The day will come when the investigator, managers or (heaven forbid) lawyers are called to give evidence in court, and this can be a daunting prospect. However, the ordeal can be made easier if the potential witness heeds the following warnings and rules. They are deliberately written in a very personal way, because at the time you may need to refer to them, the issues will indeed be very personal. Your ass will be kicked.

Principles

- Always tell the truth.
- Chances are you will get beaten to a pulp, even when you have acted professionally and done your very best.

Prepare Carefully

Always prepare carefully. Know your statement, proof of evidence or affidavit backwards, forwards and inside out, and the exhibits to which they refer. Double-check all schedules, calculations and conclusions you have made in your statement or on which you might be required to comment during your evidence. Make sure that your sources of intelligence are open and can be defended. Check your notes and the other records you may be allowed to refer to in the witness box to refresh your memory – make sure you can read and understand them. Think about the nasty questions you will be asked.

Fix the Appointment

Make sure you have a note of the date and time you are required to attend court firmly in your diary, in red ink.

Check out the Court

Familiarize yourself with the court, how to get there, and how long the journey takes (even if you have to stop every ten minutes for lavatorial breaks). If you have not given evidence before, sit in on another trial for a couple of hours before your date. Watch and get the hang of things. It is pretty awesome – lawyers are very clever.

On the Day

APPEARANCE

On the day you are required to attend, arrive early. Make sure you dress sensibly. Your wife may tell you that you look wonderful in your yellow waistcoat, pink suspenders, Gucci sunglasses and Hush Puppies, but it is doubtful that the court will appreciate them. If you are a member of the Surbiton Train Spotters' Club, however proud you might be, don't wear the lapel badge or tie. This is not impressive. All you will achieve is to mark yourself out as a plonker.

If you must have facial hair, make sure you do not look like a member of the Taliban. Also wear clothing that – unlike Tony Blair's – does not show how profusely you are sweating.

WAITING TO BE CALLED

Do not read sensitive papers in public areas, and be careful with your mobile telephone and laptop computer. Do not engage strangers in idle conversation: the delightful blonde sat next to you on the bench could be a plant by the opposing side. Do not discuss your evidence or the case with anyone else waiting around the court, and especially with a witness who has not been released. A little paranoia did no one any harm, and waiting about – and there will be lots of this – makes matters worse. This is the time to read this book or have a nap: the two things are closely related.

ENTERING THE COURT WITH PANACHE

Do not go into the court until your name is called. When this happens, your legs will buckle and the past will flash before your eyes. You will wish you had heeded your Probation Officer's advice and become a butcher. It's too late. Pick up all your belongings – *turn off your mobile telephone* – and walk into court nice and slowly. Don't panic. Take your time, and grab a few deep breaths. Wait to be spoken to, and don't go in with a cheery 'Good morning, Judge. I like your wig', or with some flippant remark to the defendant like 'Guilty bastard!'. Neither will go down well. Also, if you are truly a Freemason, don't be tempted to give members of the jury, the judge or anyone else the secret signals. This will not be appreciated, especially if you outrank them.

GIVING YOUR EVIDENCE IN CHIEF

After taking the oath (over which you must take time) or making some sort of esoteric incantation or engaging in a plate-throwing ritual (depending on your beliefs), you will be led through your evidence by counsel representing your side. He should be friendly, more or less, and he may smile from time to time and nod his head. *Don't relax.*

Direct all of your answers to the judge, and try to establish eye contact with him from time to time, but don't glare or wink. If – at any point – you are not certain of a fact, ask the judge if you can refresh your memory from your notes. Under no circumstances try to crack a joke. It will backfire on you. Counsel for the other side may jump up and down and make objections to your evidence. This is a good sign, unless he has itchy underpants, in which case it means nothing. When you have finished your evidence in chief, wait in the witness box and, whatever you do, don't look smug, because the ambush is just around the corner. Never forget: lawyers are clever and the older they are, the more clever they get.

The big problem comes with cross-examination by counsel for the other side. He will ask you lots of dreadful questions and try to trip you up, and make you appear an incompetent plonker or worse. Remember, this is his job, and he will be doing his best. It is just like being grilled by your mother-in-law after a boozy night out with the boys. Tell the truth, and if you have made a mistake, admit it. Don't argue the case or matters of law – you are not an advocate – appear impartial, concede points genuinely in favour of the obnoxious crook, and stick to the facts. Wherever possible, answer questions with a simple 'yes' or 'no' and, whatever you do, do not try to be clever or funny. This will lead to sudden death! When opposing counsel sits down, you remain standing. *Don't move.*

Next, you may be re-examined by the counsel representing your side. You can tell how badly you have been mauled in the cross-examination by the number of questions he asks. If there are a lot, you can assume you have not been too impressive. Don't worry. That's life sometimes, and lawyers are very clever.

Finally, you may be asked questions by the judge. These are really important, and take care, as judges are very clever. Simply tell the truth.

IN BREAKS AND OVERNIGHT

You can almost guarantee that you will not complete your evidence in one session, and will have to worry through an overnight or some other adjournment. George Carman QC – perhaps the leading advocate and cross-examiner of his generation – used to love this, if not contrive it. He used to say, 'It will give the witness time to worry,' and he was right.

Don't speak to anyone during short breaks. Politely ignore and avoid eye contact with members of the jury if you happen to bump into them in the pub or Lodge. Just vamoose as quickly as you can. Imagine you have a massive dose of contagious pox and that you must steer clear of everyone. This is a good rule.

During longer breaks – however attractive it might seem at the time – don't console yourself in the pub and leave without your legs. Keep off the juice overnight, and arrive at court the next day nice, fresh, and preferably celibate. Tell your wife or husband you have a migraine. This always works, and you can make up for it later.

After the Event

Chances are that at the end of it all, you will leave court feeling drained, downtrodden and with hurt feelings because unfair allegations have been made against you. Even when you know you have carried out your tasks honestly, professionally and to the best of your ability, you will still get pulped. These feelings do not get better over time, and there is no easy answer to them.

Witnesses and others involved in investigations might wonder whether the whole episode and the torture in court was worthwhile. The answer is overwhelmingly in the positive, because someone has to take a stand against fraud. As investigators, we are in the firing line, and we should be grown-up about our responsibilities. If we want an easy life, we

should become lawyers or politicians. And just to reassure you: lawyers hate giving evidence themselves.

Finally, remember that in court you are a guest, and it is lawyers' territory. They always win. That is why this book has been rude to them. Every dog has its day!

'All I said was that he looked like Lord Lucan.'

16 *Stage K: Clearing Up*

Principle

- Close the case professionally, and file all records securely.

Reach Final Conclusions

Try to make sure that all suspicions involving people and companies are cleared up, one way or the other.

Thank Helpers

Write letters of thanks to employees and third parties who have assisted in the investigation. Make sure that the personnel file of any employee who was under suspicion, but has since been cleared, is properly endorsed.

Improve Controls

Review the weaknesses that caused the problem, and put new controls in place. Document this action.

Retain Papers Securely

Retain papers securely until all litigation has been completed, and for at least seven years thereafter. It is always possible that Dracula will rise from the coffin! If you have to retain computer and structured manual records, seek the specific approval of the Information Commissioner. If she says 'no', get it in writing and wait for the disaster.

Appendices

Improving prosecution statistics.

1 *Examination of Documents*

Introduction

The analysis of documentary evidence is critical in most fraud investigations. This appendix sets out some general guidelines.

Continuity and Integrity

It is essential that the integrity of all documentary evidence (including that which might be relevant only to the defence) is catalogued and preserved, and that the chain of continuity covering the time from discovery to production in court is maintained.

- Keep a register of all documents obtained (whether they are relevant or not), and give and obtain a receipt for them.

- Normally, original documents should be placed in transparent plastic exhibit envelopes.

- The integrity of fingerprint, ESDA (which reveals impressions of writing from other documents) and other forensic evidence should be preserved. Original documents should not be written on or damaged in any way. Note: Fax paper and some photocopies quickly deteriorate when exposed to light, and documents on which there may be fingerprints or impressions of other writing become less clear for ESDA examination when enclosed in plastic. Thus documents of these types should be carefully photocopied and the originals placed in paper envelopes.

- Exhibit labels should be written up before being fixed to the extreme edges of envelopes containing the original documents. The labels should not be fixed to the envelopes and then written on, as the impressions created may compromise ESDA and other forensic tests.

- Wherever possible, documents should be preserved in the state in which they were found. Original documents should not be stapled, nor should bound books and files be broken up. If you do have to break them up, keep a note of their original state.

- Important original documents should be kept separate from the working copies, and should not be released until after the case, and any subsequent appeal, has been completed.

- Comments, exhibit numbers and cross-references should be written on the copies, *never* on the originals.

These procedures should ensure that the integrity of documents is preserved, and that their admissibility in court is not compromised.

Copying

Copy every document that could be relevant, back and front. Work from copies, and keep the originals secure.

Analysis of Documents

BACKGROUND

The analysis of documentary evidence falls into two main categories:

- forensic analysis
- detailed analysis of meaning and content.

Wherever possible, all of the documents in a case should be examined by one person, not a group of people. In this way, connections between apparently unrelated documents can be made. If the job is divided between too many people, these connections may be overlooked.

FORENSIC ANALYSIS

This analysis will be a broad one, looking for general patterns rather than for scientific proof. All original documents should be examined for:

- erased, altered or crossed-out writing
- inconsistent inks or typefaces
- impressions of writing from other documents; these can be proven by an ESDA examination
- fingerprints on documents the suspect denies he has handled
- dates of printing and lists of directors' names, to establish whether a document could have been created on the date alleged
- altered photocopy documents or faxes – a very common method of forgery is to copy an original, alter it, recopy it, and destroy the original; another method is to apply heat, using a domestic iron or hot knife, to lift off characters, much like a correctable typewriter ribbon
- altered laser print – laser printing can be altered by scraping off characters using a very sharp knife
- layout of text and typing, especially of documents which were supposedly written by different people or different companies – this is an important factor in procurement frauds, where the type or layout of bids by what are claimed to be unrelated contractors are the same
- address layouts on envelopes, to identify common patterns and authors
- similar folding or staple holes in apparently unrelated documents or documents from supposedly different sources
- postal franking machine stamps showing the origin of mail to be different from that claimed.

On this preliminary sweep, notes should be made of those documents that appear to be fraudulent or forged. Depending on the patterns that emerge, professional forensic examination should be considered.

MEANING AND CREDIBILITY OF CONTENT

Every potentially important document should be examined, and its meaning and the credibility of its content considered in the context of the worst-case theory:

- On letter headings, invoices, orders and so on, examine the list of directors, registered office, registration, VAT, telephone, fax or telex numbers, and look for inconsistencies, bearing in mind the purported date the document was produced.

- On pre-printed forms, compare the printer's codes and date of printing with the date when they were supposedly used.

- On multi-part, NCR ('no carbon required', multiple-part forms) or colour-coded forms, examine the consistency of copies taken from various files, and the completeness of numerical sequences; list any missing documents and any patterns in the periods of time, copy numbers or origin.

- Compare copies of the same document and letters recovered from different sources or different files, and list out any discrepancies, including missing documents.

- Examine all informal notes, jottings and comments on the back and front of all documents handled by the suspects.

Before the final report is prepared, and preferably before final interviews are held with the suspects, the project team should be in a position to explain every entry on every document, and to understand the significance of every piece of evidence.

'No, Jones, you cannot blame the big bad wolf for this.'

2 *Preparation of Schedules*

Introduction

Schedules are critical in most large-scale investigations, and can be used to summarize and present complex information in an easily understandable way. There are some important principles about scheduling:

- They must be accurate, and should be double-checked before being included in reports or produced in court.
- They should be easy to audit and to track to the source data.
- On preliminary or working schedules, adequate space should be left for the insertion of additional notes and columns.
- Complex schedules should be distilled into a summary form.

In all fraud cases, a diary of events should be prepared. Similarly, schedules may be prepared summarizing the main points in a bulky file of correspondence.

Diary of Events

A diary of events summarizes all actions, correspondence and so on relating to the fraud. The diary can be maintained using a simple database management system, such as *Filemaker Pro*, or *Excel*, or may be prepared manually.

When the fraud involves different time zones, the diary should show local and Greenwich Mean Time (GMT). Input to the diary of events will be taken from:

- telephone call records
- travel expenses
- diaries
- time recording systems
- the journal on personal computers
- witness and other statements
- accounting and other records.

This means that it summarizes in one place and in chronological order everything that happened during the period when the fraud took place.

Proof of Loss

Schedules proving the loss should be supported by the documentary or other evidence necessary to prove every entry. Where figures are estimated, that fact should be made clear. Most fidelity insurance policies have a clause which prohibits the use of 'inventory' or profit and loss calculations. To overcome this restriction, the evidence used to support the Proof of Loss must establish that:

- the losses were as the direct result of dishonesty traceable in the records
- there is a reliable unit count of the assets stolen
- there is a very low probability that the fraud could have taken place without the involvement of employees (even though their identity may not be known)
- there is good overall proof, with a plausible timeframe
- the losses stopped or diminished after the fraud was detected.

It should also show that enquiries were conducted by a capable and professional investigator.
     A Proof of Loss should consist of separate schedules for the following:

- an accurate statement of the losses actually incurred
- estimates of further losses, providing the basis of estimation is reasonable and made clear on the face of the schedules
- interest on the losses
- interest on estimated losses
- costs of investigation and litigation.

It is unlikely that the fidelity insurer will consider any compensation for stock losses where they cannot be specifically traced to dishonest activity by an employee.

Summarizing Important Facts

Another purpose of scheduling is to illustrate symptoms of concealment, to prove guilty knowledge, or to identify patterns of dishonesty. At the start of an investigation, the ultimate purpose of schedules may not be clear. It is not unusual for an investigator to start out producing a simple schedule of losses, only to find in the process that patterns that virtually prove the fraud, guilty knowledge and responsibility emerge.

'When in doubt, schedule' is a good rule for any fraud investigator.

3 *Selecting Investigators*

Selecting the Firm

There are probably hundreds of investigation firms in Europe, and thousands throughout the world. In general, no professional qualification is needed, and standards vary dramatically, so get answers to these questions when you are looking to retain investigators:

1 Does the firm have an outstanding reputation as a specialist?
   • What impression is given by its promotional literature?
   • What success has it had on similar assignments?
   • What good and bad media reports have there been on the firm?
   • Does it avoid publicity which could compromise its clients and assignments?

2 How are its ethical and professional standards defined and maintained?
   • policies on values and operating standards?
   • internal procedures and supervision?
   • training?
   • quality control and legal compliance?
   • membership of a professional specialist association?

3 Is the firm free of any strategic conflicts of interest?
   • independent of the company's external auditors?
   • independent of a dominant shareholder?
   • independent of insurers, bankers and others whose interests could conflict?

4 Is the firm financially sound?
   • shareholder funds?
   • profitable track record?
   • bankers' references?
   • adequate professional insurance?
   • adequate human and other resources?

Individual Consultants

Standards of competence vary dramatically within firms. Sometimes, experienced staff will be used purely to sell assignments, and may never be seen again. It is essential that the names of qualified people who will be assigned to the client are listed. Again, ask yourself these questions:

5 Which consultants would be assigned to the case?

6 Review their biographies:
- Check their educational qualifications and practical experience.
- Obtain details of their experience of similar assignments.
- Test their knowledge of the law and investigative processes.

Selection Procedure

This is written on the basis that a specific assignment is in prospect. It should be modified for pre-selection as part of a Fraud Policy.

7 Prepare a specification of the assignment in question, setting out your objectives, but keep an open mind to recommendations made by the investigators.

8 Invite two or three firms to attend an initial briefing. Each firm should be briefed separately.

9 Obtain an undertaking on confidentiality before each briefing commences.

10 Review, again, copies of the firms' promotional material, and examine them carefully:
- Are they really specialists in the area concerned?
- What is their track record?

11 Listen to the questions they ask, and their suggestions:
- Are the questions sensible and the solutions practical?
- Do the consultants have a good understanding of the relevant issues, laws, rules of evidence and disclosure?
- Do they volunteer ideas?

12 Do they answer questions sensibly and truthfully?

13 Ask for a written proposal:
- Does it contain a practical work plan which will achieve your objectives?
- Does it contain a realistic budget?
- Does it specify the names and qualifications of the consultants who will work on the assignment?
- Do they have the specialist skills and experience necessary?
- Was the proposal delivered on time and to a high professional standard?

14 In major cases, consider arranging a 'beauty parade' at which shortlisted firms make a presentation and answer questions.

15 Obtain references from two or three of their clients.

16 Select the firm based on a combination of:
- the likelihood of their successfully achieving the objectives of the assignment
- overall cost, rather than the daily fee rate
- personal chemistry and professionalism.

17 Finally, do they claim to be 'accredited investigators' under the Partners in Crime 'initiative'. If so, ask them for proof, and what they have achieved. Also ask them to explain the Human Rights problems.

18 Prepare a letter of engagement and a confidentiality agreement.

19 Set up budgetary and other reporting lines.

20 Monitor the results.

'I do believe, Mr Jones, you should have told me about your bed-wetting before we started!'

4 *Planning Interviews*

Table A4.1 Planning an interview

__OBTAINING VITAL BACKGROUND__			
Without alerting the suspects, find out as much as possible about their background			
Page	**Category**	**Action**	**OK**
157	Background	Fully **research the background** of each potential suspect and witness Work, personal and other history: • Maiden names of his wife and married names of daughters • Covertly inspect his home: look for cash improvements • Check company registration records • Check all databases	
164	Background	Obtain evidence of **minor breaches** by suspects and witnesses: • Expense claims frauds • Misuse of discretion • Other Arrange this so that it can be presented in interviews.	
87	FPA	Carry out a Fraud Profile Analysis (FPA) of all of the processes to which the suspect has access.	
80	Background	Research the background of the suspect's legal adviser.	

Continued

Table A4.1   Planning an interview – *continued*

	DETERMINE THE OBJECTIVES OF EACH INTERVIEW		
	Within the overall Investigations Plan		
	Civil or Criminal Litigation		
Page	**Category**	**Action**	**OK**
68	Legality	Understand the legal framework, and whether or not you need to advise the suspect of his rights against self-incrimination.	
	Objectives	Determine whether a confession is important. If it is not, don't push, but simply give the opportunity of explanation.	
151 & 165	Resources	Decide when, where and by whom each interview will be conducted: • Assign suitably qualified investigators to each interview • Assign and brief interpreters	

164	Exhibits – Intrerview Planning	Consider how the evidence will be presented in each interview:
		• Summarize evidence in easily understood schedules
		• Translate all important exhibits if they are not in English
		• Decide whether to display the evidence or hold it back until the suspect has given a false explanation
		• Consider enlarging important documents for display
		• Consider preparing bulky evidential files or labelling filing cabinets
		• Arrange the evidence professionally in the order in which it will be presented in interviews
		• Select the best pieces of evidence you have, and enhance their impact:
		   ◊ Enclose in exhibit bags
		   ◊ Enlarge
		   ◊ Enclose in bulky files
		   ◊ Summarize on schedules	

165	Interview Room	Prepare the interview room(s): • Ask a colleague to give you his first impressions of the room • Make sure the room is clear of distractions and audio interference • Check and replay recording equipment	
158	Notes	Decide how and by whom a record of the interview will be maintained.	

Continued

Table A4.1   Planning an interview – *continued*

		PLANNING SPECIFIC TACTICS AND QUESTIONS	
		Plan the questions you will ask in four stages. Aim directly for the truth. Throughout try to establish rapport. Carefully listen and observe. Consciously control your Transactional Role. Understand and rehearse how you will deal with counter-attacks and other problems. Aim to drive the suspect to the Pivotal Point, then turn to an emphatic approach to get to the deep truth.	
Page	**Category**	**Action**	**OK**
152	Interview Structure and Planning	Decide on your opening approach: • Introductory statement • Blocking questions • Direct confrontation • Probing approach	
166 *et seq.*		Write down and rehearse your introductory statement, and decide how you will progress, depending on the suspect's reaction.	
		Decide on the control questions you will use.	
		Determine how many topics you will cover, and in what order.	
		Decide on the summary statements you will use, and how you will support them with schedules and documentary exhibits.	
		List out the main assumptions you can make. Decide how you will phrase assumptive questions.	
		Consider using war stories to reinforce important topics. Write these down, and include them in the rehearsal.	
		Determine the questions you will ask and statements you will make to increase the suspect's anxiety to the point where he loses his confidence to continue with deception. Pay particular attention to reinforcing important questions visually with the production of exhibits.	
		Decide how you will phrase soft and direct accusations.	
		Decide how and where you might use enticement questions.	
		Decide how you will phrase rationalization statements.	
		Decide how you will deal with negotiating questions.	
		Decide how you will handle the Pivotal Point and the first admissions.	
169		List out the elements in the WORST CASE that you would like to prove.	
		List out the items you would like to recover.	
		Decide on how you will get the suspect to agree the record of the interview.	
		Decide how you will close the interview.	

Continued

Table A4.1   Planning an interview – *concluded*

Page	Category	Action	OK
		REHEARSING THE INTERVIEW *Always rehearse important interviews*	
166 *et seq.*	Rehearse	Rehearse the interview with interpreters and corroborating witnesses: • Brief the interpreter on the tactics • Brief the corroborating witness to remain silent • Also carry out a rehearsal with you taking the role of the suspect • Refine your approach	
169 *et seq.*	Final Interview Planning	Pay particular attention to how you will: • Establish rapport • Deal with refusal to answer questions • Produce important evidence • Move rapidly from one topic to another • Repeat important questions • Ask enticement questions • Use war stories • Use assumptive questions and alternatives • Use rationalization statements • Make accusations • Interject when the suspect is thinking through a lie • Phrase soft and hard accusations	
		Make a final check on the legality of your approach.	
		CONDUCTING THE INTERVIEW AND FOLLOW-UP	
158 *et seq.*	First Step	Conduct the interview as part of the FIRST STEP or otherwise catch the suspect by surprise: • Give the minimum advance notice • Keep conspirators separate so that they cannot compare their stories • Plan the time the interview is held to your advantage • Have an easy time immediately before the interview • Check everything • Arrive in the room before the suspect • Direct him to where you want him to sit • Have the interpreter sit alongside you	
162	Action	Conduct the interview: • According to the plan • If the suspect continues to lie, force him into detail and indefensible positions	
173		Close the interview	
		Agree the record of the interview with the suspect: • Oral summary • Copy of the tape recording • Joint notes • Admissions repeated before an independent witness • Statement	
123		Update the Fraud Theory and Investigations Plan.	
173		Keep in touch with the suspect in the days after the interview.	

5 Criminal Justice Act Statement Forms

WITNESS STATEMENT

(CJ Act 1967, s9 MC Act 1980 s102; MC Rules 1981 r 70)

Statement of: ....

Age if Under 18   (if over 18 insert 'Over 18')   **Occupation** ....

This statement (consisting of   page(s) each signed by me) is true to the best of my knowledge and belief and I make it knowing that, if it is tendered in evidence, I shall be liable to prosecution if I have wilfully stated in it anything which I know to be false or do not believe to be true.

Signed .... Dated ....

Signature.. Signature witnessed   **1**

WITNESS STATEMENT
(CJ Act 1967, s9 MC Act 1980 s102; MC Rules 1981 r 70)

Signature.. Signature witnessed

2

6 *Chart On the Regulation of Investigatory Powers Act 2000*

REGULATION OF INVESTIGATORY POWERS ACT 2000

and

THE TELECOMMUNICATIONS (LAWFUL BUSINESS PRACTICE) (INTERCEPTION OF COMMUNICATIONS) REGULATIONS 2000

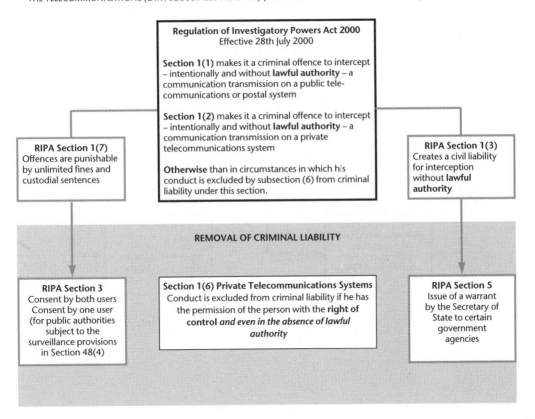

Regulation of Investigatory Powers Act 2000
Effective 28th July 2000

Section 1(1) makes it a criminal offence to intercept – intentionally and without **lawful authority** – a communication transmission on a public tele-communications or postal system

Section 1(2) makes it a criminal offence to intercept – intentionally and without **lawful authority** – a communication transmission on a private telecommunications system

Otherwise than in circumstances in which his conduct is excluded by subsection (6) from criminal liability under this section.

RIPA Section 1(7)
Offences are punishable by unlimited fines and custodial sentences

RIPA Section 1(3)
Creates a civil liability for interception without **lawful authority**

REMOVAL OF CRIMINAL LIABILITY

RIPA Section 3
Consent by both users
Consent by one user (for public authorities subject to the surveillance provisions in Section 48(4)

Section 1(6) Private Telecommunications Systems
Conduct is excluded from criminal liability if he has the permission of the person with the **right of control** *and even in the absence of lawful authority*

RIPA Section 5
Issue of a warrant by the Secretary of State to certain government agencies

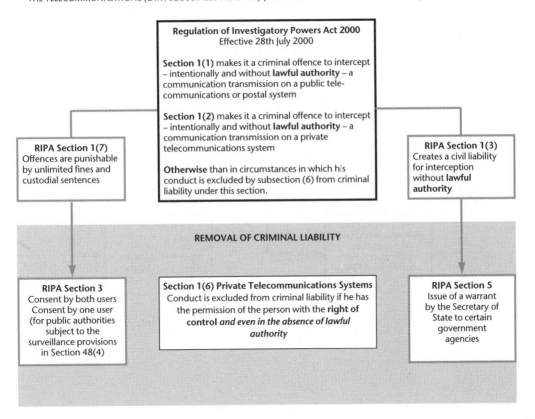

Continued

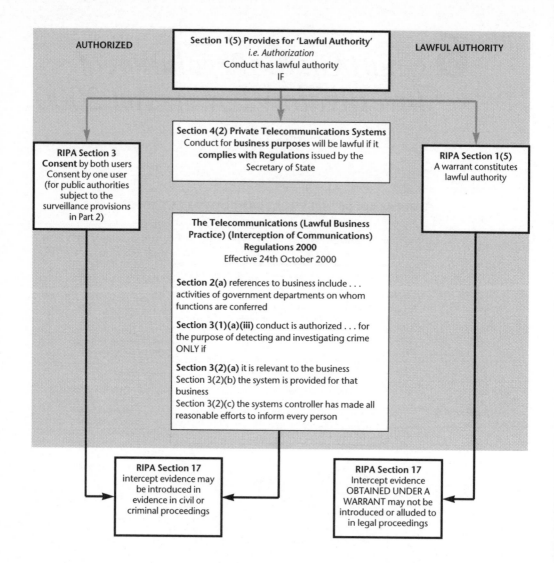

AUTHORIZED

LAWFUL AUTHORITY

Section 1(5) Provides for 'Lawful Authority'
i.e. Authorization
Conduct has lawful authority
IF

RIPA Section 3
Consent by both users
Consent by one user
(for public authorities
subject to the
surveillance provisions
in Part 2)

Section 4(2) Private Telecommunications Systems
Conduct for **business purposes** will be lawful if it
complies with Regulations issued by the
Secretary of State

RIPA Section 1(5)
A warrant constitutes
lawful authority

**The Telecommunications (Lawful Business
Practice) (Interception of Communications)
Regulations 2000**
Effective 24th October 2000

Section 2(a) references to business include . . .
activities of government departments on whom
functions are conferred

Section 3(1)(a)(iii) conduct is authorized . . . for
the purpose of detecting and investigating crime
ONLY if

Section 3(2)(a) it is relevant to the business
Section 3(2)(b) the system is provided for that
business
Section 3(2)(c) the systems controller has made all
reasonable efforts to inform every person

RIPA Section 17
intercept evidence may
be introduced in
evidence in civil or
criminal proceedings

RIPA Section 17
Intercept evidence
OBTAINED UNDER A
WARRANT may not be
introduced or alluded to
in legal proceedings

7 *Example of an I² Chart*

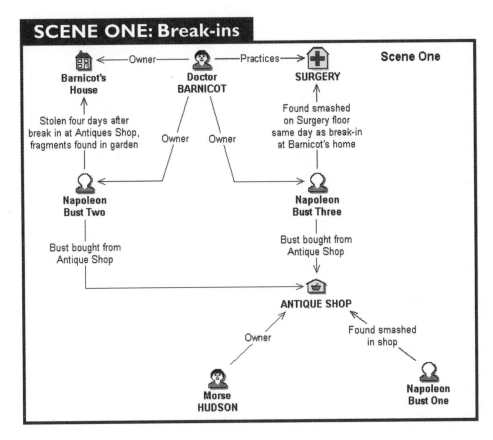

SCENE ONE: Break-ins

Scene One

Barnicot's House ←—Owner—— Doctor BARNICOT ——Practices—→ SURGERY

Stolen four days after break in at Antiques Shop, fragments found in garden

Owner   Owner

Found smashed on Surgery floor same day as break-in at Barnicot's home

Napoleon Bust Two   Napoleon Bust Three

Bust bought from Antique Shop

Bust bought from Antique Shop

ANTIQUE SHOP

Owner

Found smashed in shop

Morse HUDSON

Napoleon Bust One

Figure A7.1   Example of a simple I² chart – Further details of the case of which the above forms part can be found on <www.maxima-group.com>

Index